August 11, 2008

Dear Stan

Thank you for your interest and support.

Canada's Cool!

Warmest regards,
Jane

© Copyright 2006 Lane
All rights reserved. No part of this publication may be reproduced, stored in a retrieval system, or transmitted, in any form or by any means, electronic, mechanical, photocopying, recording, or otherwise, without the written prior permission of the author.

Note for Librarians: A cataloguing record for this book is available from Library and Archives Canada at www.collectionscanada.ca/amicus/index-e.html
ISBN 1-4120-8897-6

Printed in Victoria, BC, Canada. Printed on paper with minimum 30% recycled fibre. Trafford's print shop runs on "green energy" from solar, wind and other environmentally-friendly power sources.

TRAFFORD
PUBLISHING™

Offices in Canada, USA, Ireland and UK

Book sales for North America and international:
Trafford Publishing, 6E–2333 Government St.,
Victoria, BC V8T 4P4 CANADA
phone 250 383 6864 (toll-free 1 888 232 4444)
fax 250 383 6804; email to orders@trafford.com

Book sales in Europe:
Trafford Publishing (UK) Limited, 9 Park End Street, 2nd Floor
Oxford, UK OX1 1HH UNITED KINGDOM
phone 44 (0)1865 722 113 (local rate 0845 230 9601)
facsimile 44 (0)1865 722 868; info.uk@trafford.com

Order online at:
trafford.com/06-0653

10 9 8 7 6 5 4 3

I would like to say a special thank you to my sister

Kelly Roberts

for her assistance and never ending encouragement for this project and a harbour to work from. I would also like to thank my brother

Cameron Roberts

for putting his artistic skills to work on the development of the book covers. I love it. Thank you!

Dear Fellow Canadians,

I am Canadian! This well publicized phrase implies the word proud. Like so many Canadians, I am proud to be Canadian. When I attended the University of Alberta I took all the history courses I could on Canada. When I began teaching I liked to teach about our country but found over time that some things I had been taught were incorrect. I had been taught that Mount Robson was Canada's highest mountain but discovered that in fact Mount Logan is. I began to wonder what else had been errantly taught or omitted. I began studying Canada and read everything I could on the topic. I soon found other facts that were little known or not known at all.

The first story that struck a chord in my heart was Janis Babson. She was such a brave little girl and with what she did for the organ donor program should be heralded as much as we worship Terry Fox. I began to uncover more great Canadians.

As a result of my research I decided to write a book on Canada. I thought writing an encyclopedia would be a great challenge so I set my mind to that task. The huge encyclopedia's compiled by Mel Hurtig, McClelland and Stewart and others have great stories hidden in the multitude of pages. I wanted my encyclopedia to uncover what is Canadian. It is an excellent accessible way to find out about things and people that are Canadian. There is not much information about any person or event but it puts the information at your fingertips so you can discover who is who and when things happened. If you want detailed information then the regular Canadian encyclopedias and books written on the various topics are good once you know what to look for. *Canada's Concise Encyclopedia* is the best source to get you started in your quest to find out all things Canadian.

I felt that I needed more than an encyclopedia on Canada for though it outlines Canada nicely it does not tell the great stories that could be contained in so many of the short entries. I decided to take some of the best little known stories I came across and make them into short stories so others could enjoy them like I have. Harold Johns, Reginald Fessenden, The *Empress of Ireland,* Alan McLeod, Elijah McCoy, William Osler, Mona Parsons and Louis Slotin are a few that I decided to highlight. Still it was stories like the great Edmonton Commercial Grads basketball team and Johnny Bright, two stories that occurred right in the city I am proud to call my birthplace, that surprised me a most because I would have thought that this information should have been taught and discussed in the public school system but it remains buried deep within the pages of history.

When I came across the story of Sir John Thompson and found out one of our Prime Ministers died in front of Queen Victoria in Windsor Castle I was astounded. I started to ask my colleagues about the event and found that no one was aware of this leader of ours much less the circumstances of his death. This particular story I decided should be one of the featured stories in my book for I think it is a shame that NO Canadians have the foggiest idea about this event in Canadian history.

I feel that *Stories from the Heart of Canada* will enlighten Canadians about our heritage and history and introduce them to a number of great Canadians they have never heard about. I feel that after reading my books Canadians will proudly say, "I am Canadian and now feel that I know something about my wonderful country" and if they don't know about some person or event they will look in these resources to see if it is there. If it is I will smile. If it isn't then perhaps it should be so please contact me at laneagan@telus.net. Tell me what I missed because I know I could not have covered the entire country through my research. Besides new stories and future great Canadians are emerging right in front of our eyes. I would also like to know what you think about my book(s). Please email me!

Stories from the Heart of Canada
Table of Contents

1. Pamela **Anderson,** Canada's Most Photographed Beauty p. 1
2. Janis **Babson,** Organ Donor Saint p. 3
3. Frederick **Banting,** Miracle Man p. 6
4. Captain Robert A. **Bartlett,** Arctic Adventurer p. 9
5. Alexander Graham **Bell,** Inventor Best Know for the Telephone p. 11
6. **Beothuk,** Lost Civilization … Lost Peoples p. 23
7. Norman **Bethune,** Mobile Doctor of the People p. 25
8. George 'Buzz' **Beurling,** Falcon of Malta p. 29
9. Len **Birchall,** Savoir of Ceylon p. 34
10. Billy **Bishop,** The Lone Hawk p. 35
11. **Blondin,** Tightrope Walker Extraordinaire p. 38
12. Father Jean de **Brébeuf,** Jésuit Missionary Martyr p. 41
13. Johnny **Bright,** Helped Coin the Word Racism in United States p. 43
14. Kurt **Browning,** Ya Just Gotta Love The Guy p. 45
15. Étienne **Brûlé,** Canada's 1st Coureur de Bois p. 48
16. Tommy **Burns,** Canada's only World Heavyweight Boxing Champion p. 50
17. **Canadian Caper,** Kenneth Taylor Canadian Ambassador to Iran 1980 p. 59
18. Ethel **Catherwood,** The Saskatoon Lily p. 61
19. Don **Cherry,** Grapes p. 63
20. **Crowfoot,** Chief of the War Eagles of the Plains p. 64
21. Samuel **Cunard,** Shipping Magnate p. 66
22. Louis **Cyr,** The Strongest Man in the World p. 68
23. John **Diefenbaker,** Just Call Me 'The Chief' p. 70
24. Céline **Dion,** Voice of an Angel, a Diva, an Icon p. 71
25. Adam **Dollard des Ormeaux,** Canada's Davy Crockett p. 76
26. Tommy **Douglas,** Canada's Political Saint p. 78
27. Gaétan **Dugas,** Patient Zero in the AIDS Epidemic p. 80
28. Ben **Dunkelman,** Great Soldier Who Just Wanted to Come Home p. 81
29. **Early History** p. 83
30. **Edmonton Commercial Grads,** Greatest Team in Canada's Sporting History p. 86
31. Bob **Edwards,** Editor Who Would Open Your Eye p. 88
32. *Empress of Ireland,* Tragedy on the St. Lawrence p. 91
33. Reginald **Fessenden,** Greatest Wireless Inventor of His Age p. 95
34. Michael J. **Fox,** Small for his size BIG for his cause p. 98

35. Terry **Fox,** 'Marathon of Hope' Runner p. 102
36. Northrop **Frye,** Tower of Literary Power p. 106
37. Igor **Gouzenko,** Russian Defector's Revelations Starts Cold War p. 109
38. Nancy **Greene,** 'Tiger' on the Hill p. 113
39. Wayne **Gretzky,** The Great One p. 117
40. **Halifax** Explosion p. 121
41. Rick **Hansen,** 'Man in Motion' p. 123
42. **Hillcrest,** Canada's Worst Mine Disaster p. 126
43. Judith **Jasmin,** Television Pioneer Who Covered the 'Quiet' Revolution p. 129
44. Harold **Johns,** Cobalt-60 for Cancer Patients p. 132
45. Pauline **Johnson,** Quill of Her People p. 133
46. Ruby **Keeler,** Innocent Blue Eyed Bombshell p. 136
47. Frances **Kelsey,** Thalidomide Heroine p. 139
48. William Lyon Mackenzie **King,** Commonwealth's Longest Standing Prime Minister p. 140
49. **Klondike Gold Rush** p. 142
50. Albert **Lacombe,** Prairie Missionary p. 145
51. Sam **Langford,** The Boston Tar Baby p. 148
52. Marie de **La Tour,** Heroine of Acadia p. 150
53. Wilfred **Laurier,** Follow My White Plume p. 152
54. Tom **Longboat,** Greatest Distance Runner of All p. 154
55. Elijah **McCoy,** The Real McCoy p. 155
56. Sir John A. **Macdonald,** Canada's First Prime Minister p. 157
57. Angus **Mckay,** Farmer with a Mission p. 160
58. Alexander **Mackenzie,** from Canada by land July 22, 1793 p. 162
59. Willie **McKnight,** Bright Light McKnight p. 164
60. Alan **McLeod,** Courage on the Wing p. 166
61. **Maskepetoon,** Tongue of Peace p. 169
62. **Métis** p. 171
63. **Mount Logan,** Canada's Highest Mountain p. 173
64. Emily Ferguson **Murphy,** Janey Canuck p. 174
65. **Northern Dancer,** The Little Horse that Could p. 176
66. William **Osler,** Teacher of Doctors p. 178
67. Mona **Parsons,** Canadian/Dutch Resistance Fighter p. 180
68. Lester B. **Pearson,** Winner of the Nobel Peace Prize p. 185
• David **Pelletier** - see Jamie Salé p. 216
69. Oscar **Peterson,** Jazz Giant on the Keyboard p. 187
70. Mary **Pickford,** America's Sweetheart p. 193
71. **Piskiart,** The Lone Warrior p. 201

72. Jacques **Plante,** The Man with the Mask p. 203
73. **Poundmaker,** Great Chief with a Lost Cause p. 205
74. Louis **Riel,** Champion of his People - Martyr for their Cause p. 211
75. Marguerite de la **Roque,** Isle of Demons Castaway p. 214
76. Jamie **Salé** and David Pelletier, Figure Skating Pairs Event Fiasco p. 216
77. Sir Charles **Saunders,** Canada's Wheat King p. 218
78. Norma **Shearer,** Silent Silver Screen Star Who was a Gold Mine for MGM's 'Talkies' p. 219
79. Joshua **Slocum,** 1st to Sail Around the World Alone p. 225
80. Louis **Slotin,** Tickling the Dragon's Tail p. 232
81. **'Snoopy'** was a Canadian … Roy Brown and Wop May p. 233
82. **Springhill,** Nova Scotia Greatest Endurance Feat in Canadian History p. 236
83. Sam **Steele,** Lion of the Yukon p. 242
84. William **Stephenson,** The Spy called 'Intrepid' p. 244
85. Dorothy **Stratton,** *'Playboy* Tragedy' p. 251
86. Maurice **Strong,** Custodian of the Planet p. 253
87. **Superlative Canadian Geography** p. 256
88. David **Suzuki,** Environmental Guru p. 260
89. Frederick 'Cyclone' **Taylor** p. 261
• **The Water Rats,** The Taking of the Scheldt Estuary p. 264
90. Sir John **Thompson,** Prime Minister who died in Queen Victoria's Castle p. 265
91. Ross **Tilley,** Guinea Pig Doctor p. 270
92. Pierre Elliott **Trudeau,** A Red Rose in His Lapel p. 274
93. Shania **Twain,** She is the One p. 277
94. Joseph Burr **Tyrrell,** Dinosaur Slayer p. 279
95. **Underground Railway,** Last Stop Canada p. 283
96. Marie Madeleine Jarret de **Vércheres,** Heroine of Castle Dangerous p. 286
97. James Morrow **Walsh,** Sitting Bull's Mentor North of the 'Medicine Line' p. 287
98. Angus **Walters,** Captain of the *Bluenose* p. 296
99. John **Ware,** Bronco Busting Cowboy p. 300
100. Mike **Weir,** Becoming a Master p. 310
101. Percy **Williams,** World's Fastest Man p. 311

My Poetry of Canada

From *Love Lane poetry from my heart and soul*

Canada 'The Promised Land p. 314
Christmas 1792 p. 315
Canada's Peace Poem p. 317
Hockey p. 319
How Steep the Price? p. 321
Yonder Hudson Bay p. 323
Oath to Canada p. 325

Bibliography p. 327

Pamela Anderson
Canada's Most Illustrious Beauty

Canada is the birthplace of many of the world's most beautiful women.

Pamela Anderson was born in Ladysmith, British Columbia on July 1, 1967 earning her the title 'The Centennial Baby' for which she received cash prizes and awards. Her father Barry was a furnace repairman and mother Carol was a waitress. The family moved to Comox, B.C., and a photographer captured her picture amongst a hundred other students. It was copyrighted and placed in all the libraries in British Columbia.

She had braces, excelled in sports and was called 'Rubber-Band' for her flexibility. Her favourite sport was volleyball and she loved to play the saxophone whenever she could. In her yearbook she aspired 'to be a California Beach Bum.'

In 1988, Pamela moved to Vancouver and was working as a fitness instructor when her close friends invited her to a CFL game. The Lions were playing the Toronto Argonauts in B.C. Place. Between plays Pam's bright smiling face was broadcast on the jumbotron screen and the stadium erupted! She was wearing a Labatt's T-shirt her friend had given her. She was soon modelling for Labatt's for their promotion *Blue Zone*, she became the 'Blue Girl' and her posters were plastered all over Canada in bars and restaurants.

Ken Honey, a freelance photographer, took a few pictures and convinced Pam to send them into *Playboy*, which he later did on her behalf. *Playboy* liked what they saw and Pam moved to Los Angeles in October of 1989. By November she was on the cover of *Playboy* for the first time.

She hit the television screen in 1991 as Lisa, the Tool Time Girl on *Home Improvement* with Tim Allen. She has experienced great popularity and really stole some hearts when she first appeared on *Baywatch* in 1998.

Apart from all the television and movie appearances, Pamela had time to fall in love with Tommy Lee, the drummer for Motley Crue. After meeting in a bar one night in 1995 he followed her to Cancun, Mexico and after four days of partying and courting they were married on the beach. When they returned to L.A. they had wedding rings tattooed on their fingers. Pamela's says Tommy's and vice versa.

Pushed to exhaustion filming *Baywatch* and *Barb Wire* she got pregnant for the first time but suffered a miscarriage and to make matters worse their honeymoon video was stolen.

She has two children with Tommy Brandon and Dylan. She claims to be a vegetarian and often speaks for People for the Ethical Treatment of Animals (P.E.T.A.).

As Queen of the cover of *Playboy* she has graced it no less than 12 times: November 1989, February '90, February '91, July '92, August '93, November '94, January '96, September '97, June '98, February '99, July 2001 and May 2004. She wrote a book called *Star* in 2005 that is published by Simon and Schuster. She has certainly got her share of publicity and attention in her short lifetime.

Janis Babson
Organ Donor Saint

In 1951 Janis Babson was born in Windsor, Nova Scotia. Her father Rudy, a Mountie, was transferred to RCMP headquarters in Ottawa when Janis was still a baby. They moved to the suburban area of City View.

This touching story began to unfold when Janis saw a television program during White Cane Week. She was very moved by the program, learning that eyes donated to the Eye Bank could give someone the 'gift of sight.' Tears welled up in Janis's eyes when she said, "Mom, when I die, I'm going to give my eyes to the Eye Bank."

Her mother, Rita, said, "That's very nice dear but you may change your mind when you grow up."

Janis excelled in school and although she was a normal child in most ways, she did possess a remarkable compassion for people and replied emphatically, "No I won't."

One afternoon in February Janis struggled along the road with a load of books. Rita looked closely at her child and was frightened by the pallor in her face. Rudy and Rita decided to take Janis to the doctor the next day.

The family physician, Dr. Whillans said to Janis, "Well young lady, is this a new way of getting out of school?"

Janis answered light-heartedly, "No, it's a new way for Daddy to get out of work."

Rudy remembers that moment vividly for it was the last honest laugh he had for a long time. The doctor examined Janis and took a blood sample. The doctor stiffened when he saw the high white blood cell count under the microscope. A more thorough examination was needed so Janis was booked into the Ottawa Civic Hospital and came under the care of one of Canada's leading haematologists, Dr. Alexander English.

Janis laughed about being a 'pin-cushion' for the many blood samples they needed. It became apparent to Dr. English he had the terrible task of telling the Babsons that little Janis had a sub acute form of leukemia that was always fatal.

For some reason the bone marrow in Janis' body had gone berserk and were producing leukocytes, white blood cells, at a fantastic rate. The cells spread throughout her body invading healthy tissues and breaking them down. Drugs such as methotextrate and steroids helped to slow down the wild leukocyte multiplication. After a month in hospital receiving treatment, Janis was ready to go home but unknown to Janis she was only on a short-term loan to her family. The things Rita and Rudy had always meant to do 'sometime' with the children, they now did, for 'sometime' had arrived.

Janis went back to school but the Babsons decided not to tell her about her leukemia. They gave Janis anything she wanted. They went to Disneyland, camping, movies, in fact - Janis's wish was their command. Every Thursday at about eleven o'clock she would burst into the clinic - like a ray of sunshine. She gained weight and seemed so healthy. She was so concerned about her mom and dad that she decided to serve them breakfast in bed one Saturday. This became a weekly occurrence thereafter.

Brave Janis had a smile for everybody but she was racked with pain as the rioting cells attacked her spine. Massive radiation treatments left her crippled and the end was very near at hand.

One morning Janis learned the truth when a young intern and a nurse new to the floor came to her room. The doctor asked gaily, "What's wrong with you my pretty?"

Before Janis could answer the nurse read from her chart book, "She has leukemia." The intern flashed a furious look but the damage was done.

That afternoon Janis confronted her mother. Rita stood ashen-faced and felt like fleeing but said, "How would you feel if you did have leukemia? Would it frighten you?"

Janis shook her head. "If that is what I have, I've been praying so hard to get better and I always wondered why I didn't. Now I know, because God didn't mean for me to get better. He wants me."

All these months Rita had steeled herself to see Janis through this moment. Now the moment was here and Janis was seeing her through it.

On Saturday May 6, 1961 Janis told her mother she wanted to make a will. "People do that before they die, right?" Janis prepared for her last journey by giving her worldly possessions to those she loved. She included her classmate Elizabeth Hays who challenged her for top honours and even included Ricky Lewis who chased her home one-day after school. The last item was her wish to give her eyes to the Eye Bank.

Through her last days Janis always carried her rosary beads. She prayed to Sister Therese whom she was sure was waiting for her. She was not known to cry but when the pain was very intense, like when they had to stick a needle into her hipbone to draw bone marrow, she would pray loudly crying out to God.

She briefly went into a coma and when she came out of it she asked her mother if she had something for her. Her mother couldn't think what that could be. Janis asked if she had to sign something from the Eye Bank. This forced her mother to go and look for a form. Janis went into another coma but when she came out again her mother had the form and Janis signed it.

On May 12, 1961 Janis got all dressed up with a ribbon in her hair. She was ready but wanted her mom and dad to stay close by. She drifted in and out of coma. In the late afternoon, as though struggling out of a bad dream, she opened her eyes and spoke clearly, "Daddy! Have you made the arrangements with the Eye Bank?"

About 9:00 P.M. Janis suddenly struggled to sit up and stared straight ahead. "Oh, is this heaven. Mommy! Daddy! Come quick!" Rita and Rudy were amazed by her sudden strength. Then there was none at all. She was on her journey and by 9:25 so were her eyes.

One of Janis's best friends Tricia Kennedy missed the funeral for they had recently moved away to Chalk River, Ontario. A local reporter asked some questions of this newly arrived family for a meet-your-neighbour page. He asked if they knew any interesting stories to round out the article. Tricia piped up and told about her very best friend, Janis Babson, who died of leukemia and had pledged her eyes to the Eye Bank. Tim Burke of the *Ottawa Journal* picked up the story and the day after it ran, 27 Ottawans signed pledges donating their eyes, a one-day record. It was almost immediately broken when, at a Kinsmen meeting, 50 members spontaneously bequeathed their eyes. Not long after 175 Mounties and their families did the same including the entire Babson family. From 1959 until Janis' death, 644 eyes were promised and in the two years after her death 1,170 pledges were taken, most of them in the Ottawa area. It is a shame that the story of such a precious little heroine was kept an Ottawa secret.

Finally, in Toronto, a retired druggist Abe Silverman read about Janis. He was so moved that he established the Janis Babson Memorial Endowment Fund at Hebrew University in Jerusalem for prizes in leukemia research.

Frederick Banting
Miracle Man

Frederick Banting was born on November 14, 1891 in Alliston, Ontario. He made good progress through school and was in medical school in 1915 when World War I shattered his world. He rushed off to enlist as a private. When they found out he was a medical student they ordered him back to the University of Toronto to get his medical degree. In 1916 he enlisted as a doctor.

He served in the army corps of the 44th battalion. Shells burst and men stared from the mud of Cambrai where limbs and bodies of fallen soldiers lay everywhere. Frederick said of the war, "It was like the ingenious technique of a Great Surgeon gone mad." He honed his surgical skills in the line of battle.

One day a shell burst nearby knocked him out and pelted him with shrapnel. When he woke, he was not in a trench but in a hospital. Around him men lay wounded. He felt the throb of pain. He heard the sound of the army doctor saying, "Hello, son. We've got to operate."

He turned to the doctor and said, "You're not going to take my arm away from me. Not if I can help it, sir!"

"We must amputate, my boy. Otherwise we may not be able to save your life."

"Oh no, not my arm. I'll risk the chance of dying. You see doctor, I'm a surgeon myself and I need all the limbs God gave me for service," Banting cried.

The doctor shrugged his shoulders and moved on to other beds of wounded soldiers. Banting risked the chance of dying and lived. He had another chapter to add to this fascinating story.

He returned home after the war and began work at the Toronto Children's Hospital as a resident surgeon. He tried to set up his own practice in London, Ontario but in the first 30 days only one patient called and his income for the month was 4 dollars. He accepted a position in the Western Ontario Medical School as a 'part time' lecturer in pharmacology. One day he was asked to give a lecture about diabetes. He researched the subject but found that for the millions of sufferers the result was always fatal for this was a disease with no known remedy.

What he observed was that patients who died from diabetes had a shrivelled up pancreas with 'island spots' floating in it. He felt that these islands contained the secret. He went to his superior Professor Macleod and asked if he could carry out some experiments. His laboratory was little more than a bench in a room. He was provided with some dogs for the experiments. To aid in his research he was given a young assistant with an aptitude in chemistry, Charles Best. Banting would do the surgical work and Best would analyse the blood and urine.

His theory was that the island cells supply the fuel that burns up the excess sugar in the body. When this fuel fails, the sugar multiplies and the body becomes diabetic. He operated and tied off the pancreases of 10, 20, 50, up to 90 dogs with no results. When they experimented on their 92nd dog a miracle happened. In this dog Banting removed the pancreas and reattached all the tubes with no pancreas at all. In a very short time the dog went into convulsions. Soon the dog would be in a coma. In a flash of brilliance Banting grabbed a syringe and went to the dog's pancreas on the bench and inserted the syringe tip into the 'island cells' to extract some of the fluid from each cell. He took this fluid and injected it into the convulsing dog. In a few hours the dog was on his feet, barking and wagging his tail. They were jubilant. The 'island' extract was the substance they were looking for. The dog died 20 days later and the miracle cure remained elusive.

The substance in the island cells appeared to be the remedy for diabetics but it was unattainable in large quantities. Having been born on a farm Banting realized that these juices could be extracted from slaughtered cattle and from newborn calves. He found that given enough extract, they named isletin, a dog could be kept living for an indefinite time. There remained one single question to be answered, would isletin work on human beings.

A friend and fellow medical student named Joe Gilchrist was dying from this disease. One day Banting invited him to his laboratory. He injected some of the isletin into his friend. They conducted some experiments but his blood sugar changed little. Banting could not bear to look at his friend. He gave Best some instructions and left for his farmhouse. It was here that the telephone rang. An excited Joe Gilchrist on the other end said, "Right after you left yesterday I started to breathe easily. My head cleared. My appetite returned. Today, to be sure, my legs are dragging again. I'm tired but I'm not worried, I'm coming back for another shot of the extract…the elixir of life…"

It was renamed insulin and though there was a shortage of it, the life giving substance was miraculous. Diabetics in comas could be completely revived and restored to complete health. Banting's discovery saved the lives of some notable men, King George V, George Eastman and H.G. Wells. Dr. George Minot was spared and he went on to discover an equally great gift of mercy, the treatment for the fatal liver disease, Pernicious anaemia.

In 1923 Frederick Banting and John Macleod received the Nobel Prize in Medicine. As soon as Banting received the prize he sent half to his assistant, Charles Best. In the telegram that accompanied the cheque he wrote: "You are with me in my share - always."

In 1924 Frederick married Marion Robertson and they had one son the named William. They would later divorce

Banting lived a peaceful life of glory. He took up painting and escaped the little cubicle of a laboratory. In 1939 he married Henrietta Ball but later in the year all this came to a sudden halt when World War II broke out. He went to enlist again and asked the officer in charge, Colonel Rae, to assign him to a medical unit with the lowest rank possible. Rae gave him the rank of captain. He protested asking to be a private so Rae raised him to the rank of major. He protested violently. Rae threatened to raise him to rank of colonel so Banting consented to serve as a major. "A man can try his best," he said, "even in an exalted post."

He flung himself at the enemy and became dedicated to the war effort. On February 21, 1941 he was flying to London when the plane crashed in Newfoundland and though he did not die upon impact he died shortly afterwards. A great man left this world a better place to live.

Captain Robert A. Bartlett
Arctic Adventurer

On August 15, 1875 Robert Abram was born to Mr. and Mrs. William J. Bartlett in Brigus along the shelter of Conception Bay in Britain's oldest colony, Newfoundland. He was one of eleven children.

In the little fishing village Bob soon learned to sail and fish. Usually in the month of May the whole family moved to Turnavik, an island about 800 kilometres, along the Labrador coast. It was here that the Bartlett's did their cod fishing.

His parents, devoutly religious folks, had decided that Bob should become a minister and sent him to the Methodist College at St. John's. Robert's heart was in the sea, a fact that his parents soon came to realize and by the age of seventeen Bob was given command of the schooner on the summer expedition to Turnavik.

Robert was not merely content to command a fishing vessel, he wanted to get the papers as a Master of British ships, so he could command any ship, anywhere. At eighteen he launched upon a six-year period of training. His first voyage as an apprentice took him from St. John's to Pernambuco in South America and ended in a shipwreck on the south coast of Newfoundland on the return voyage. That was but one of twelve shipwrecks which he experienced in his fifty years on the sea.

In time he became a master mariner. As fate would have it, at this time Admiral Peary, who later conquered the North Pole, was going north on one of his expeditions. Robert was persuaded to go along as mate by his uncle, the commander of the *Windward*, John Bartlett. The journey made him a lover of the Arctic. In later journeys to the Arctic he set himself to studying the ways of the North so that he would be as capable on the ice as in command of a ship. He learned how to survive in the cold with the help of an Inuit guide. He ate raw seal meat and found out how to mix blubber with his diet so he could stand the cold better. He could drive a dog team forty to ninety kilometres per day, learned to avoid avalanche areas and how to find his way through drifting snow.

When Admiral Peary went to conquer the North Pole in 1908-09 Captain Bob Bartlett went along as commander of his ship the *Roosevelt*. It was due to Bartlett's skill as a navigator that the ship was taken far enough north for Peary to make the rest of the journey with a dog team across the ice. The Captain broke trail for Peary to within two hundred and thirty-two kilometres of the Pole. Here Admiral Peary sent Bartlett back and he was not present on April 6, 1909 for the Polar conquest.

Bartlett captained the *Karluk* when the Canadian government sent an expedition into the Arctic. In January 1914 the *Karluk* was caught and crushed by ice near Wrangel Island, 600 kilometres north of the Arctic Circle. With the ship lost, Bartlett set out with 25 members of the expedition and succeeded in crossing the ice to the island in about a month of difficult and dangerous travel. He then took his Inuit guide and set out to find a means of rescue. They crossed three hundred kilometres of swiftly flowing ice to Siberia and over eight hundred more to Alaska. He secured a rescue ship and returned to Wrangel Island to rescue the remaining eleven survivors only eight months later. The Royal Geographic Society honoured him for conspicuous bravery and leadership.

He sailed the Arctic from 1926-41 in his own schooner *Effie M. Morrissey*. By the time Robert Bartlett died on April 28, 1946 the aeroplane had come into use as an instrument of Arctic exploration and rescue. Captain Bob was one of the last of the older school explorers. He had more than forty Polar voyages to his credit and over 320,000 kilometres of sailing in the Arctic.

Alexander Graham Bell
Inventor Best Known for the Telephone

Alexander Melville Bell fell in love and married Eliza Grace Symonds. On March 3, 1847 Alexander Graham Bell was born in Edinburgh, Scotland. At eleven years old Aleck invented a tool that cleaned the tough husks from wheat kernels. He found an old vat with a rotating paddle wheel inside. He lined the vat with a rough surface and found the husks were effectively removed. The vat was still in use fifty years later.

His grandfather taught speech and was a superb elocutionist and wrote a book called *The Standard Elocutionist*. As a boy Aleck taught their Skye terrier to speak by manipulating his tongue and jaw. The dog was quite a novelty in the neighbourhood. His father also was interested in speech and perfected his Visible Speech system in 1864. His mother was a painter of miniature portraits and loved to play the piano.

Aleck began to suffer from headaches and sleeplessness that would affect him for his entire life. He became interested in a young lady named Marie Eccleston whom he proposed to but she rejected him.

In 1867 his younger brother Edward was found to have tuberculosis a common ailment in the crowded, smog-chocked cities. He died in 1867 and then in 1870 Melly (Melville), his older brother died from the same disease. His mother and father begged Alex, who was also frail in health, to come with them to Canada and in August 1870 they arrived in Brantford, Ontario.

Aleck landed a job teaching at the Boston School for Deaf Mutes and with the success he had teaching Visible Speech he landed a position as a professor of vocal physiology at Boston University.

He was soon teaching a young lady by the name of Mabel Hubbard and she made astounding progress.

Aleck investigated pitch and found each vowel had a unique rate of vibration. His experiments duplicated the work of the famous German scientist Hermann von Helmholtz. He concluded from the diagrams that Hermann had transmitted vowel sounds through a wire. It was a mistake but led him to believe that sounds could be transmitted electrically that led him down the path of experimentation that led to the invention of the telephone.

By 1872 the limitations of the telegraph were clear. It was obvious to inventors like Thomas Edison that sending multiple messages through the telegraphy would improve communication and make the inventor rich. There was no better place than Boston for the city hummed with ideas, inventors and enthusiasm. Another inventor, a dentist named Mahlon Loomis, was awarded U.S. patent No. 129,971 and was hailed as the father of wireless.

Aleck taught during the day and experimented at night. He found that many messages could be sent through the telegraph using different pitches. At his parent's home in the summer of 1874 he was trying to improve the phonautograph that drew shapes of sounds by tracing their vibrations with a pen. It would help him discover the principle of the telephone. He wrote, "If I could make a current of electricity vary in intensity precisely as the air varies in density during the production of sound, I should be able to transmit speech telegraphically."

Aleck suggested that the complex rising and falling human voice could be converted into a continuous rising and falling undulatory electric current. The father of his star pupil Gardiner Greene Hubbard helped fund supplies and other resources. He was a patent attorney and he wrote to Bell on November 24, 1874, "Whatever you may recall any fact connected with your invention jot it down on paper as time will be essential to us, and the more things actually performed by you at an earlier date the better for our case. You must not neglect an instant of your work, so that we may file the application for a patent as soon as possible."

A key player was Thomas Sanders, a merchant, who supplied the investment capital.

Thomas Watson became Aleck's assistant in 1875. He was a skilled craftsman and electrician. The two men perfected Bell's vibratory circuit breaker, a key component in his design for a message recorder. He filed for a patent on April 6, 1875 and was issued Patent No. 161,739. His application was suspended pending another patent application from Elisha Gray that conflicted with Bell's claim.

Hubbard responded reassuringly, "You are...worth more than all the other men put together - for they stumble on their inventions - you work on them scientifically - you will come out ahead yet so do not be discouraged or disheartened."

Bell got an audience with Professor Joseph Henry, the nation's most respected theorist on the properties of electricity at the Smithsonian Institution. After seeing Aleck's device he advised him to postpone publishing and work out the difficulties. He said, "Get it." Bell renewed his efforts and forged ahead with revived determination.

He was competing with other notable inventors. He tried dozens of combinations of electric current and materials to transmit speech.

Progress was painfully slow and failed experiments filled notebooks but progress was being made.

The Western Union President William Orton invited young Bell to New York to demonstrate his multiple telegraphy system. His transmissions went like clockwork but Orton disliked and distrusted Hubbard and would not make a deal. The next day Bell returned feeling he had been had. He demanded his equipment back and accused Orton of spying and that the entire exercise had been to benefit his rival Elisha Gray whose multiple telegraph system was in the back room.

It seemed unfathomable to Bell that people in power wanted only the ability to send more Morse Code messages through a cable and seemed uninterested in voice transmission. Never the less there was a great deal of money to be made for the person who could send multiple messages through an iron line.

On June 2, 1875 Aleck and Watson were 'tuning' the reeds in the multiple telegraph transmitters and receivers when an accident happened. The reeds were thin metal strips made to produce a single, pure tone. Watson plucked the reed on the receiver and Aleck heard a very faint sound coming from the receiver. Aleck knew instantly the reed could induce the undulatory current needed to transmit the complex sounds of the human voice. Because of his prefect musical pitch and sensitive hearing Bell heard what most people would have missed. He quickly sketched out a machine he called the gallows telephone. Watson soon built a pair of them. Though they couldn't carry conversation they did transmit complex sounds.

Bell was ecstatic and wrote his parents and Hubbard. His parents were unimpressed and Hubbard dismissed it altogether encouraging him to concentrate on multiple telegraphy.

By this time Aleck was smitten with Mabel Hubbard and he told his parents and hers. Both families objected to the union. His parents were concerned about the young ladies deafness and were reassured she was not born deaf but lost it after a bout of scarlet fever as a young child. Her parents thought Aleck was too old though he was only twenty-eight at the time. They thought he was ten years older than he was. Aleck was asked not to startle her by his confession and to wait a year.

The very day he told his parents Bell finished building the first two telephones he designed. No batteries were needed and the vibration of the sound itself was enough energy to induce the current. July 10, 1875 Bell spoke, sang and shouted into the device while Watson listened downstairs. He heard a voice that was muffled but unmistakably human. Bell wrote his father, "When sounds are received upon another stretched membrane - instead of a steel spring which can only vibrate to certain pitches - it is highly probable that the 'timbre' of the voice may be perceived. I feel that I am on the threshold of a great discovery."

Mabel was not that smitten with Aleck and she wrote, "...we should not speak of love. It is too sacred and delicate a subject to be talked about much and till I know what it means myself I cannot understand or fully sympathize with the feeling. Only if you ever again need my friendly help and sympathy it is yours." Taking heart that she had not completely rejected him he turned his attention to inventing with a new purpose - to earn enough money to get married.

Bell made a deal with a Toronto businessman and newspaper publisher George Brown to file a patent in England in return for a share of the rights. Brown sailed for Britain on January 25, 1876. Brown was advised that Bell's patent was worthless, lost interest and did not file the application. He did not inform Bell of his decision.

Aleck's mentor Mr. Hubbard insisted he patent his device. On February 14, 1876, he beat Elisha Gray's cabeat patent application by two hours. The Examiner discovered Mr. Gray's application and judgement was delayed. Bell was told by the Examiner the point at issue. It was how Gray made a sudden change in the intensity of the current without actually breaking the circuit and the Examiner thought this constituted an undulatory current. Bell explained it did not and even if it did he had mentioned the same thing in his application filed in February of 1875. The Examiner handed Bell the papers and he was able to point out the exact passage. Since the Examiner thought this was an important case it had to go to Washington.

Aleck picked up a point from Gray's caveat that featured a variable-resistance liquid transmitter and undulating current for voice transmission. Bell returned to Boston to resume his experiments.

His sweetheart Mabel responded in wonder at the course of events and convinced Alec to drop the 'k' from his name.

His patent was approved March 3 and issued on March 7, 1876. Bell would have exclusive rights to make and sell telephones in the United States for the next 19 years. It was an invention that would change the world but would require millions of dollars to develop and protect.

March 10 with the newly constructed liquid transmitter Alec said, "Mr. Watson, come here, I want to see you." These were the first words ever spoken on the device.

That night Alec wrote to his father, "Articulate speech was transmitted intelligibly this afternoon. I have constructed a new apparatus operated by the human voice. It is not of course complete yet - but some sentences were understood this afternoon…I feel that I have at last struck the solution of a great problem - and the day is coming when telegraph wires will be laid on to houses just like water or gas - and friends converse with each other without leaving home."

May 25 Bell demonstrated a functional telephone for the first time in public at the Massachusetts Institute of Technology. June 25 Bell demonstrated his telephone at the International Exhibition in Philadelphia's Fairmont Park. Even Elisha Gray was astounded and couldn't believe the voice was transmitted electrically.

The first long distance phone call was between Brantford and Paris, Ontario. William Orton dismissed the bell telephone as a toy. Western Union was offered the patent rights for $100,000 but turned down the most profitable invention in recorded history. Orton decided to steal the invention and told Tomas Edison to focus on telephones. Edison made a new transmitter that had a carbon piece secured to a metal diaphram and it was much louder and clearer.

Thanks to intervention by Mabel's mother on Thanksgiving Day November 25, 1876 they became engaged much to Alec's delight.

By July 4, 1877 there were at least 200 telephones in service. By August 1 the figure had risen to 778. By the end of August, three homes were hooked up on a single wire – an early party line. Bell's father connected the Prime Minister's home with the Governor General's.

July 11, 1877 nineteen year old Mabel Hubbard married thirty-year old Alexander Graham Bell. They took a honeymoon to Niagara Falls and stopped over in Brantford and Mabel met Eliza for the first time. In August they traveled to England and Queen Victoria was given a demonstration. They stayed in England where their first baby Elsie May Bell was born on May 10, 1878.

Western Union was using Edison's carbon-button transmitter and Bell Telephones stock prices stayed low at $50. Western Union were buying Bell stocks and they were the bully on the block. A patent infringement suit was set to go to trial in 1879. Bell's testimony was critical. His photographic memory coupled with his natural speaking ability made him a terrific witness. The death knell was struck in the form of a letter from Elisha Gray to Bell that gave him credit for inventing the telephone. Western Union decided the risks were too great to continue its defence. By October 10, 1879 Bell shares were selling for $500. Bell Telephone held a successful monopoly with fourteen years left to run.

Mabel gave birth to a second baby girl Alec wanted to name 'Photophone' after his latest invention. They settled on Marian though they called her Daisy.

On July 2, 1881 Charles Guiteau shot President James Garfield in the back. Bell was working on a metal detector and was summoned to find the bullet lodged in the president's back. Alec was unsuccessful and due to so many doctors investigating the wound with unwashed hands he died after seventy-nine days of suffering. Later in the year their son Edward was born prematurely and died several hours later.

In 1878 Bell wrote to Hubbard about Edison's phonograph, "It is a most astonishing thing to me that I could possibly have let this invention slip through my fingers…"

Bell began to experiment with a cylinder of wax that was an improvement over Edison's work with tinfoil. In the end Edison had to buy the rights to Bell's patent to develop the phonograph commercially.

For a holiday and to get away from his celebrity and fame the Bell's traveled on the *Hanoverian* to Nova Scotia and Bras d'Or Lakes. The ship wrecked in the fog but all were saved. The *HMS Tenedos* took the stranded passengers to the city of St. John's, Newfoundland.

Thomas Watson would accumulate sixty patents in telephony during his Bell Telephone career. He developed a ringer. By 1881 there were 132,600 phones. There were many problems like crosstalk and interference from various electrical sources like lightning, trolley cars and an expanding electrical power grid. For the time being reception was poor until lines were rerouted and insulated and more metallic circuits were installed.

Alec even caught his father-in-law Gardiner Hubbard siphoning assets and power into his own company. He sent Gardiner a blistering letter accusing him of stealing from his own grandchildren.

In 1882 Bell was working on a respirator he called the 'vacuum jacket.' The device revived a sheep that had drowned in some water and was unconscious. Philip Drinker developed the iron lung on the same principle in 1928.

In 1882 the company heard about Thomas Doolittle's new hard-drawn copper wire. It was strong enough to hang from telephone poles and was a much better conductor than iron lines. Unfortunately the local Indian tribes admired the shiny copper that glowed in the sun and they took the lines right off the poles to make jewellery. They replaced the lines with copper dipped in tar and they remained intact.

Long distance calls became more profitable as the customers were charged by the call. In 1885 American Bell spun off American

Telephone and Telegraph (AT&T) to build a national long-distance network. More powerful long-distance transmitters were developed.

In late summer of 1885 the Bells returned to Baddeck and rented a cottage in Crescent Grove. They were looking for land to purchase. They purchased a place they would call 'Beinn Bhreagh' or 'Beautiful Mountain' in Gaelic. Alec loved the solitude and fresh air. The children loved the free, wild life and bathing in the lake.

Bell was also very involved in the progress of the *National Geographic*. He supported it and helped it along the way. By 1905 the *Geographic* no longer needed Bell's annual $1,200 contribution as the magazine was making a surplus. The non-profit society would serve as a model for such publications as *Smithsonian, Audubon, National Wildlife* and *Natural History*.

Alec and Elsie traveled widely and wherever he traveled Bell took special pleasure in visiting schools for the deaf and discussing teaching methods with teachers.

When rates were raised by the Bell company and a per call charge was levied there was an eighteen month boycott by many users that ended May 12, 1888. By 1893 there were only 230,000 telephones. With the patents running out many companies were prepared to enter the markets ignored by the Bell company. They would cut prices and compete for customers bringing phones to the farmers and middle class. Alexander Graham Bell's prophesy was about to come true.

In 1889 Almon Strowger made a mark on the industry by inventing the dial telephone. In 1897 Milo Kellogg introduced the Kellog Switchboard. The job of telephone operators, a vital, respected cultural link was threatened but it would take years to eliminate them. A patent in 1899 on a device called a loading coil extended the range of long-distance calls. By 1905 eavesdropping had become practically a national sport and there was no privacy in the system.

November 1, 1901 Bell's first grandchild arrived and was named for his great-grandfather Melville Bell. Eventually he had nine grandchildren who adored him. He always had a jar of hard candy on hand for his beloved children.

By 1907 there were 6,118,578 customers. Dial phones sold by the Automatic Electric Company were the rage and it was one of the first changes Theodore Roosevelt made in the White House when he took office.

On October 23, 1900 Elsie Bell married Gilbert Grosvenor in London. Her husband built the *National Geographic Society* and as the 'first lady of geography', Elsie, read hundreds of manuscripts and examined tens of thousands of photographs.

Bell was fascinated by the prospect of flight. He would follow the developments closely and would be one of the first to congratulate the Wright Brothers on their successful flight in 1903. Alec continued to experiment with flight believing he could make it safer. At Brenn Bhreagh his kites grew larger and some were so large they actually could lift a person off the ground.

A young lad that was always around the Bell residence named Douglas McCurdy exploded a firecracker made with his father's gunpowder. Doctors feared he would lose an eye and they wanted to amputate his right hand that became gangrenous. Bell persuaded the doctors to postpone surgery and the lad recovered saving his hand. McCurdy invited a friend named Casey Baldwin to the Bell residence and he hit it off right away with the Bells.

Alec was fascinated with the tetrahedral design in architecture and built an observation tower on a near by hill. The triangular design would be used in space-frame architecture and offered advantages in constructing lightweight flying machines.

Bell purchased a sixteen-horsepower motor from Glenn Curtiss. Alec found the motor underpowered and overweight. He challenged Curtiss to design and build a larger engine. He soon had a twenty-horsepower engine and joined the group of aeronautic experts Bell was assembling. A U.S. Army lieutenant named Thomas Selfridge joined them. Elsie thought these young engineers would help her husband in his quest. She provided $20,000 in capital and the men formed the Aerial Experiment Association (AEA) with Bell serving as chairman without salary.

The AEA developed their first plane they named *Red Wing* because its wings were covered with red silk. On March 17, 1908 Casey Baldwin climbed aboard and the blood-red machine climbed ten feet into the air and flew 319 feet and the assembled crowd witnessed the first public flight of an airplane in North America. Five days later they took the plane up for another flight. It was caught by a side wind, crashed and was irreparably damaged.

By May 14, 1908 they had another plane ready for trial. The wings were covered with white muslin and they named it *White Wing*. It had ailerons and a three-wheeled gear for landings and take offs. May 18 Casey Baldwin made the first flight. A few days later Curtiss flew up to 1,017 feet. May 23 McCurdy crashed the plane but walked away uninjured.

The AEA built their next aircraft they named the *June Bug*. Glenn Curtis was the principal designer and on July 4, 1908 he flew 5,090 feet on his second try in upstate New York. They won a prize put up by the *Scientific American*. Bell's daughter Daisey exclaimed, "…the actual sight of a man flying through the air was thrilling to a degree I can't express. We all lost our heads and shouted and I cried and everyone cheered and clapped and engines tooted." The *June Bug* would fly successfully 150 times without crashing.

September 17, 1908 Thomas Selfridge accompanied Orville Wright in a flight. There was a loud crack and a piece of the propeller blade flew off. Unbalanced the propeller cut a wire to the rudder and Orville lost control of the plane. It did a nose dive and hit the parade ground. Orville was badly hurt and Selfridge never regained consciousness. He died a few hours later the first person to die in the crash of a powered aircraft.

The AEA built its forth and final airplane designed by Douglas McCurdy. It was covered in a new silver-coloured coating used for weather balloons so it was called the *Silver Dart*. On January 9, 1909 it lifted off the ice at Baddeck Bay and 150 townspeople stared in disbelief. It reached thirty feet and flew at forty miles an hour. It was the first powered flight in Canada. After there was a celebration with tea, coffee and Bell's favourite drink watered-down raspberry vinegar made from wild raspberries from Beinn Bhreagh. The AEA had fulfilled it historic objective and was disbanded March 31, 1909.

Curtiss would build a new plane called the *Gold Bug*. He competed with leading European aviators as well as the Wright entrée for the Gorden Bennett Trophy before a huge crowd of 200,000 at Rheims, France and won.

In 1914 the Wright brothers sued Curtiss to prevent him from building airplanes without paying them a royalty. Though Bell supported Curtiss he refused to take an official position.

On August 16, 1912 Lee de Forest, Ban Etten and Logwood stumbled upon a circuit that was revolutionary. They looped the signal through the amplifier several times each time noting an increase in its output. It would eventually revolutionize electronics strengthening all kinds of weak signals making them loud enough to hear thousands of miles away. De Forest demonstrated his new amplifier to Western Union and Bell Laboratory on October 30 and 31, 1912.

Harold Arnold, a Bell engineer, perfected the amplifier using newly designed German vacuum pumps to remove excess gas from de Forest's Audion tubes making them more reliable. The electronic telephone repeater was sufficiently powerful and reliable to make a transcontinental telephone line possible. On July 17, 1914 the line was completed when the wires were spliced together at Wendover, Utah on the Nevada border. The federal government collaborated with the formation of a telephone monopoly heralding the end of two and three telephone companies that made communication fraught with petty rivalries. This would lead to a universal telephone service.

At 4:30 P.M-1:30 San Francisco time on January 25, 1915 Alexander Graham Bell picked up the telephone in New York and used the greeting he always preferred, "Hoy, hoy, Mr. Watson are you there? Do you hear me?"

On the other end his one time assistant Thomas Watson replied, "Yes Mr. Bell, I hear you perfectly. Do you hear me well?"

"Yes your voice it perfectly distinct. It is as clear as if you were here in New York instead of being more than three thousand miles away. You remember, Mr. Watson, that evening, thirty-eight years ago when we conversed through a telephone on a real line for the first time?"

The spliced a replica of the 1875 membrane telephone into the circuit and continued their conversation. Recounting the historic event of March 10, 1876 Bell spoke the words, "Mr. Watson, come here. I want you."

Watson replied, "It would take me a week to get to you this time."

President Woodow Wilson came on the line from Washington, D.C. and congratulated the men. Every newspaper carried the story of the historic conversation.

A call from New York to San Francisco for three minutes cost $20.70. The service was soon extended north and south. Theodore Vail convinced the country that it was fitting and proper to have a telephone monopoly again.

In his declining year Bell's energy never waned. He explored ideas in energy conservation, salt-water distillation, solar heating and wrote about the threat of global warming which he named the 'greenhouse effect.' He encouraged progress in woman's suffrage and civil rights. He supported Maria Montessori and designed experiments to teach science to school-aged children. Her philosophy of teaching appealed to Bell for she encouraged her students to learn for themselves.

July 12, 1913 Bell opened the 'Children's Laboratory' in a Beinn Bhreagh warehouse. He argued, "The system of giving out a certain amount of work which must be carried through in a given space of time, and putting children into orderly rows of desks and compelling them to absorb just so much intellectual nourishment, whether they were ready for it or not..." was not efficient. He preferred to let children experiment and come up with their own answers. He felt it "...develops their reasoning powers and arouses their interest."

His wife became the president of the Montessori Educational Association and conveyed the message of liberty to mothers and children. Other members of the family thought the elders knew best and children should not be left to just dabble with their learning experience.

The Montessori method declined and came under attack. It would be years before it was rediscovered.

In July 1912 Casey Baldwin got the first full-sized hydrofoil off the water at Baddeck Bay. It was called the *HD-1* and it reached 30 miles per hour. By 1915 the *HD-3* reached a speed of 50 miles per hour.

Alec hated to waste time or be disturbed when thinking. He constructed a system of ropes on his sleeping porch that enabled him to open and close windows without having to get out of bed. He even taught his favourite horse, Champ, to go automatically to the laboratory if he clapped once and to return home if he clapped twice.

In Washington the hot, muggy weather was unbearable for the Scotsman. In the attic he had a tank constructed that he had filled with ice. A canvas windpipe led down to his study and his 'ice stove' made his environment quite comfortable and he used the cooler for many years.

Mabel was a devoted wife who managed the family and finances. She knew his strengths and weaknesses and understood him well. Next to her the person closest to the inventor was his valet and butler Charles Thompson. He was a man of colour who was employed after a fire in the household. Charles sorted through Bell's precious papers and organized them so well Alec hired him permanently and he remained with the family for thirty-five years until Bell's death.

Charles was so highly respected he got married on the Bell estate and over the course of his employment was treated with dignity. When he was discriminated against in Baddeck, a large meeting was held and he was soon told that there shall not "...be a coloured line of this sort in Canada."

Another employee, a maid named Maria Fortune, was told by her abusive, alcoholic husband to quit her job. Her husband took it to court. The matter was eventually settled and the family helped Maria get a divorce. She remained a devoted employee long after Alec's death.

With the opening of World War I Bell converted his property into a place where they built lifeboats destroying the natural beauty of the area in the eyes of his wife.

On October 24, 1917 Brantford, Ontario unveiled an elaborate monument to Bell. He said, "I came to Brantford in 1870 to die, having been given only six months to live....(I) conceived (the telephone) in Brantford in 1874 and (it) was born in Boston in 1875."

In 1920 Bell returned to Edinburgh, Scotland and was celebrated from one end of the country to the other. By 1922 there were 14,346,701 phones in use in the U.S. connected by 37,265,528 miles of wire and generated $553,263,801 in revenue.

Alexander Graham Bell had been diagnosed earlier in his life with diabetes. Now it advance to pernicious anemia that immobilized him. In the early hours of August 2, 1922 Mabel sat holding his hand when he quietly passed away.

The news quietly filtered out and condolences flooded in from around the world. At Baddeck the switchboard was kept open round the clock for three days to handle the huge volume of incoming messages. The American Telephone and Telegraph Company sent a large wreath of laurel (for victory), wheat (for the gathering harvest) and roses (for greatness and sweetness). Furthermore there was a telegram stating that on the day of Bell's funeral service that AT&T in North America would be silent for one minute to honour Bell's passing.

Interestingly enough a Canadian named Frederick Banting was on the verge of cracking the mystery of diabetes with his discovery of insulin.

Bell's beloved wife Mabel died from cancer on January 3, 1923.

Beothuk
Lost Civilization ... Lost Peoples

The Beothuk were native to Newfoundland and it is speculated that they numbered from 2,000 to 5,000. Their natural enemies were the Micmac and Labrador Inuit. They had friendly relationships with the Naskapi and Montagnais in Québec. Due to a short growing season the Beothuk did not grow crops, instead they were semi-nomadic hunters and gatherers. Though there were caribou to hunt inland, the coast had the world's richest bounty of fish, seals and other seafood. They were skilled canoeists who hunted with harpoons.

They were known to love the colour red for they mixed red ochre with oil or animal grease and applied it to everything including their faces, hair, bodies, personal possessions and tools. The Micmac referred to them as Red Indians. It was more than likely due to this group that the Indians of North America became know as 'Red Skins.'

When the Vikings landed at L'Anse aux Meadows in Newfoundland in about 1,000 A.D. they encountered the Beothuk that they called Skraelings. It is thought that they probably traded with them and occasionally engaged in armed conflict. It is believed that as the climate became colder the Vikings pulled up their stakes and left. Another Viking tale is told about how the Skraelings harassed them in their canoes as the Norse men desperately pulled on their oars while trying to protect themselves from the barrage of arrows with their shields. One enterprising Beothuk fired his arrow high into the air. It cleared the phalanx of shields and smashed into the head of a Viking who eventually died. Such was the ending of the first foreign invasion into Beothuk lands.

Newfoundland was not rediscovered until John Cabot visited it in 1497. It took some time but by 1519 English and Portuguese fishermen started to make an annual summer pilgrimage to Canada's east coast. They began to come ashore to dry their fish on bawns. The fishing was so phenomenal that by 1578 more than 400 vessels congregated in the area. Some built rudimentary houses but no one was willing to stay over the winter. The Beothuk developed a pattern of avoidance during the summer months. When the Europeans left they would go and pilfer anything they found of value. Eventually they became more brazen and would steal anything that was not nailed down. This bred distrust, contempt and even hatred.

The French also claimed Newfoundland as a result of Jacques Cartier's 1535 explorations. Sir Humphrey Gilbert attempted to establish a colony in 1583. There were few objections except from France. In 1610 John Guy established a settlement at Conception Bay and managed to trade with the Beothuk. He arranged to meet them there in the future. Unfortunately he did not make arrangements with the next captain who was terrified when hundreds of 'Red Skins' surrounded the ship eager to trade. The captain fired his cannons at them and white men would never regain their trust. Settlements forced the Beothuk inland away from their rich fishing ground, but because they avoided the Europeans they avoided the ravages of epidemics that killed so many other tribes at this time.

The Treaty of Utrecht in 1713 gave Britain control of Newfoundland and the French began to build a fort in Cape Breton called Louisbourg. There was little mention of the Beothuk during this time as the French and English fought each other. As hostilities cooled the British settlements spread along the north coast cutting the natives off from the sea. The worst enemy was starvation and by 1768 it is believe there were fewer than 400 left. Most were confined along the Exploits River Valley on the north side of the island.

Relations worsened over the years. The Beothuk continued to steal from the invading settlements and in turn the settlers began to shoot them on sight like they were some kind of vermin. One detailed account tells how the crew of a fishing vessel weighed anchor in a cove where the Beothuk were washing their clothing. They began shooting the men, women and children who scrambled for their lives. One of the men said it was like shooting fish in a barrel. There were even some punitive expeditions into the interior.

In 1810 the British government issued an official proclamation protecting the Beothuk. In fact between 1819 and 1823 many British expeditions were led. One such venture saw the British taking several prisoners including Mary March and Nancy Shawnadithit. All prisoners perished except Nancy Shawnadithit. W.E. Cormack, who founded the Boeothick Institution, took the sole survivor, Shawnandithit, to his home in 1827. The government insisted that Nancy be returned to her tribe and that same year an extensive search for her kin was initiated but to no avail. Nancy was the last known member of her tribe. She died of tuberculosis June 6, 1829. Since this date no First Nations tribes have resided in Newfoundland.

Norman Bethune
Mobile Doctor of the People

Norman Bethune was born into a deeply religious family in Gravenhurst, Ontario on March 3, 1890. From an early age he showed intelligence, ambition, artistic skill, and an unwillingness to compromise against principles regardless of the consequences. As a student at the University of Toronto he began to demonstrate a compassion and commitment to helping the less fortunate and this trait would become a dominant feature in his work.

He interrupted his studies twice. In 1911-12 he worked as a lumberjack and at night taught the men labouring in the camp. In August 1914 he enlisted in the Canadian army and served as a stretcher-bearer in the First World War. In April of 1915 he was severely wounded in the leg by shrapnel in the Second Battle of Ypres. Following the six months it took to recover from his injury, he completed his medical degree. Before the war's end he returned to France as a medical officer with the Canadian airmen.

After the war he entered post-graduate studies in London, England and served at the famous Great Ormond Street Hospital for Sick Children. In 1922 he completed his extensive training in surgery at the Royal College of Surgeons in Edinburgh. It was there that he met Frances Campbell Penney. They were married in 1923. After an extensive honeymoon that lasted for six months the broke couple returned to America and Bethune opened a practice in Detroit, Michigan.

He faced mounting debts and an uncertain marriage. He tired easily and in the summer of 1924 was diagnosed with tuberculosis in both lungs. The finest sanatorium in Canada was Calydor located in his birthplace, Gravenhurst. He stayed there only a month before entering the Trudeau Sanatorium in Sarnac Lake, New York.

By this time Frances had decided to leave him. Still suffering from tuberculosis, for which rest was the only known cure, Bethune came across a little known and seldom-used treatment called artificial pneumothorax. It required inserting a needle into the chest cavity and pumping air into the collapsing lung. Bethune insisted the doctors try it on him. Miraculously it worked and on December 1, 1927 he left the sanatorium.

Dr. Edward Archibald, a pioneer in the struggle against tuberculosis, invited Bethune to Montreal's Royal Victoria Hospital. Archibald was a leading thoracic surgeon and Bethune became adept at this discipline even inventing a variety of surgical instruments that were widely used throughout North America. In time their once harmonious relationship became strained for Bethune could be impolite, arrogant and showy. He disliked regulations and freely spoke his mind. He painted and wrote poetry and stories. He was an admirer of the authors D.H. Lawrence and Katherine Mansfield both of whom suffered tuberculosis.

Ostracized by society due to his arrogant attitude, he opened his downtown Montreal apartment to artists, writers and poets for parties that became the talk of the town. It was here he discovered politics and heard the voices of dissent.

In 1935 he sold his car to finance a trip to the Soviet Union to attend the International Physiological Congress. He was impressed with the Soviet medical model that treated all patients without regard for their ability to pay.

He returned to Canada and spoke in Montreal before the Medico-Chirurgical Society about medical treatment for all classes. He later published *"Take the Private Profit out of Medicine"* attacking the Canadian medical establishment.

He openly complained that manufacturers make more clothing than they can sell but thousands go wretchedly clothed. Likewise he contended that millions are sick, hundreds of thousand suffer pain and tens of thousands die prematurely through lack of medical care. "As we practice it," said Bethune, "Medicine is a luxury trade."

He exhorted doctors to not ask, "How much have you got" but rather "How best can we serve you!"

When civil war broke out in Spain in October 1936 Bethune sailed looking for the roughest waters. German and Italian military troops and equipment poured into Spain to back Franco's legions. Russia also sent tanks and planes to help the failing government forces.

Bethune was soon visiting hospitals in Madrid and began to plan a mobile blood transfusion service. For him thought and action were virtually synonymous. He believed in a system by which the blood could be taken to the wounded. Within days the Canadian Blood Transfusion service was receiving donated blood. Unable to buy a vehicle in Spain or France he picked up a station wagon for 175 pounds sterling in London.

Into the vehicle he installed an Electrolux kerosene refrigerator, gas auto clave for sterilizing, glassware, flasks, drip bottles, 3 complete blood transfusion sets of the latest English model (Froud), chest instruments, serum for testing blood groups, hurricane lamps, gas masks, and other items. Bethune was pleased that he had an outfit that was superior to the International Red Cross for his was mobile.

During the Spanish conflict thousands are killed and many more thousands were wounded. Norman stationed himself near the front line and came upon both soldiers and citizens cut down and on the verge of death. Using his mobile unit he tests and administered life saving transfusions of blood. Soon he found that his unit was causing considerable interest among the Foreign Press and Bethune envisions the creation of two more mobile units.

On February 7, 1937, the civilian population of Malaga begin a march along the Malaga road to Almeria. It was two hundred kilometres of misery, as planes strafed and bombed the wretched and weary. They took to hiding during the day and walking at night. Bethune used his Mobile Blood Transfusion vehicle to transport the most desperate cases to the Almeria hospital, a 500 bed facility, that removed its red crosses because it was bombed so frequently. The war's wanton destruction further intensifies Bethune's faith in the Republican cause.

Despite the chaos, the Spanish civilians impress him, as there is no looting and property is as respected as life. An American news crew creates and films *Heart of Spain* that tells the story of Bethune's blood transfusion service. He is elevated by the Spaniards to the rank of major. Shortly after Bethune is injured and is ordered to return to Canada.

On June 6 he begins a speaking tour of the United States and Canada showing the film and raising funds for the mobile unit. At the end of the three-month campaign he announces in Winnipeg that he is a Communist.

On July 7, 1937 an incident at the Marco Polo Bridge near Peking sparked a war between the Chinese and Japanese. The 'Rape of Nanking', as it came to be called, saw the Japanese troops indiscriminately murdering, raping, plundering and burning the village.

Again Bethune had a cause and he was soon on his way to China. Initially he did not have a mobile blood transfusion vehicle but instead provisioned donkeys with what he could and treated all the injured he came across in a days travel. He was soon named Director of the International Peace Hospital.

Bethune's active engagement amazed the Chinese who were accustomed to foreigners letting the Chinese do the dirty work. Bethune was willing to jump out of a truck and sink up to his ankles in mud to help the others push. He applied to the International Red Cross for a grant for artificial legs and called for an Amputation Centre and Rehabilitation Hospital for Discharged Soldiers. He was also instrumental in organizing Mobile Operating Units

An important part of his work in China was training other doctors, nurses and orderlies. He had pamphlets printed on the treatment of wounds as well as an illustrated book on military medicine. He became concerned about a perceived lack of care by some of the doctors on the front line and went to the front to instruct them in the field under actual combat conditions. He then went to conferences where he openly criticized medical procedures in his forthright manner.

On September 15, 1938 he opened the Model Hospital where he invited his colleagues and protégé to embrace the communist paradigm. He admired China for their glorious struggle against Japanese imperialism. He felt they were fighting for the happiness and prosperity of millions and not for the enrichment of the few. He often quoted an old saying, "A doctor must have the heart of a lion and the hand of a lady."

Unfortunately the hospital was soon destroyed and rendered useless. This simply confirmed that in modern warfare mobile medical teams were what was needed. He felt that the time was past where doctors wait for patients to come to them. Doctors must go to the wounded and the sooner the better.

He had boundless energy and showed an inventive capacity to fashion equipment, instruments and medicines from the resources at hand. All this came to a grinding halt when he cut his finger during a hurried operation. His gaunt body slowed and his physical condition worsened. He did not have the strength or the antibiotics to fight the infection. Bethune died twenty minutes past five on the morning of November 12, 1939.

It was not until the creation of the People's Republic of China in 1949 that people outside of the country learned of his selfless devotion. In 1952 the Norman Bethune International Peace Hospital opened in Shijiazhuang, capital of Hebei Province. In front of the hospital stands an immense statue of him.

In 1973 the Canadian government purchased Bethune's house in Gravenhurst. It was restored to its original condition and on August 30, 1976 the Bethune Memorial Home was opened to the public as a national museum. The People's Republic of China donated a wooden sculpture that is on permanent display.

George 'Buzz' Beurling
Falcon of Malta

Most people know that Canada's #1 ace of World War I was Billy Bishop but few people know who Canada's #1 ace of World War II was. The top allied ace with 41 victories was Marmaduke E. St. John of South Africa who flew for the RAF. Ninth on the list was a man from Canada with 31 1/3 victories. His name was George Beurling and this is his story.

On December 6, 1921 Hetty and Frederick Beurling had their first son, George, who was the third of five children. George was born in a wood frame house not far from the St. Lawrence River in Verdun, Québec. His parents were very religious and were members of the Plymouth Brethren. He was not a distinguished scholar as he failed grade five and completed grade nine with only a 57% average. He did not complete high school, which was a disappointment to his father who was a painter. He was fascinated by planes from a very early age and built model aircraft. At nine he had his first ride in a real plane with Ted Hogan. From that moment on he said, "The world will never be the same." In 1939 at the age of eighteen, he made his first solo flight in a Curtiss Rambler.

In that same year George hopped a freight train like thousands of other homeless Canadians making his way to a small airfield north of Toronto. He hoped to work for room and board and to build up some flying time. He found employment as a co-pilot but found the job monotonous as he considered himself more of a stevedore than a pilot. When he heard that pilots were being hired to fight in China against the Japanese, he hopped a train to the west. He visited an uncle in Merritt, B.C. who generously gave him $500 to continue his travels. He continued on to Vancouver and used the money to get more flying time. On Dominion Day 1939 George headed for San Francisco to enlist having logged 120 hours of solo flying time. He hopped a southbound freight train and by nightfall was in the hands of the U.S. Immigration authorities for attempting to enter the United States illegally. He was held for two months. He was escorted back to Canada and was given a one-way ticket to Montreal September 1, 1939 the day Germany invaded Poland.

As soon as he arrived in Montreal he went to enlist in the Royal Canadian Air Force (RCAF). Despite all his flying time, they turned him away because he lacked formal education. George brooded over the rejection but persevered in his pursuit of flying. He hung around the airports and quite literally did chores for airtime. In May 1940 he heard that the Royal Air Force (RAF) was accepting experienced pilots in Britain. He went to the Montreal docks and got passage on the *Valparaiso* as a deck hand. To his delight the RAF found his qualifications more than acceptable but they required his birth certificate, which in his haste he had left at home. No problem. He hopped another ship and returned home, got his birth certificate and worked his way back as a deck hand. By September he was a legitimate member of the Royal Air Force.

In training he survived his first crash with his instructor at the controls. Of all of 'Buzz's' skills the one that set him apart was his shooting ability. His first shot at a target drogue separated it from the aircraft towing it. His training complete he found himself behind the throttle of the Vickers-Supermarine Spitfire, possibly the best fighter of World War II. On Christmas Day 1941, he flew his first combat mission, it turned out to be uneventful. After four unproductive months with the 403rd Squadron he transferred to Squadron 41. He accepted the 'tail end Charlie' position and soon peeled off from the squadron to shoot down an enemy F-W with a short burst. He was reprimanded for breaking formation. He continued to be rebellious and because he didn't smoke or drink he became isolated from his wing mates. He wanted to escape the squadron. When he overheard a pilot bemoaning the order to send him overseas, Buzz asked to be the man's replacement. Squadron 41 was glad to see the brooding Canadian leave.

Buzz was soon on his way and he and a number of new Spitfires were loaded onto the aircraft carrier *Eagle* headed to Malta. Eventually Buzz arrived at the RAF station at Takali. A veteran pilot, 'Laddie' Lucas, soon took Buzz aside and harshly reprimanded him for peeling away from the formation. He explained the need to fly in pairs to cover each other's tail and thus the need to search 180 degrees instead of 360. Lucas said, "You've got absolute trust from me provided you do this. But if you let me down - and make no mistake about this - you're on the next damn plane to the Middle East. Well?"

"Boss," said Beurling, "That's good enough for me." Within a month he would become a legend.

Buzz had remarkable eyesight. The story is told that one day he said, "Thirty-six flying fortresses headed this way." Sure enough within five minutes exactly 36 bombers appeared. This uncanny ability allowed Buzz a few minutes to get into position before the enemy knew he was there. Another day he said to a wing mate that a lady two blocks away had pretty blue eyes. They approached her and sure enough his eagle eyes were right.

Buzz was a perfectionist who took every aspect of flying seriously. Though he rebelled against authority he was deadly behind the controls of a Spitfire. He was always ready for battle and often volunteered for missions. He was dedicated to the job and spent his spare time going over the black book he kept of all his kills and misses. He would also go and hunt lizards to keep up his shooting skills, never shooting at less than 500 feet, the usual distance used in combat. He perfected 'deflection shooting', the art of figuring the speed of the enemy, sometimes 400 mph and shooting in front so the plane and bullets would collide. It was very much like shooting clay pigeons at the target range. The volley must be aimed where the pigeon will be when the shot arrives. Day after day the pilots battled with the usual odds being about 4 against 20. Many of his wing mates went down and for this reason he refused to form friendships for he thought it might affect his judgement.

The blond Canadian ace got raked several times during combat and on October 14, 1942 he was hit by cannon fire from a Messerschmitt and shrapnel struck his chest, left heel and leg. He plunged from 16,000 feet with the controls shattered. At 2,000 feet with the cockpit engulfed in flames he crawled onto the wing of his plane and pulled the ripcord at 500 feet to escape his fourth crash.

He received the Distinguished Flying Medal, Distinguished Service Order and Distinguished Flying Cross but his days of glory were now over. He had 29 victories when he was ordered back to Canada to take part in a war bond drive. His wing mates carried him from the hospital for a celebration. "Screwball", as his comrades called him was disheartened to leave his element.

On the Liberator flight to Gibraltar the plane went down killing all aboard except two fighter pilots Donaldson and Beurling, who escaped by jumping into the water just before the crash. He returned to Canada in triumph. He was a celebrity.

His reputation as a ladies man began with his Victory Bond tour across Canada. On the tour he met Diana Eve Whittall, a west cost debutante. Just before he left for duty overseas he proposed to her and she accepted.

He found his new RAF task of escorting mass bomber formations about as exciting as herding sheep. He continued to break formation, once going into such a steep dive with the powerful Spitfire Mark IXb that he blacked out coming to just in time to save his skin. As a result of this manoeuvre he popped every rivet in the aircraft, which had to be scrapped. Some said it was a miracle he was able to coax the aircraft home. He longed for the freewheeling Malta-style combat in which he excelled. On the eve of D-Day having added only two more victories to bring the number to 31 1/3 as his official total, Beurling retired from the RCAF bitter and unforgiving.

On November 24, 1944 he married Diana, but surprisingly, no members of either family attended the ceremony and there were no guests. They spent their days skiing at Sainte-Marguerite then in the higher hills of Mont-Tremblant in the Laurentians. While Diana learned on the lower slopes Buzz met Vivian Stokes, an American debutante, on the upper slopes. They were both married but that did not stop the romance.

Buzz still longed for combat so he tried to enlist with the RCAF for the Pacific front but was turned down. His record of skirmishes with authority, incidents of turbulent service and rejection of promotion was just cause for finding him unsuitable as a regular officer in the RCAF. He bought a Tiger Moth and gave flights to anyone who would pay for a ride with the war hero. He hung around Montreal nightclubs and restaurants drinking Coca-Cola. Diana began divorce proceedings and he continued to see Vivi.

Buzz was out of his element in civilian life. He longed for the intoxicating thrill of battle. World War II was over but the way things were going in Palestine it looked as if there could be some excitement there. Machal recruiters came in contact with the ace and he was more than willing to battle for the Jews in Israel. Being well versed in religion he was able to convince Sydney Shulemson he wanted to fight for the cause as a matter of principle. He was whisked to New York where he spent some time with Vivi before flying to Rome.

On May 20, 1948 Buzz was flying a Canadian-built Norseman aircraft with Leonard Cohen. They were coming in for a landing when a blue flame surrounded the aircraft. It soon stretched the length of the plane. As the wheels touched down the flames burst around the cockpit, the first inkling to the pilots that anything was wrong. The plane turned violently to the left and there was a thunderous explosion killing both Buzz and Cohen.

The authorities did a very poor job of investigating the accident. No one came to claim the body after a grand funeral, which was not attended by one person Buzz knew. When his lover Vivi Stokes went to see his grave she found out he was still not buried. She selected a grave near the poets Keats and Shelly, and on a cross she had engraved "And Thou...hast all/The all of me."

Two and a half years after his death Beurling's widow gave permission for his remains to be disinterred and removed to Israel. Finally he was buried in Zahal Cemetery near Israel's northern port city of Haifa.

Len Birchall
Savoir of Ceylon

On April 2, 1942 amidst World War II Len Birchall was the pilot of a Canso Catalina flying boat on patrol south east of Ceylon. He was at the end of his range, about 350 miles out, when he noticed dots on the horizon. Len took the Catalina to investigate. They encountered four battleships, five aircraft carriers, troopships and numerous cruisers and destroyers. They quickly transmitted the information to their base before a Mitsubishi 'Zero' fighter intercepted them and blasted them out of the sky damaging the radio and severely wounding Birchall, who still managed to crash land on the water. A Japanese destroyer picked up the survivors who were beaten and interrogated. Although the crew denied sending a radio message the allies were alert and ready for action when the Japanese attacked Ceylon. Winston Churchill called this, "One of the most important single contributions to victory."

Billy Bishop
King of the Clouds

On February 8, 1894 a baby boy named William was born to Margaret and Will Bishop in Owen Sound, Ontario. Billy had an older brother named Worth and a younger sister named Louise. Billy's school days were undistinguished other than the fact that sometimes he could be found skipping school to play some billiards.

In 1911 Billy decided to apply for entrance to the Royal Military College (RMC) and to pursue a military career. He thought that he could do well, though his scholastic record was mediocre. He passed, was accepted, and wrote home that the new recruits were "the lowest form of military life." The college was a real test for Billy. He was always getting into trouble and in fact cheated on the final exam - and was caught. He was expelled and would not return to the RMC as the First World War had begun in Europe. Canada was short of officers and Billy's training, albeit incomplete, won him acceptance into the Mississauga Horse, a Toronto militia regiment.

When the first contingent of the Canadian Expeditionary Force sailed from Quebec City on October 1, 1914 Billy was in a military hospital with pneumonia. He transferred to the Seventh Canadian Mounted Rifles and prepared for overseas duty and just prior to sailing he proposed to Margaret Burden. She accepted although Billy had neglected to buy a ring. June 23, 1915 the *Caledonia* and Billy sailed into Plymouth Harbour in thick fog. He was soon stationed at Shorncliffe. This he described as, 'military hell' as the rain makes the place an incredible morass of muck and mire and when the ground dries out the dust is even worse.

One day a trim little fighter plane emerged out of the low clouds and landed in a nearby field. Then and there Billy decided the only way to fight a war was up there above the clouds. Billy overheard some pilots talking one day in a local pub. He listened in and questioned the men about becoming an airman. One of the pilots suggested Billy contact a chap named Cecil - Lord Hugh Cecil. It took several weeks but eventually Billy did get an audience with Lord Cecil, which was a somewhat historic event, since it got Bishop into the air force even though he had to enter as an air observer, rather than a pilot.

His first training flight was September 1, 1915 in a primitive old Avro two-seater. By Christmas Billy's training was complete. He seemed to be prone to getting all kinds of bumps and bruises, and on the first day of leave Billy cracked his knee when he slipped off the gangplank. He did not let this bother his spirits but on the last day of his leave he found the pain so unbearable that he hobbled into a hospital. While there he met Lady St. Helier, a noblewoman of influence who was able to get Billy an extended leave. He used this extra time to return home to visit his family. During the visit, Billy gave his fiancée Margaret a diamond ring. He was firm about not getting married, however as he was determined to become a fighter pilot and his chances of survival would be less than 50/50.

When he returned to England in September 1916 he was shaken to find that his Suicide Squad had lived up to its name and was practically wiped out. He was also having trouble being accepted as a pilot trainee, but with a word to Lady St. Helier he began training as a pilot October 1, 1916. Previous experience as an observer led him to the top of his class. After only three hours of flying Billy was to make his first solo. It was a successful flight except for the belly flop landing which would become a Bishop trademark. He said in later years, he destroyed as many Allied planes as the German ace Manfred von Richthofen because of his heavy-handed landings.

Billy shot down his first airplane of the war on March 25, 1917. By April 20 he had shot down 7 Huns and was awarded the Military Cross. On April 30 he was promoted to captain and shot down his 14th hostile aircraft. On May 8th just prior to another furlough he was awarded the Distinguished Service Order. When the leading ace Albert Ball was shot down Billy became an instant celebrity when he donned the title on May 26th Billy returned to work shooting down his 20th and hatched a plan for an early morning solitary raid at the Estourmel aerodrome. He knocked off 3 Albatrosses and was awarded the Victoria Cross for his daring single-handed feat.

The knight of the skies would fly from dawn till dusk always ready to add another victory to his tally. In fact he refused to take every 3rd day off for he wanted to keep his skills sharp and keen. His Nieuport fighter with the blue propeller spinner on the nose was on a winning streak and Billy felt invincible. June 27th Billy traded in his ragged Nieuport for a spanking new S.E. 5. This new aircraft had a more powerful engine and came equipped with a Lewis gun on the top wing and a Vickers gun on the engine cowling directly in front of the pilot. It even had his familiar blue nose cone freshly painted. His first flight out he engaged seven Albatrosses and sent them fleeing.

The next day he chased a pair of two seaters over a barrage of anti-aircraft fire and one shell exploded under the plane. Billy heard a sharp clang, felt a sickening lurch and immediately his engine sputtered and slowed. He turned toward his own lines, losing height, his engine barely idling, he pushed the throttle cautiously open, hoping to coax a little more power from the damaged motor. Instead it shook violently and burst into flames, which began to blow into the cockpit. Billy immediately kicked right rudder and pushed the stick to the left putting the plane into a sideslip to sweep the flames away from the cockpit. A drenching rain was falling and he could barely make out a field just beyond a barrier of poplar trees. He pulled back on the stick to clear the trees but crashed into them as the flames licked about the cockpit. The plane stopped in mid air and flipped upside down hanging in the branches of the tree. Billy fainted. The young air warrior was rescued by two soldiers who happened to be driving by and survived without a scrape or burn as the driving rain extinguished the fire. Billy survived his most harrowing experience but it reinforced his fear of ground fire. He was soon back at the airfield and took charge of another new S.E. 5.

He found out that he had won the Victoria Cross on August the 10th. On August 16th he knocked down his 47th victory and he was given his leave orders. King George awarded him the MC, DSO and VC saying that no one had ever been awarded three such prestigious awards on a single day.

He returned to Canada to a hero's welcome. He thought his flying days were over and that he would be offered a desk job. He married Margaret and took her to England with him. He finally was given the task of recruiting his own squadron. He called them the Flying Foxes and he knocked down his 48th victory May 27, 1918. His wing mates and buddies fell like flies but Billy was blessed and seemingly invincible. He was daring and reckless. June 19th he secured his 72nd victory and was again ordered on leave. While he was absent a pilot named Mick Mannock took over the Flying Foxes and exceeded Billy's mark by one before the end of the war. But when Billy retired from flying he was the world's #1 living ace exceeded only by the 'Red Baron's' mark of 81. Billy won the newly created award, the Distinguished Flying Cross, and even received awards from other countries. When he ceased active service he trained Allied pilots in Canada. He had a son they named William Arthur. The King of the Clouds died peacefully September 10, 1956.

Blondin
Tightrope Walker Extraordinaire

Jean Françoise Gravelet was born in St. Omer, France on February 28, 1824. His father was an acrobat and thus his parents were pleased to enrol him in École de Gymnaste at Lyons. After only a few months' instruction he made his first public appearance as 'The Little Wonder.' In a few years the boy became a distinguished member of the European acrobatic team and in 1851 the celebrated gymnast, Gabriel Ravel, offered to take him to America. Blondin, his stage name, signed a two-year contract, which was later extended to eight years. In 1858 the troupe appeared in Buffalo and Blondin visited Niagara Falls with Ravel on his Sunday off.

Standing on the precipice of the thundering falls he turned to his colleague and exclaimed, "What a splendid place to bridge a tightrope."

Ravel thought he was joking but soon realized his seriousness as Blondin cast his eyes about seeking a likely anchoring spot for the rope. Ravel blew his top, heated words were exchanged and Blondin pretended to drop the idea. His contract was up in a year and he was prepared to bide his time. As soon as his contract lapsed, he headed straight for Niagara.

His first problem was to get a rope and it would cost thirteen hundred dollars alone. He had no money nor would any sane man advance money to an obvious lunatic. He finally uncovered Mr. Hamblin who put up the money in cash but then proceeded to plead with Blondin not to jeopardize his life. Blondin would not listen to reason and proceeded on the considerable engineering problem.

The *Maid of the Mist* was procured to drag a cable 5/8ths of an inch thick across the river. To this a second cable was attached and finally a third. The main rope was Manila hemp around a steel core. It was three inches in diameter. To fasten the cable, holes were drilled into the solid rock of the cliffs. Horses heaved and strained to pull the rope taut. Once the rope was stretched across the gorge it was evident that Blondin could not make a level crossing. The rope's own weight caused it to sag fifty feet at midpoint. To prevent it from swaying, guys were attached and anchored. Sand bags were attached to help prevent the rope from blowing upward as the wind roared through the gorge. The stage was prepared for Blondin's great feat.

On June 30, 1859 the betting was frenzied with sums large enough to make sabotage profitable. Blondin checked and rechecked each rope. He stepped out onto the rope on the American side before a crowd of about 25,000. Slight and agile, the five foot five inch, one hundred and forty pound daredevil casually strolled down to midpoint. The crowd was silent as he sat down on the rope and surveyed them. He rose, advanced and then lay down on his back. The crowd gulped and held its breath. Suddenly he turned a back somersault, landed on his feet and swiftly walked upward to the landing stage on the Canadian side. The roar of the crowd drowned out the sound of Niagara.

He crossed the gorge on a number of occasions that summer - on July 4, July 14 and August. Each time out the stunts grew more daring. He bicycled across, pushed a wheelbarrow, stood on his head and crossed the gorge at night. People complained that they couldn't see him at night so he crossed blindfolded. Still people were not satisfied. They wanted to see him at night so one night he crossed after dark in the glare of a locomotive headlight. It was said that he cooked an egg for lunch and even walked part way across on stilts. He intended as his last feat, to carry someone across on his back. He advertised for someone to take his dare and make $500. He upped the reward but still there were no takers. He turned to a one-time whaler and his manager Harry Colcord. All wondered how he convinced Harry to participate in such madness but participate he did. Never before and never since has so much humanity thronged to the Gorge of Niagara.

For this last stunt Blondin appeared on the American side of the falls dressed in pink tights. He tantalized the crowd with headstands, somersaults and a trip across without a balancing pole. After a fifteen-minute rest, he appeared with Harry who was formally dressed.

"Harry," said Blondin, "Be sure and let yourself rest like a dead weight on my back. If I should sway or stumble, on no account attempt to balance yourself." Colcord listened carefully, after all his life was at stake.

They started off. Blondin moved with maddening slowness. Step by careful step down the long incline. The worse was to come. Blondin required periodic rests to gather his strength. Colcord would slip off Blondin's back onto the taut, vibrating rope and stand while it swung to and fro, hundreds of feet in the air while holding on for dear life. The least false move or loss of presence of mind could plunge both into eternity. Harry would then climb on Blondin's back and this was repeated seven times.

Half way across the gorge it appeared as if Blondin was losing his balance. He worked the pole as if they were a pair of wings. Some suspect that Blondin was in total control but was giving the crowd the extra thrill he always provided. Blondin ran along the rope, momentum keeping him upright, the pole thrashing madly until he reached the nearest guy wire. He stepped on the line to steady himself. The crowd gasped as the guy wire snapped and the corresponding guy on the opposite side jerked the manila rope sideways. Blondin recovered himself enough to continue his run to the next brace of guys where he halted and said to Colcord, "Get off, quick."

A dastardly attempt had been made to kill them, probably by some unscrupulous, gambler trying to save his stake. Now it was time for the long climb up the rope to the American side. At the last stop Colcord realized that there was real danger from an unexpected source. The people, excited to frenzy, were capable of rushing towards the two men and might crowd them right over the bank. They decided to make a rush and drive right through them. This they did and he etched his name indelibly into the history book as they became over night heroes.

Father Jean de Brébeuf
Jésuit Missionary Martyr

Jean de Brébeuf was born at Conde sur Vire, France on March 25, 1593. At twenty-four he entered the Jésuit novitiate in Rouen, France. He became the most robust of all Blackrobes, as he was a giant of a man physically and spiritually. He was 6' 7" or 6' 8" with broad shoulders and lived up to his Huron name, *Echon*, 'he who pulls heavy load.' He was ordained as a priest in 1622.

He sailed from Dieppe to Québec in 1625. After a brief apprenticeship among the Algonquin his superior Father Charles Lalemant, sent him to Huron country.

After three years of service he was forced back to France when David Kirk, a British captain, captured Québec.

Brébeuf returned to the New World in 1634. He had a gift for languages and wrote the first dictionary of the Huron language. He also translated prayers and wrote the *Huron Carol*. He contributed to *Relations de Jésuits* in 1635 and 36. He was among the first witnesses during this period of 'first contact' with the natives of the new land.

Unlike the Roman Catholics who cloistered in their fortified forts and spoke Latin, the Jésuits believed in taking the word of God to the people in their language in their camps and villages. Although this made them vulnerable, the work they did was outstanding. The various tribes were to soon regard them with reverence. Though Brébeuf might have seen the native's spiritual practices as pagan he never the less poured out his love, help and care.

He spoke a number of native languages. He could preach, pray and sing with his brethren no matter the tribe. Of all the languages he was most proficient in Huron. Still conversion was very slow work because in Brébeuf's estimation immorality, attachment to customs and prevalence of epidemics discouraged them. When smallpox broke out in 1637 the natives had little immunity and rightly attributed the scourge to the Europeans. They tore down crosses and vandalized the church. Brébeuf's flock deserted him and their newly embraced faith.

He wrote: "Your life hangs by a thread. Of calamities you are the cause - the scarcity of game, a fire, famine, or epidemics…you are the reason, and at any time a savage may burn your cabin down or split your head…what you suffer shall be of God."

He was heedless of pleas to flee. March 18, 1649 when the Iroquois attacked the weakened Huron, Brébeuf remained with them ministering and giving them their last blessing as they died. Brébeuf did not attempt to defend himself and was taken prisoner.

Heedless of the Iroquois mission, Brébeuf continued to bless and pray for the Iroquois in their language. Brébeuf and Father Gabriel Lalément were taken to be tortured to death.

Brébeuf was stripped naked, his fingernails torn from his fingers, he was beaten with sticks and bound to a stake all the while praying, "My brothers God loves you and forgives you as do I, for you know not what you do."

He exhorted other captives to suffer patiently and promised heaven as their reward. They secured his feet so he could not extinguish the flames they started in the twigs they lit at the base of his feet. A Huron renegade, once baptized by the missionary, poured boiling water over Brébeuf's head symbolically returning the favour. Still he unfalteringly preached. They placed the dreaded 'collar' around his neck. Six tomahawks, heated white-hot were lashed with green whippling. When hung over the shoulders of the victim the sizzling iron sank into the flesh. Any other mortal would have screamed in pain but Brébeuf now in a deep trance and didn't seem to notice as he continued to bless his torturers with his very heart. This seemed to further enrage the Iroquois who tore strips of his flesh off, roasted it and devoured it before his eyes. Still he prayed so unwavering and loud that one of the young braves unable to bear the brave words of mercy and forgiveness rushed up, grabbed Brébeuf's tongue and cut it off. Still he prayed until his lips were sliced off in the hope of forever silencing the brave missionary. They thrust a glowing iron shaft down his throat. The torture lasted more than three hours when they scalped him. Seeing him near death they laid open his breast and devoured his heart, liver and blood that they thought would impart some portion of his courage unto them.

Father Lalément was then tortured for eleven hours before his frail body was relieved by death. Brébeuf and Lalément's deaths rank amongst the most atrocious in the history of Christianity.

Johnny Bright
Helped Coin the Word Racism in United States

Johnny Bright was born in Fort Wayne, Indiana on June 11, 1931. He attended Drake University and played football where he became a power running back and in his senior year was in contention for the Heisman Trophy that no black man had ever won. When Drake took on Oklahoma A&M in 1951, a play would come to stand in infamy. Johnny was tackled and fell out of bounds on his back. As he tried to get to his feet Wilbanks Smith came in well after the play was over and crushed his elbow into Johnny's jaw, breaking it. At the time helmets did not have face shields or guards. A photographer won a Pulitzer Prize that year for the picture showed the sheer savagery of the attack. The word racism was widely used to describe the 'Johnny Bright incident.'

Johnny went back to the huddle and called for the ball the next play. He threw a touchdown pass but due to his injury was forced to the sideline and did not return for two weeks. He did not win the rushing title or the Heisman that year and the Philadelphia Eagles drafted him in the first round.

As a result of that vicious hit, facemasks and mouth guards were then mandated. In subsequent incidents there was the Rosa Parks bus incident in 1955. Martin Luther King and his *'I Had a Dream'* speech (1963), Selma, Alabama 1965, and the continuing emancipation of the black man in America.

Bright chose to sign with the Calgary Stampeders for the 1951-52 season rather than help break the 'colour' barrier in the NFL. The next year he was traded to the Edmonton Eskimos where he stayed until 1964. In the 1956 Grey Cup he gained a record 171 yards. In 1957 he had eight consecutive 100-yard games and in 1959 he won the Schenley Award as the CFL's most outstanding player, the first black athlete so honoured. With the help of Jackie 'Spaghetti Legs' Parker they led the Eskimos to Grey Cup wins in 1954-56 over the Alouettes. He once held the CFL record for most playoff touchdowns, most yards gained in Grey Cup game, most consecutive games played 197, and rushed for 10,909 yards. Not surprisingly he was inducted into the CFL Hall of Fame in 1970.

When he retired from football he became the principal of Bonnie Doon High School and head basketball coach for the Lancers. I personally knew Mr. Bright from his Eskimo days. I was on the Salisbury Sabres basketball team and his talented team beat us. I didn't know then what I know now...he was a very special person in more ways than I could then fathom.

Kurt Browning
Ya Just Gotta Love The Guy

Jack Browning married Gladys Stewart in 1921 and they settled in Caroline, Alberta population 389. They had a son Wade in 1955 and daughter Dena in 1958. Kurt was more or less an accident as he was born in Rocky Mountain House, Alberta on June 18, 1966.

Kurt was in grade two when he made his figure-skating debut at an annual ice carnival as a skunk. He loved to play hockey but was only 5' 7" and 145 pounds. To get more skating time he figure skated and his first partner was Michell Pollitt. They won some prizes in ice dancing. His teacher Karen McLean saw some potential in her student.

Kurt met Michael Jiranek aka 'Mr. J.' at the Royal Glenora Club in Edmonton. He taught Kurt to jump for that is what Kurt wanted to do most. Mr. J suggested Kurt move to Edmonton so he could get the coaching he needed. Kurt opted to finish grade 10 at home and proceeded to Edmonton for grade 11 and the skating club.

He was terribly home sick and headed home every weekend for a time. His parents gave him undying support telling him to put all his energy into training and they'd handle the rest.

Kurt roomed with his cousin Jennifer and a friend Wade. He cycled eight miles to the club most of the time as cross training. He met Joelle Tustin and they dated for two years and parted friends. Jiranek gave Kurt a great deal of freedom allowing him to be responsible for his own training and progress. Mr. J would keep things in perspective, when what he needed to do and the demands of the media often clashed with his objectives and that drove him bananas.

In 1983 at the Canadian championships in Montreal Kurt won the gold medal in the novice division. He met Donald Jackson, an international Canadian figure skater, for the first time and got a small taste of media attention.

The next year in early January Kurt was in a minor car accident that jarred him, threw him onto the floor, covering him in glass. He did not do well later that month at the championships in Regina. He placed seventh and was not happy, nor was Mr. J.

He met Tracey Wainman, the three time women's senior champion, who helped Kurt with his compulsory figures. Kurt struggled with his compulsories and cut his right foot when the left blade pierced his boot and foot during a Lutz. He received five stitches and had to take ten days off.

In June 1985 he was invited to an international event Coup d'Excellence in Montreal. Chris Bowman of the States won and Kurt placed a respectable fifth. He also met Christine 'Tuffy' Hugh and they dated for a while. Kurt flew to Europe in August to compete in France and West Germany. While in Paris they stayed where other Canadian team members had left messages from previous years. As was the tradition they wrote on the bottoms of the dresser drawers. Kurt says it was like a time capsule being opened.

Kurt placed second in St. Gervais and ninth in the next competition. In October he competed at the Skate America competition in St. Paul, Minnesota and placed eighth. Poland's Jozef Sabovcik won, Brian Boitano second, Viktor Petrenko third with Christopher Bowman forth. This was his first real taste of the big league.

Kurt finished high school and entered Alberta College. He did not complete college for he had bigger things on his mind. In August 1986 he landed his first triple Lutz in competition as well as triple flip in the same program. He won a silver medal.

Kurt's skating was now taking him all over the world. He met Katarina Witt the German ice princess and met the diminutive skating star from Japan named Midori Ito. He was even chastised by his mother for 'stealing' some Japanese cotton robes from one hotel they stayed in and as a result Kurt didn't give her one.

The Axel in named for Axel Paulsen. It is the only jump that you enter going forward. Kurt loves this jump and calls it the king of jumps. The Salchow is named after Ulrich Salchow and you enter it going backwards. That makes it easier to learn. The Lutz is named after Alfred Lutz and is the least natural. Kurt has injured himself with this jump on three occasions and had a total of 15 stitches to remind him of the difficulties of this jump. A 'waxel' is a failed jump and on one occasion he put his teeth though his upper lip requiring a few more stitches. Kurt says when you jump you don't have to jump hard. It's all in the technique and timing. Try too hard and you're doomed.

October 1987 at the Skate Canada meet, Kurt placed fourth behind Orser, Boitano and Petrenko.

David Dore of the Canadian Figure Skating Association (CFSA) challenged all team members to produce, "Medals, medals, medals." Without corporate and other donors the competitors could not travel to other countries for competitions. Kurt calls him Super Dave.

The funny thing about the 1988 Calgary Olympics for Kurt was that he associated the event with exotic and distant places and here it would be in his own backyard just a stone's throw away from his hometown, Caroline. The Jamaican bobsled team and Eddie the Eagle, the kamikaze English ski jumper got more than their share of the press coverage that year. Brian Orser lost to Boitano in the 'Battle of the Brians' and Kurt placed eighth. That was the year Elizabeth Manley took the silver in the women's event.

At the World Championship in Budapest, Hungary, Kurt earned his name into the *Guinness Book of World of Records* for completing the first competition quad toe-loop. Kurt went on tour with Stars on Ice and became enamoured with Katarina Witt.

Kurt was thrilled when at the 1989 World Championship in Paris, France he won his first international gold medal. He would retain the crown in Halifax in 1990 and in Munich in 1991.

His Olympic heartache continued in 1992 when he placed sixth. He did however go on to Oakland and the World Championship where he won the silver. One day a team-mate said to Elvis Stojko, "Do your impersonation of Kurt."

Stojko stamped his feet like an angry bull and struck Kurt's opening pose. He took off waving his arms like a windmill, punching the air, super-speedy movements and bouncing all over the ice. Kurt was touched by the impersonation, for Elvis had obviously been working on it for quite a while he was so accurate.

Again Kurt took the gold in the 1993 Worlds in Prague, Czechoslovakia and he hung in there for the 1994 Olympics. In fact he carried the flag for the team at Lillihammer in Norway although he placed a disappointing fifth while Elvis Stojko won the silver. Kurt had said Elvis was amazing and was proud of his team-mate's accomplishment.

Kurt was the only figure skater to win the World Figure Skating Championships with and without compulsory figures. He loves to skate, finds it magic and relishes it most when there are no rules and regulations. He has been on the ice with all the great skaters, Hamilton, Boitano, Orser, Cranston and many others. The Russian Viktor Petrenko even gave him the nickname 'Kurtrinka.' He is proud to be a Canadian and spent a great deal of money in legal fees to ensure that athletes have the right to control their own trust funds.

Kurt has a sense of humour and likes to do things slightly risqué and flirtatious. His heart however belongs to Sonia Rodriquez who he met at Wayne Gretzky's place and they married June 30, 1996. They have a child named Gabriel.

Étienne Brûlé
Canada's 1st Coureur de Bois

In the early 1600's a young man came to Canada to become Samuel de Champlain's servant. He was very much an adventurer and was soon on one of his many journeys into the virgin woods of America.

Étienne Brûlé took to the wild woods like a duck to water and in his life accomplished many firsts. He was one of the first courier de bois to search waterways for furs and other treasures. He was the first white man to 'shoot' the Lachine Rapids in a birch bark canoe. He longed to be on the move and paddle in hand he fixed his eyes on the farthest horizon. He was the first to ascend the Ottawa River thus establishing the route to Huron country. He was the first to set eyes on Georgian Bay and Michilimackinac and onto the waters of 'Grand Lac' or Lake Superior. In fact he was the first white man to see all the Great Lakes with the possible exception of Lake Michigan.

One can imagine this French man, strong and powerful, tanned brown with sun-bleached hair and a glint in his eyes that was wild and untamed. He had gone 'native', living as the natives lived. His friend, Father Gabriel Sagard said of Étienne that he was "much addicted to women."

Étienne Brûlé was much loved by both the natives and French. Champlain often consulted him about the fur trade routes and the vastness of the inner continent. The task of being a French coureur de bois was risky, but Étienne truly enjoyed the lifestyle. After a long expedition he returned to Québec to find that English warships had blockaded the St. Lawrence and Champlain was about to surrender to Captain David Kirk. Champlain quickly recruited Brûlé's help to go seek food and find some allies to help with the defence of the fort. Étienne hastened to a nearby tribe but when he arrived in the village a great feast was prepared for him as they had not seen him for some time. After the festivities a party was finally put together to go and alleviate the situation in Québec City. By the time they returned to the fort it had been deserted and Samuel de Champlain was on his way to England as he had surrendered having only one tub filled with potatoes and roots.

As a result of his late return the fortunes of Étienne Brûlé took a sudden turn, for Champlain was also a much-loved man both amongst the various tribes and French. He roamed the forests but was not welcomed as he once was. Finally in 1633 the Huron of Tonaché killed, quartered and threw him into a huge pot. They proceeded to eat him. That might have been the end of this story but in the year that followed the tribe contracted smallpox and 2/3 of the village died. They thought the 'spirit of Brûlé' had decimated the village. It was burned to the ground and forever abandoned.

Tommy Burns
Canada's only World Heavyweight Boxing Champion

Noah Brusso was born in a little log cabin in Hanover, Ontario on June 17, 1881. He was the twelfth of thirteen children born to Sofia and Frederick Brusso. Five of his siblings would die before they reached adulthood.

He loved to fight and eagerly joined in the schoolyard free-for-alls. He also excelled in lacrosse, hockey and skating. While working on a passenger boat on Lake Erie he trounced a burly second mate. Hoping to fight more seriously he jumped ship in Detroit and joined the Detroit Athletic Club and began to train in earnest. He trained for six months under Sam Briddle and one night went to a Jack 'Tiger' Cowan fight. When Cowan jumped over the ropes into the ring he collapsed with a twisted ankle. Brusso's buddies pushed him into the ring to fight in his place. He knocked out the six foot 170 pound Freddie 'Thunderbolt' Thornton in the fifth round. The year was 1900. On the streets he was shunned and discovered it was because Freddie was black and whites aren't supposed to fight the inferior race.

There was real discrimination in boxing at the time. Title holds were all white and they refused to give any coloured scum a shot. That is why Sam Langford, one of the great boxers of the era, never got a title shot in his entire career. (see Sam Langford)

Noah had a chip on his shoulder and was always an under dog so he felt a kinship to the Negro boxers whom he refused to draw the line on. As a result, the records he set have been discredited and little noticed because he dared to cross the colour line in his sport.

Burns fell in love with a lovely young girl named Nellie Sweitzer who was a cashier at a confectionary shop. He thought marriage would hinder his boxing career so he called it off. It was a regrettable decision he would admit later in life.

His parents were German Methodists and despite a strict up bringing young Tommy started fighting regularly and after five knockouts he was the middleweight champion of Michigan when he KO'd Eddie 'The Bay City Brawler' Sholtreau in one minute and 35 seconds of the first round. Reporters started to call him 'Brusso the Bruiser.' He accepted a rematch with 'Thunderbolt' Thornton but held out for a $100 purse reasoning that the racial factor would sell the event out and it did. It was held in Detroit's posh Windmere Hotel on January 16, 1902.

Tommy decked him in the fifth round just as he had the previous time. In the lobby a woman slapped him in the face and said, "Nigger lover."

Not to be intimidated Brusso took on another black boxer named Harry Peppers from Chicago three weeks later. There was a large police presence. Peppers was flat-footed and Tommy ran circles around him. Peppers refused to come out of his corner for the third round. Only two days later on March 5, 1902 he faced George Steele who was outclassed and resorted to low blows that led to his disqualification after the second round.

On May 16, 1902 Brusso faced 'The Bay City Brawler' again. He piled on the points in the early rounds but in the fourth was stunned by a blow that knocked him off his feet for the first time. He took the full nine count and resumed the fight. With tenacity he hung in there until the tenth round and won the decision. It was a valuable lesson. He needed better conditioning if he was going to rise through the ranks.

After the fight he met Irene Peppers, more than likely the sister of Harry Peppers, and they eventually got married on November 2, 1903. They were divorced within in six months at a time when the marriage bond was rarely broken. Now he had to face public disapproval on yet another score. He liked to gamble, liked to sing and had a love for music. He also dressed in the best suits money could buy complete with silk top hat and even a walking stick. He enjoyed the company of youngsters and was an incurable practical joker. He was also religious and attended church regularly.

December 26, 1902 Brusso faced Tom McCune for the Michigan championship. They tapped gloves at centre rig and McCune's supporters chanted, "Kill the nigger lover." Brusso knocked Tom down in the forth and put him down twice in the fifth. In the seventh the end came with unexpected suddenness with a left hook to his jaw that stunned McClure. He followed with another left and then dropped him with a straight right. He came up inside the count but was easily dropped again and the referee stopped it with 20 seconds to go in the round.

January 16, 1903 Noah faced southpaw Mike Schreck and Noah was put down in the eighth round. He was up by the count of nine but was clearly losing. He rallied in the ninth and pressed in the tenth but it was too little too late. He lost the decision.

February 13 he defeated Jim 'Elbows' O'Brien. He took on two opponents March 25. He put Dick 'Bull' Smith down twice in the third round and the referee stopped the bout. Jim 'Reddy' Phillips started out fighting dirty and it got worse. With Brusso getting the better of him anyway Phillips kicked him in the groin and was disqualified. Twenty-four days later he knocked out black heavyweight Earl 'Hercules' Thompson in the third round.

Before the end of the year Brusso faced his sixth black man Jack 'Big Boy' Butler whom he dispatched in the second round. December 31 he closed out the year in Detroit with a victory over Tom McCune.

January 28, 1904 Noah faced Ben 'Gorilla' O'Grady. He put him down twice in the first and three times in the second round. Early in the third round Brusso drove his right straight on the point of his jaw and he was out before he hit his head on the mat. The dragged O'Grady to his corner but were unable to bring him around with water or smelling salts. They carried him into his dressing room and a few minutes later cried out, "Is there a doctor in the house." A physician named Gurney rushed to his side and concluded he had suffered a concussion. Ben slipped into a coma and lay unconscious.

Brusso was handcuffed and led away by police. He was charged with assault that would be upgraded to manslaughter if O'Grady died. Noah was inconsolable and vowed if the man died he would never fight again. On the fifth day O'Grady pulled out of the coma but he suffered permanent brain damage and would never fight again.

Noah's mother was humiliated by the negative publicity and begged him to abandon the sport. As a result Noah opted to change his name, he chose an Irish alias 'Tommy Burns.'

February 26 Burns defeated George Shrosbree and fought an old foe Mike Schreck to a draw the very next night. He took on Toni Caponi on March 18 and obtained a draw. He faced him again April 9 and won. At a poker match he won the deed to a gold mine in Alaska.

He struck out for the distant land and took on Klondike Mike Mahoney who announced he would fight 'lumberjack style' and that included both punching and kicking. Burns was 158 pounds while Mahoney was 208. Tommy got the better of him in the first two rounds. In the third Mike drove his right foot into his solar plexus and Tommy went down. He was paralysed for a couple of minutes and the referee stopped the bout and declared it a draw. When he became the world heavyweight champion he sent Mike a card saying, "To my friend Klondike Mike Mahoney, the only man who gave me a KO to the solar plexus."

In a dance hall in Portland, Oregon he met Julia Keating whom he courted and married in 1904. 'Jewel' as he like to call her was a good cook and Burns soon weighed an astonishing 185 pounds and sarcastic reporters referred to him as 'blubberweight.'

Burns had to get into fighting form. Never up before eight, he would walk briskly and sprint for 100 yards or so and would cover about five miles. Following a rub down and shower he would have a light lunch. He would rest until three and would hit the gym. He did all manner of exercises but he felt the key was to avoid a boring routine. The most remarkable part of his routine was sparring. Instead of sparring for the traditional three-minute rounds he'd go for six solid minutes. He would use three partners so he was always up against a fresh opponent. The workouts were tough but it prepared him well for his fights.

He took on another black fighter named Billy Woods September 16 in Seattle. Burns 'trash talked' calling him a nigger and yellow. It went fifteen gruelling rounds and it was called a draw. Burns record now stood at 27 wins, 4 draws, and 1 loss with 22 knockouts.

On October 4 Burns took on 'Foxy Jack' O'Brien who had fought 133 bouts and had won 85, tied 11 and lost only 3. The rest of his contests were 'no decisions' as both boxers agreed ahead of time no verdict would be rendered unless there was a knock out. He had 24 knockouts. At a shade under six feet and 171 pounds he was a formidable opponent. His promoter assured Tommy it would just be an exhibition bout. O'Brien attacked in the first round with punches that would fell an ox. Burns weathered the storm and fought back but lost the decision on points. Burns vowed to get the double-crosser.

He started the New Year out right knocking out a native American heavyweight named 'Indian Joe' Schildt in the sixth round in Ballard, Washington on January 31, 1905.

With his marriage to Jewel agreeing with him Burns found it very difficult to maintain his weight at the 158 pounds required to fight in the middleweight division. He often entered fights weak and his results were not good securing two draws with Hugo Kelly and another with Jack 'Twin' Sullivan who would defeat him in a decision on October 17.

In 1905 the popular James Jeffries retired as world heavyweight champion with a record of 18 wins (15 by knockout) and 2 draws. He had refused to fight the two best black fighters - Jack Johnson and Sam Langford.

Jeffries passed the crown to Marvin Hart. Hart had to defend his new title. Looking over the field of contenders he decided Tommy Burns would be an easy opponent. He underestimated the five-foot-seven 175-pound rock from Canada. As Burns prepared for the fight of his life he had 30 wins, 7 draws and 3 losses with 24 knockouts. Tommy was about to enter the land of the giants.

Burn's defeat was a forgone conclusion. The 29 year-old Hart was five inches taller and 40 pounds heavier. He had lost only 3 of his 36 bouts and thought he could tear Burns to pieces. The odds were 17-to-1.

The match took place at the Pacific Athletic Club in Los Angeles, California on February 23, 1906. A collective gasp went through the crowd when Hart stepped into the ring. The size difference was startling.

Referee Charles Eyton summoned the boxers to the centre of the ring. Hart noticed Burns was wearing several layers of tape around his hands and demanded it be removed. Burns taunted him and poked Hart in the chest shouting, "Get out of my corner, you cheese champion!"

Hart went berserk calling him "a little rat" and threw a punch that Tommy easily ducked. The referee stepped between the two and guided Hart to his corner as the crowd booed and hissed. They thought Hart was a bully for throwing the unwarranted punch.

Hart bolted from his corner when the bell rang determined to teach Burns a lesson. Burns was much faster and avoided the rushes while peppering long lefts into Hart's face. He kept Hart boiling by taunting him. In the third round he nailed Hart in the nose, blood flowed and it kept running almost every round there after. In the fifth Burns closed Hart's right eye. From then on Burns danced in the direction of the blind eye and belted the champion at will.

Hart won the tenth and twelfth rounds but Burns staggered him in the fourteenth with a right and left to the jaw. Burns attacked and hammered Hart about the face and forced him to cover up.

Burns could sense a knock out but Jack 'Twin' Sullivan cautioned him that he couldn't lose the fight now unless Hart knocked him out. Hart also knew he needed a knockout and attacked frantically but Burns easily sidestepped every rush and scored a number of telling counter-punches. Both men were standing at the end of the twentieth round but there was no doubt who had won. Hart was bleeding and bruised and one reporter wrote Burns didn't have a mark on him. The referee raised Burn's right arm into the air and it didn't take long for the stunning news to flash around the world.

Reporters wanted to know if Burns would defend his title against all comers. He stated he would take on all regardless "colour, size or nationality. I propose to be champion of the world…If I am not the best man in the heavyweight division, I don't want to hold the title."

In San Diego he met two challengers in one night and knocked both Jim O'Brien and Jim Walker out in the first round. He took on 'Fireman' Jim Flynn who outweighed him by 30 pounds and was a solid puncher. After fifteen brutal rounds, Burns landed a shattering right that knocked Flynn to the canvas, ending the fight with a knockout. Flynn took 10 minutes to get up. He fought American Jack O'Brien, the light heavyweight champion and broke his nose in the fifth, delivered a punishing blow to his jaw in the eighth and opened a nasty cut over is left eye in the tenth. The bout was called a draw, though reporters insisted that Burns won on points. In a rematch May 8, 1907 Burns dropped a bombshell declaring 10 minutes prior to the bout that O'Brien had tried to fix the fight but that all bets were off and the fight was on. The fight was a marathon because O'Brien ran and Burns chased. Tommy landed more blows to his back than anywhere else and Burns won a 20 round decision. It was one of the strangest bouts in the history of championship fights.

After the fight a reporter pointed out since both fighters weighed under the 175-pound limit, Tommy was both the heavyweight and lightweight champion of the world. Burns said, "Forget it, I don't want that thing. Let O'Brien keep it." Just the same the championship was uncontested in this division until 1912 when Jack Dillon beat Hugo Kelly replaced Burns as the new lightweight champion.

On July 4 Tommy finished his U.S. tour knocking out Australian Bill Squires two minutes and eight seconds into round one.

Burns embarked upon a worldwide tour determined to prove that he deserved the crown despite his size. Burns now turned his attention to Europe and sought new challengers. The English found Burns arrogant and his conduct offensive. They hoped their countryman, Gunner Moir, could silence the cocky Canadian but Burns knocked him out in the tenth round. He also knocked out Englishman Jim Palmer in the fourth.

Jack Johnson followed Burns to England and was demanding a fight. Tommy said he would provided he got 75% of the proceeds win lose or draw. Johnson said he would declare himself the champion. The threat was laughable. Never the less Burns was popular amongst African-Americans because he publicly renounced the colour line. Though it was not publicly known an agreement was reached when Australian promoter Hugh McIntosh agreed to pay Burns $30,000 for a bout with Johnson at a time of his choosing. Burns would be risking his purse for the Johnson bout but he continued to fight though he wanted a good payday for his effort.

He took on the Irish champ, Jem Roche who was an inch taller and 28 pounds heavier. The match took place in Dublin on St. Patrick's Day March 17 at the Theatre Royal. The city was in a frenzy and great crowds swirled around the venue that was of course sold out. The moment the bell rang Burns jumped to the centre of the ring and stared at Jem. Roche annoyed struck down Burns' arm and covered his face with both gloves. Burns feigned with his left and then crushed his right fist into Jem's jaw and the Irishman dropped to the canvas like he had been shot. He lay for several seconds and tried to get up but couldn't before the count of ten. It was all over after only one minute and 28 seconds. It was the fastest knockout ever recorded in a world heavyweight championship match. It still stands a century later.

Tommy helped him to his corner and the groggy Irishman asked, "I'm not beat, am I Mr. Burns?"

"I'm afraid you are Jem."

One other winner that unforgettable night was a quick-thinking Irish fan who ran out of the Royal waving his ticket declaring he couldn't bear to witness the event claiming Roche was murdering the champion and offered to sell his ticket for two pounds. The clever thief got his money and disappeared before the buyer discovered he had been conned.

Burns got another attractive purse to fight Joseph 'Jewey' Smith the 'Champion of Africa.' On April 18, 1908 he faced him in Paris in front of an exuberant crowd and knocked him out in the fifth round. Seconds later panic erupted as a photographic apparatus exploded setting fire to the flags and decorations. Spectators leaped to their feet prepared to run but were prevailed upon to remain in their places and the fire was quickly extinguished.

Baron Rothschild, one of the riches men in the world, had visited Burns just prior to the fight and invited him and Jewel to his home. Burns accepted and when he arrived was amused that his host was dressed in black tights down to his knees. He shadowboxed with the old gentleman a few rounds and they had their pictures taken together.

His astonishing European tour ended June 13th in Paris when he took on Billy Squires once more. It would not be a first round knock out this time as Squires won the first five rounds, stunning Burns at the end of the fifth. Burns rallied and scored a knockout in the eighth round with a powerful stomach blow.

He sailed to Australia ready for the showdown with Jack Johnson. Perth, gave him a hero's welcome. The man who had defeated the best boxers in North America, Australia, Europe and Africa received deep appreciation from the Aussies for he had traveled half way around the globe to be with them. He was David who had slain a whole host of Goliaths.

Burns traveled across the continent to Sydney with adoring fans along the track all the way. Eight thousand people met him in Sydney at the station

On August 24th Burns took on Billy Squires again in a 25,000-seat stadium being constructed for the Burns-Johnson battle at Rushchutter's Bay. They shut down construction and 20,000 fans got the treat of a lifetime. Burn's looked to be heavy and not closely trained. Squires landed a devastating shot to the mouth in the third and landed another jackhammer left in the fifth. Tommy was in deep trouble. In the seventh round he came to within an eyelash of being knocked out. Burns fought back until the eleventh when he was tagged with three right uppercuts followed by a staggering left to his nose. Tommy was groggy and staggered to his seat.

The crowd was roaring non-stop in the blazing sun and there was almost pandemonium as they sensed an upset in the making. Burns changed tactics and no longer tried to slug it out but became elusive sidestepping and dodging his opponent until he landed two lightening punches putting Billy on the defensive. Squires was exhausted and Burns made him taste canvas two times in the thirteenth round. Burns implored Billy to stay down but the proud Aussie insisted on staggering to his feet. Burns had no choice but to knock him out. It was the toughest fight of his life.

Burns set another record when he faced 'Killer' Billy Lang in Melbourne on September 7, 1908. Lang knocked Burns off his feet in the second round with a heavy swing. In the third Burns got in close and cut him down to size with shattering body punches and sent Lang to the canvas for a count of 9. Burns took charge and knocked the challenger down several more times before he was counted out in the sixth. It was his 44th victory and 8th consecutive knock out in defence of his crown. No heavyweight has surpassed that mark even to this day.

It was billed as the first great battle of the inevitable race war. Burns called Johnson a 'nigger' on several occasions and later expressed regret for his shameful conduct. They met on Boxing Day 1908 in Sydney. With Burns guaranteed $30,000, it was the first of the championship's 'golden gate' fights. There was bedlam outside the stadium as forty thousand had showed up hoping to buy a ticket from a scalper.

Johnson was a giant standing six feet tall and weighed 196 pounds. Burns was 5' 7" and weighed only 163 pounds. He was fighting influenza or perhaps a form of jaundice. Not that he complained but he had tried to postpone the bout but McIntosh insisted it must go on as all the tickets were sold.

At 11:15 A.M. the gong sounded and the fight of the century was under way. Both sprang from their corners like panthers. They fell into a clinch and the referee tried to pry the fighters apart grabbing Burns' left glove. As he did so Burns was tagged with a dynamite uppercut that landed on his jaw lifting him off his feet. He hit the canvas with a thud. He was sent to the canvas again in the second round, suffered a swelling left eye and he was bleeding from the mouth. In the fifth Tommy ran from his corner and delivered a powerful right to the challenger's head. Later in the round Burns also landed six crunching blows to Johnson's ribcage. In the seventh a punch raised an ugly lump under Burn's right eye and another dropped the champ for the third time. In the fourteenth round a heavy right put the Canadian down for a fourth time but Burns managed to get to his feet by the count of eight but police officers stepped in to halt the fight. It was over and for the first time ever the heavyweight-boxing champion of the world passed into the hand of a black man.

Tommy Burns had defended his title 10 times in 3 years and was one of the smallest heavyweight champions ever. Jack Johnson went on to become one of the greatest heavyweight champions of all time defeating Jim Jeffries who came out of retirement. It took place in Reno, Nevada on July 4, 1910. The 'Boilermaker' hit the canvas for the third and final time in the fifteenth round. That night there were riots all over the States and seven black men were killed. The next night the blacks struck back and a few white folks were killed. In some cities troops had to be called in to restore order.

Burns had more time for Jewel and their four girls – Margaret, Patricia and twins Mary and Helen. In 1918 Burns filed for a divorce and received custody of the children at a time when it was almost automatically awarded to the woman. There was something wrong with Jewel.

Burns only fought sporadically after his defeat and his last bout was July 16, 1920 against Joe Beckett. His record was 48 wins, 5 losses, 9 draws and 1 no decision with a amazing 39 knockouts. No doubt his most enduring feat was the fact that he was the first man to allow men of colour to cross white racist barrier into the arena of professional sport. For this alone he should be lionized and given his fair due.

Burns did well until the stock market crash in 1929 when he lost much of his wealth. He got severe arthritis in both shoulders. He even fell in love with Nellie Vanderlip, a widow he married at age 65. He became an ordained minister in 1948.

Tommy died in poverty in Vancouver, British Columbia in 1955.

Canadian Caper
Kenneth Taylor Canadian Ambassador to Iran 1980

Mohammed Reza Pahlavi was the Shah of Iran from 1941 to 1979 with the exception of a brief period in 1953 when Prime Minister Muhammed Mosaddeq staged a coup. Mosaddeq's reign was short lived as the Shah, with the military assistance of the United States, regained power over the country. The U.S. involvement would prove to be hazardous in the years to come.

In 1979 when Ayatollah Ruhollah Khomenini over threw the Shah and called for his capture for his brutal treatment of his people. President Jimmy Carter gave asylum to the Shah so he could he receive some medical treatment at a New York hospital. In fact the U.S. was harshly condemned for their support and assistance of this regime.

This condemnation escalated on November 4, 1979 when street demonstrators outside the U.S. embassy in Tehran stormed the compound taking all the personnel inside captive.

Six Americans evaded capture, as they were not in the compound at the time and they sought asylum through the Canadian embassy. The Canadian Ambassador to Iran, Kenneth Taylor, contacted Prime Minister Joe Clark and negotiations began, under a cloak of secrecy. Pat and Ken Taylor harboured fugitives, Joe and Kathy Stafford. He asked Zena and Don Sheardon to hide Bob Anders, Mark and Cora Lijek. Lee Schatz was initially sheltered by the Swedish ambassador Sundberg and would join them later.

Through diplomatic channels President Jimmy Carter was contacted and the Minister of Foreign Affairs Flora Macdonald makes arrangements. To conceal their identities they decide on the 'Hollywood Option' and secure passports and other pieces of identity. To do so required a Special Order in Council in Parliament, so at end of day they made it the last item on the agenda, Clark says, "No need for discussion" and the passports are issued.

Bob Cidell, a Hollywood make up artist, forms Studio 6 with 6 characters and a script named 'Argo.' They courier the Canadian passports to Iran and they pass through CIA agent Antonio's hands who forges the Iranian stamp on them. The six American's go though mock interviews and numerous rehearsals similar to what they might expect to face at the customs office.

January 28, 1980 they go to the Tehran Airport to catch a Swiss Air flight after 79 tense days. There was a moment of intense anxiety when the customs officer leaves while processing their passports but he returns with a cup of tea much to everybody's immense relief. They are soon on their way out of the country and out of danger.

When they returned to American soil there is a celebration and outpouring of affection from American citizens toward Ken Taylor and Canadians. Mohammed Reza Shah Pahlavi died July 27, 1980. Fifty-two American hostages are held for 444 days, but Canada was pleased that they could come to the assistance of a superpower.

Kenneth Taylor received the Congressional Gold Medal from President Ronald Reagan on January 16, 1981.

Ethel Catherwood
The Saskatoon Lily

Ethel Catherwood was born in Hanna, North Dakota on April 28, 1909. Despite her talent and fame, the details of her life remain sketchy. Her early years remain a mystery but her trail is picked up in late August 1926 when she entered the Saskatoon city championships and equalled the Canadian record for the high jump with a jump of 1.511 metres. On Labour Day, September 6, 1926 in Regina she broke the world high jump record held by Phyllis Green of Great Britain. When all other competitors had been forced to quit Miss Catherwood continued to jump and soared gracefully over the bar at 1.586 metres to better the World record by more than an inch. The *Saskatoon Phoenix* reported that her performance overshadowed the championship events for men and even the auto races failed to furnish the thrill the spectators derived when she set the new record.

The new star on the Canadian athletic scene went to Toronto and made a quick impression on the city's sports writers. "The instant this tall slim graceful girl from the Prairies tossed aside her cloak of purple and made her first leap, the fans fell for her. She had a flower like face of rare beauty above a tall, slim body clad simply in pure white...she looked like a tall lily - and she was christened by the crowd 'The Saskatoon Lily.'"

Philanthropist mining millionaire Teddy Oke took Ethel under his wing. Oke insisted that Ethel and her sister, Ginger, stay on as members of his Parkdale Ladies Athletic Club. He sent them to business-college and found them jobs in his brokerage firm that was already brimming with women athletes. He hired Walter Knox, the greatest professional athlete of his day to coach. With Oke's backing and Knox's coaching, Ethel Catherwood was in peak form.

On July 2, 1928 at the Olympic trials in Halifax, Nova Scotia, Catherwood jumped a record 1.60 metres to reclaim her world record from Marjorie Clark of South Africa and set a mark that would stand as a Canadian record until 1954.

Carrying her rag doll and a ukulele, Catherwood was soon sailing for Amsterdam. However, just before the Olympics a new world mark was set for women with a jump of 1.605 metres by the new queen of high jumping, Carolina Gisolf of the host Dutch team. She would be one of the twenty-three contestants Ethel would be facing in the final.

The running high jump, as it was then called, was held on the final afternoon of the games. The weather was cold and the number of entrants large. No new records were set. Catherwood emerged from beneath her Hudson Bay blanket to jump 1.588 metres to claim victory. The most photographed girl at the Olympic games was jubilant after her gold medal win. She was lifted to the shoulders of the Canadian athletes and spectators alike. She waved her arms to the cheering crowd and smiled again on the podium as the Canadian flag soared to the top of the Olympic pole as a tribute of her victory. Miss Catherwood's success was received with more enthusiasm than any other Canadian win except that of Percy Williams who won the gold medal in the men's 100 metre and 200 metre events.

It is an unfortunate fact that Ethel Catherwood essentially disappears after her success at the Olympics. She is known to have married James McLaren, only to divorce him and then marry Byron Mitchell. She died September 26, 1987.

Don Cherry
Grapes

Don Cherry was born in Kingston, Ontario on February 5, 1934. He grew up a hockey-obsessed kid. He had a shot in 1955 when he played a single playoff game for the Boston Bruins. The next year he was injured dashing his hopes of NHL success. He turned to coaching first in the minor leagues then joined the Boston Bruins in 1974. He looked good and his antics were admired but he was traded to Colorado and fired for good in 1980.

Smarting from his dismissal he took a bit part on live hockey broadcasts with the CBC. He provided 'expert analysis' on the game but no one could have predicted he would reinvent the role. He cheered for his favourite teams, complained about 'brutal' refereeing, liked fights and just loved the game. His ratings were so high he was given the *'Coach's Corner'*, a four and a half minute show between periods of Saturday night games.

His face would get beet red as he shouted and pointed his finger, "How many times do I have to repeat it? Fightin' is parta da game. What 'ave we come to? You kids out there, you listen to me: you never pass the puck out blind like that!"

He was outrageous, sometimes offensive with slang and sloppy grammar that raised more than a few eyebrows. He never offered an apology and dressed in gaudy suits with high-collared shirts. He looked like a cartoon mobster but among fans he was a hit. More people watch Cherry than the game itself. Perhaps we watch him to see if he will go too far, but he has endured and knows how to capture the spotlight as he did in the recent strike year scalding the hides off of everybody.

Crowfoot
Chief of the War Eagles of the Plains

In 1821 the great chief of the Blackfoot was born somewhere south of the Red Deer River. His oldest brother was destined to be chief of the tribe until he visited the Snake tribe with peaceful intentions and was murdered. Crowfoot led a war party to avenge Crow Big Foot's death. He was bestowed with his brother's name after his victory and some pioneers believed that the Police Scout Jerry Potts was responsible for the shortening of the name to Crowfoot.

As a young brave he had a reputation for courage and success in battle. This man, who was destined to shape the future on the Plains, was a man of great wisdom. At the peak of his influence he could be seen riding the plains with his beloved umbrella, which he carried for protection from the sun, rain and even snow. He was a man of striking appearance, penetrating eyes, chiselled features and long unbraided hair. He fancied clothes with bright colours. Riding his white or pinto horse he enlivened the prairie scene of the day.

Reverend John McDougall had been commissioned to inform the natives that the North-West Mounted Police were coming and their intentions were honourable. The force arrived at Oldman River October 13, 1874 after their long trek from Manitoba. Before accepting the strangers with their bright red uniforms and shining guns he wanted to know more about them. While the fort was being constructed he came and stood boldly. He was neither friendly nor hostile. He came with an open mind. Colonel James MacLeod, with the scout Jerry Potts to interpret, explained to the chief the government's intention to end whiskey trading. They intended to punish anyone, white or Indian, who refused to obey good laws.

Crowfoot's reaction was favourable as he said, "My brother...I listen to you not only with my ears but with my heart also. In the coming of the Long Knives, with their firewater and quick shooting guns we are weak and our people have been woefully slain and impoverished. You say it will be stopped. We are glad to have it stopped. We want peace. What you tell us about this strong power which will govern with good laws and treat the Indian the same as the white man, makes us glad to hear. My brother, I believe you and am thankful."

When a member of the Blackfoot tribe faced a criminal charge, the chief attended the trial. After following the proceedings carefully, he nodded approval, saying, "There is no forked tongue here. When my people do wrong, I shall send them here to be tried."

In 1876, the same year that Alexander Graham Bell was testing the first telephone, Sitting Bull slaughtered Custer and all his men at the Battle of Little Big Horn. Hands bloodstained, the Sioux warriors fled to the 'Medicine Line' where a lone Mountie, James Morrow Walsh, met them. One can imagine this brave man laying down the law as pronounced on Canadian soil. The Sioux invited Crowfoot to smoke with them but he rejected their offer. Threats were made against the Blackfoot tribe but the NWMP assured Crowfoot that Canadian forces would defend all Canadian Indians who might be attacked from outside the country. Crowfoot then told the Mounties that if they needed any help, Blackfoot warriors were willing to fight to keep the peace. He said, "Tell the great White Mother that we are loyal." Peace prevailed and Sitting Bull and James Morrow Walsh became close friends during the five-year exile of the Sioux in the Cypress Hills area on the Alberta/Saskatchewan border.

Crowfoot's proudest moment came October 22, 1877 at Blackfoot Crossing, near, Cluny, Alberta. He said, "The Mounted Police have protected us as the feathers of a bird protect it from the frosts of winter. I wish all my people good and trust that all our hearts will increase in goodness from this time forward. I am satisfied. I will sign the Treaty." And sign he did - last - for as he said he would be the last to break it.

In 1885 Louis Riel and Gabriel Dumont tried to get the Blackfoot to join the Northwest Rebellion. As the railway tracks stretched across the prairies the Indians became concerned about their rights as the iron link cut through their reserves. Father Albert Lacombe assured the chief a new agreement would be negotiated. Crowfoot remained loyal and refused to support the rebellion. For their effort and loyalty they both received lifetime passes on the CPR. When Crowfoot went east on the ribbon of steel, he returned believing revolt was impossible for "the whites are as thick as flies in summertime."

Crowfoot, 'The Greatest Chief of All', made his last speech on his deathbed. "A little while and I will be gone from among you," he said. "Whither, I cannot tell. From nowhere we came; into nowhere we go. What is life? It is the flash of a firefly in the night. It is breath of a buffalo in the wintertime. It is the shadow that runs across the grass and loses itself in the sunset." He died April 25, 1890. He was buried at Blackfoot Crossing with his best horse, saddle, rifle, well-seasoned stone pipe and a finger from each of his three wives. His tombstone reads 'Father of His People.'

Samuel Cunard
Shipping Magnate

The records of the Cunard family in the New World go back to 1683 when Thomas Kunders arrived with a party of Quaker immigrants. They settled on a tract of land granted by King Charles II of England to William Penn, now in the State of Pennsylvania.

When, a century later, the Thirteen American Colonies revolted against Britain the great-grandson of Thomas Kunders, Abraham Cunard, moved to Halifax to live under the British flag. He fell in love with Margaret Murphy and they were married in 1783. November 21, 1787 Samuel Cunard was born.

Samuel was a good student but it was business that attracted most of his attention in his boyhood. While attending school he would spend his late afternoons gathering dandelions to sell by the basket. With the money he earned he would attend auctions in the evenings and buy articles he thought were being sold at bargain prices. These articles he would try to sell later at a profit.

Halifax was a booming port at the turn of the 19th century. It was in this area that Samuel became interested and his business talents would shine. He joined his father, who was a carpenter, and they built the Cunard Wharf, which soon became the centre of shipping trade in and out of Halifax. He was soon a wealthy and prominent citizen. He bought his parents a farm and settled them there to enjoy their declining years. He diversified and started a lumber business in New Brunswick, bought land in Prince Edward Island, founded the Halifax Banking Company and helped support the project of building a canal across the Isthmus of Chingnecto.

Civic honours were showered upon him. He became the Fire Warden, Commissioner of Lighthouses; Administrator of Bounty for destitute Emigrants and in 1830 was appointed to the Legislative Council.

Still, shipbuilding was his main concern and when the *Royal William* arrived in Halifax on August 31, 1831 Samuel was an interested observer. The *Royal William* was the first ship built in Canada that was powered by steam. This was a new innovation during the golden age of shipping. With his foresight Samuel realized how practical a powered ship would be. As a businessman he appreciated punctuality. These new ships could be scheduled for they were not dependent upon the unpredictable winds that the great sailing ships relied upon. Canadian politicians such as Joseph Howe were pushing Britain to develop a passenger and mail service between London and Halifax. In 1838 when the government advertised for tenders for the regular conveyance of the mail across the Atlantic by steam vessel Samuel Cunard bid on the contract. He won the contract and proceeded to build the *Britannia*, a paddle-wheel steamer. July 4, 1840 the *Britannia*, with Samuel aboard, steamed out of Liverpool inaugurating the first regular trans-Atlantic steamship service. When the *Britannia* arrived in Halifax on July 17 a celebration was in order. Cunard Lines would become the largest ship company in the world and build great ships such as the *Queen Mary*, *Queen Elizabeth* and *Queen Elizabeth II*.

In 1854 Cunard moved to London and rendered effective service when Britain became involved in the Crimean War in 1854. He put all the company streamers at the service of the British government for the transport of materials and men. For this service Queen Victoria knighted him in 1859.

The Cunard Company had a perfect record in the conveyance of mail and passengers, due in large measure to the care and thoroughness with which Samuel Cunard conducted his business affairs. He died in 1865 but the tradition of safety lived on in the annals of the company, which in 1934 merged with the White Star Line to form Cunard-White Star Limited.

Louis Cyr
The Strongest Man in the World

Louis Cyr was born in St. Cyprien de Napierville, Québec on October 10, 1863. At the age of twelve he left school and went to work at various jobs and then as a lumberjack. He built up his strength and was determined to be a strong man. In that age, exploits of the professional strongmen were followed as avidly as those of the movie stars today. Louis challenged the strongest man in Canada at the time, David Michaud. They lifted stones with Cyr finally winning by lifting a boulder weighing 480 pounds, which Michaud was unable to budge.

In 1885 Cyr joined the Montreal police force and patrolled the tough Ste. Cunegonde district. His enormous figure in uniform had a sobering effect on the young hooligans of the city. He once broke up a street fight and hauled the fighters off to jail, one under each arm. After he was attacked with an axe he resigned from the force. However, his exploits had reached Richard Fox, the leading fight promoter in New York. Fox signed up Louis and promoted him with the billing 'The Strongest Man in the World.' He offered anyone who could match his strength $5,000. Cyr defeated all comers including the world's most renowned strongmen of the time: Otto Ronaldo, the German champion; 'Cyclops,' the Polish strongman; and the Scandinavian champions Johnson and Montgomery.

Fox sponsored Cyr on a twenty-three month tour of England; it was a triumph and Cyr became a household name in the Western world. The highlight of his performance was January 19, 1889 at the Royal Aquarium Theatre in London before a packed house and in the presence of the Prince of Wales. He lifted a 551-pound weight with one finger, lifted a platform weighing 4,100 pounds with a back lift. He also lifted a 273 1/4 pound weight with one hand to his shoulder and then above his head.

At a luncheon in Cyr's honour the Marquis of Queensberry suggested that one of his driving horses should be hitched to each of Cyr's arms and if Cyr could hold them to a standstill, he could take one of the horses back to Canada. Cyr won the wager and for many years after drove the nobleman's horse about the streets of Montreal.

Cyr continued to tour the United States and Canada giving exhibitions and challenging local champions. One performance will remain in the record books as his best feat. In Boston in 1895 he lifted what was claimed to have been the greatest weight ever lifted by one man

- 4,337 pounds. He accomplished the feat using the method, for which he was most famous, the back lift.

When not on tour Louis made his home in Montreal where he operated a tavern on Notre Dame Street. He amused customers by tossing around 300-pound beer kegs or by lifting his 120-pound wife, Melina, on the palm of his hand. Louis's appetite matched his enormous size. A good dinner included at least six pounds of meat. Unfortunately overeating ruined his health and he died of Bright's disease at the early age of forty-nine. All Québec mourned his death and Montreal gave him one of the biggest funerals in the city's history. The great French muscleman was dead but his legend still lives on in French Canada.

John Diefenbaker
Just Call Me 'The Chief'

John George Diefenbaker was born in Neustadt, Ontario, on September 18, 1895. His parents were of German and Scottish decent. His father was a teacher and they were homesteaders. He studied law at the University of Saskatchewan and after briefly serving in the Great War he returned to Canada and graduated in 1919. He set up a law practice in Wakaw, Saskatchewan, and defended 18 men who faced the death penalty.

In 1925 and 26 he ran for a seat in the House of Commons but lost. He tried provincially in 1929 and 38 with no luck. He ran for mayor of Prince Albert in 1933 and lost. He was elected leader of the Conservative party in Saskatchewan in 1936 but the party won no seats in the 1938 election. In the 1940 election Diefenbaker finally won a seat in the House of Commons as a member of the Opposition, which he held through the King and St. Laurent governments.

In the 1957 election he showed his remarkable campaign style and the Conservatives won a minority government. The next year they were returned with the greatest majority of seats in Canadian history up to that time sweeping 208 seats.

He improved social programs and his Agricultural Rehabilitation and Development Act helped many farmers. He found a new market in China for Canadian wheat. He appointed the first woman federal cabinet minister, Ellen Fairclough. In 1960 he gave Status Indians the right to vote and the first Canadian Bill of Rights. In 1961 his anti-apartheid statement contributed to the withdrawal of South Africa from the Commonwealth. 'Dief the Chief' did not support the Americans in their hostilities with Cuba.

High unemployment, devaluation of the dollar and the cancellation of the Avro Arrow project eroded the Conservative popularity and in 1962 they were reduced to a minority government. In the 1963 election they lost to the Liberals led by Lester B. Pearson. The Chief held his seat and was last elected in 1979, three months before his death.

Céline Dion
Voice of an Angel, a Diva, an Icon

Adhémar and Thérèse Dion had fourteen children: Denise, Clément, Claudette, Liette, Michel, Louise, Jacques, Daniel, Ghislaine, Linda, Manon and twins Paul and Pauline. Then the baby of the family Céline, came along on March 30, 1968 in Charlemagne, Québec. She was named after a popular French song, called *'Dis-Moi Céline.'* The eldest child Denise, was twenty-two at the time of Céline's birth.

At this time René Angélil sang for a popular group called the Baronettes. They did songs by Paul Anka, Ertha Kitt and the Beatles. However by the early 70's with the Front de Libération du Québec and the political and social upheavals that followed, club going declined. Then René's gambling problem got out of hand.

He soon left his wife Denise and their son Patrick for he had fallen in love with singer Anne-Renée.

Instead of performing Angélil began to promote and in 1974 he sponsored René Simard who won first prize at the Yamaha Popular song festival in Tokyo. He had a meeting with CBS Records and demanded a million dollar contract for his rising star. CBS said they would get back to him, they never did. It was another hard lesson for Angélil.

In 1976 he was looking for another musician to propel his career. He was having limited success and really needed a boost to save his career.

Céline had a manager Paul Lévesque but he was unable to get anywhere. At Mrs. Dion's urging he sent a demo tape to René Angélil but they never heard back. In the spring of 1981 Michel Dion contacted Angélil urging him to listen to the tape made by his twelve year old sister. After listening he asked to see her and when she sang *'Ce n'etait qu'un rêve'* (It Was Only a Dream) a tear came to his eye. He took her on as a client. Incidentally, Céline's mother and brother Jacques wrote the song.

This young girl was not only talented but Céline was the nicest star on the scene. She was direct, uncomplicated, approachable and concerned with others.

René knew that everything she recorded had to be different, distinct and exceptional. Céline sang at Montreal Expo baseball games and Angélil took out a $30,000 mortgage on his house to finance Céline's first two albums. Soon René's wife, Anne-Renée, was also helping Céline by boosting her confidence and introducing her to the world of high fashion.

Early in her career she played in small theatres with only several thousand seats. She soon left her formal education without completing high school with René saying, "You sing and I'll take care of the rest." He didn't quibble or haggle over fees for her performances and knew what she needed was exposure. Monetary rewards would come with stardom.

Eventually she started playing in amphitheatres in the U.S. moving on to bigger and bigger venues. Initially the songs were better known than she was but with Eddy Marnay's compositions for her, she blossomed.

Dr. Riley, a voice physiologist, recommended a number of exercises she should do every day. The results of this regiment of training took five years to come to fruition. Céline was diligent in her training and did them regularly.

Later Céline took singing lessons from Tosca Marmor, a Holocaust survivor, and in 1982 won the thirteenth Yamaha World Popular Song Festival in Tokyo.

In 1983 she was still unknown in France until her stunning triumph at the MIDEM competition in Cannes. She sang with the Montreal Symphony Orchestra at the annual Québec Cystic Fibrosis Association gala, as her niece Karine suffered from the disease. Her albums began selling well, her team grew fast and she soon had an entourage.

On September 11, 1984 she sang in front of Pope John Paul II and 60,000 people in Montreal's Olympic Stadium.

As René's marriage fell apart Céline took a year off, wore braces to straighten her teeth and learned English while rumours flew about in her absence. Sometimes René Angélil would lose a round but with Céline he seemed to end up winning bigger. When he was turned down he ended up with a better offer elsewhere. Céline grew as an individual and a performer and made the transformation from a child to a butterfly. She was like a chameleon, her material was diverse and her sound was changing as much as her look.

René got a deal with CBS Records and hooked up with Luc Plamondon the hottest songwriter in the French-speaking world. He was impressed with the way she could hit the high notes without falsetto or straining her voice. He felt there was something spectacular and very touching about singing very high. With the help of Luc and others Céline, released *Incognito* April 2, 1987. At a CBS staff party held in the Laurentians, Céline sang a duet with Dan Hill and got a standing ovation.

At the Juno Awards Céline sang a new song called *'Have a Heart'* and received thunderous applause.

Still the critics hammered away at her criticizing the themes of her songs saying that they were too syrupy. Still they had to acknowledge her extraordinarily powerful, supple and sensuous voice, the quality of her stage presence and how she charmed the audience with her charisma. She always left them begging for more.

Céline had been in love with René for a long time and one can only speculate as to when the two became intimate but some believe it was after her stunning Eurovisions success April 30, 1988. Rumours about their romantic liaison began to whirl but they kept it hush, hush.

The acclaimed producer David Foster began working with Céline on her first English album. She was thrilled to be in the recording studio and enjoyed the anticipation of a song that is about to be born. A catchy slogan emerged about her, 'Remember her name because you'll never forget the voice.' In 1989 she released *'Where Does My Heart Beat Now'* and it was her first hit to make the billboard charts.

On April 4, 1990 her new album *Unison* was launched and *Incognito* had gone platinum. She crossed Canada promoting the album though it was gruelling and tiring. Despite the promotion the album did not take off. September 21 she appeared on *The Tonight Show* with Jay Leno and sang *'Unison.'* In December her voice failed her and she was instructed to remain silent for three weeks. She communicated on the telephone by tapping her nail on the receiver.

In 1992 Céline's *'Beauty and the Beast'* song for the animated film soared to the top of the billboard charts. It became her signature song and gave her a big international breakthrough. She sang it at the Oscars that year and it won Song of the Year. April 29 René suffered a heart attack in Los Angeles. A journalist said she almost lost her second father to which Céline replied, "My father is my father… René is my heart. He's the one who makes it beat."

With the Québec referendum looming Céline weighted in supporting a united Canada. In October she appeared on *Tête-à-tête* with host Lise Payette, she talked about her family and burst into tears when asked about her love life.

On April 2, 1993 René placed a box between them on the dinner table. Céline opened it to discover a diamond and she broke into tears for at last their love would be known. May 3 her favourite niece Karine died in Céline's arms, she was only sixteen.

The Colour of My Love was launched November 8 and David Foster claimed, "Céline is the future." At the end of her performance she kissed René squarely on the lips amid shouting and applause at the Métropolis.

They were married December 17, 1994 in Montreal's Notre Dame Basilica. Present were many celebrities including Prime Minister Brian Mulroney and his wife Mila. It was a spectacle Québec will not soon forget.

Céline sang at the opening of the 1996 Atlanta Olympic Games. The audience was estimated at 4 billion.

The press asked repetitive questions: does she want to have a baby, what about her husband, is she anorexic. Céline was always kind in her responses.

By 1997 she was performing in Europe's largest stadiums in cities like London, Copenhagen, Amsterdam, Zurich and Berlin. The set up and performances of her shows are a thing of beauty. Each technician wears a different colour: the carpenters wear black T-shirts, the cameramen are in blue, the soundmen in green and the lighting people in yellow.

Céline's concerts are a symphony of sound and she is like the subject of an artist's canvas as smoke swirls around her. Lighting is an essential material for creating stage effects. Lapin creates striking visual effects that Picasso or Rembrandt would cherish. He surrounds her with clouds, makes golden rain fall and at times flashes lightning across her face. Céline never sees the effects Lapin creates for she is at the very heart of the magic kaleidoscope.

Some shows are pure magic and Céline can feel something in the air but you never know when it is going to happen. She says it is as if her voice takes on a life of its own, it is as though it is out of control, she is no longer the master and her voice possesses her. This is what she hopes for every time she sings; an intensity, heartrending inflections that seem to come of their own accord unrehearsed, unexpected, always dynamic and moving.

Céline also receives from her audiences. On the last chord of *River Deep, Mountain High* the music shatters into a million pieces just as the lights go out. There is an instant of darkness and a moment of silence then the applause. The British stomp their feet, the French cry, "Un autre! Un autre!", the Scandinavians shout, "Ohey, ohey." But it was the audience in Zurich who truly moved her. They spread their fingers wide, pulsated their hands hiding their faces and it looks like a windswept field of flowers. They cry, "Ahhh" that is soft at first but it swells until it fills the stadium.

The Bee Gees wrote a song for her called '*Immortality*' and of course she reached another pinnacle with the epic song '*My Heart Will Go On*' from the movie *Titanic*. Evidently it is the most heard song in history. Céline built a stage to perform on in Las Vegas and with her husband's pension for gambling it is a match made in heaven for them.

Céline and René had a son the was born on January 25, 2001 at 1:00 A.M weighing 6 pounds 8 ounces and they named him René Charles.

Céline has been to the Grammys, the Junos, the American and World Music Awards, sung in fifty cities, on four continents, appeared on David Letterman, Jay Leno, and Oprah, set a precedent singing two songs at the Oscars and kicked off the Olympics. What will she do for an encore?

René likes to say, "Just wait. You haven't seen anything yet."

Adam Dollard des Ormeaux
Canada's Davy Crocket

Adam Dollard des Ormeaux was born in France around 1635. He sailed to Canada in 1658 and was the commander of the garrison at Ville-Marie (Montreal). Approximately 1,000 Iroquois braves united in force planning an attack on Ville Marie and Trois Riviére. Recognizing the situation Adam took action. He approached the governor of New France, Sieur de Maisonneuve Paul de Chomedey, proposing that he and a small force of volunteers set up a defensive position at the junction of the Ottawa and St. Lawrence Rivers at a place called Long Sault. He was granted permission. By the end of April 1660 sixteen young men had come forward. The task of Dollard and his men was to die so the ones they loved could live. All seventeen made out their wills and received the last sacrament in the chapel of Hotel-Dieu.

After an arduous journey of two weeks the men reached Long Sault and found an abandoned stockade. Forty Huron under their chief, Anahotaha, as well as four Algonquin joined them. After only two days Huron scouts spotted and ambushed two Iroquois canoes. Unfortunately one Iroquois brave escaped to warn the main Iroquois party.

Soon forty or fifty canoes arrived and the Iroquois rushed the stockade. Dollard and his men fired volley after volley into their attackers forcing them to retreat. Second and third attacks were staged before the Iroquois withdrew to hold a council of war.

For five days there is a lull. Renegade Huron fighting for the Iroquois taunted the Huron fighting for Dollard and they soon abandon Dollard and jumped the barricade to join the Iroquois. Only the gallant Anahotaha remained.

They lacked water and food and were dulled from lack of sleep. Escape or rescue was impossible but they fought for their families.

On the fifth day 500 Iroquois warriors arrived to conduct a final assault. They spent three days preparing while they harassed Dollard's little band day and night. On the morning of the ninth day they assaulted the stockade but were miraculously beaten back. A second assault was able to set a fire to the fort. Desperately Dollard tried to push a grenade made from a gunpowder barrel filled with musket balls over the stockade into the midst of the attackers. It teetered on top of the barricade and fell back into the fort. It exploded killing some of the defenders and blinding others. In the hand-to-hand fighting all his men were cut down, as was Dollard. The epic battle of Long Sault was over.

The Iroquois reasoned that if Dollard and his few followers could cause them so much trouble, an attack on Ville Marie would be far too costly and they went home. Their plan worked, Dollard and his men had sacrificed their lives but in the end they saved many more.

Tommy Douglas
Canada's Political Saint

Tommy was born in Falkirk, Scotland on October 20, 1904 to a working class religious family. His father, an ironworker, was a Labour Party supporter. As a young boy Tommy had suffered from osteomyelitis, a bone disease that often has its sufferers face limb amputation. Tommy's legs had been spared through sheer luck and he didn't think others should be forced to rely on good fortune. This early experience remained with him for a lifetime.

His family developed ties to the All People's Mission run by the social measures lobbyist James S. Woodsworth. He would become Douglas's role model. Tommy began his career as a printer's apprentice in 1924 but soon left to further his education. He entered Brandon College receiving degrees in arts and theology. In 1930 he became the pastor at Calvary Baptist Church in Weyburn, Saskatchewan. It was here that he would be transformed into a social activist. It was 1930 and the Great Depression loomed before the country. These factors brought bankruptcy and even starvation to many Canadians. His church became a distribution point for the unemployed, sick and hungry.

Drought, wind and grasshoppers and the devastation they wreaked, brought him to the realization that the kingdom of God could not be achieved on earth without political action. He joined the Co-operative Commonwealth Federation (CCF) in 1933. He ran in the 1934 provincial election and lost but ran in the 1935 federal election and won. He soon earned a reputation as a strong debater who was both eloquent and humorous. He pushed for social legislation without much success. He returned to Saskatchewan from Ottawa and became the CCF provincial leader and in 1944 won a huge majority sweeping forty-seven of the fifty-three seats in the Saskatchewan legislature. He would win five successive elections.

He was instrumental at introducing rapid change: the extension of state-operated electric power, telephone service to rural areas, government automobile insurance and the introduction of free hospital care. Through the 50's he paid off the provincial debt, which happened to be the highest in Canada at the time. He urged the federal government to introduce state-run health insurance but to no avail so in 1959 he decided to go it alone. In 1960 he introduced the Medicare system, which would become the model for the entire country.

In 1961 Tommy resigned as premier to lead the newly created New Democratic Party (NDP). His new successor, Woodrow Lloyd, faced a doctors' strike July 1, 1962 that lasted for 23 days. There was great international attention but the system worked and within a decade Ottawa would extend it to everyone in Canada. It was Douglas's greatest achievement.

Tommy was defeated in the 1962 election due to a backlash to his Medicare legislation, however he won a seat in a by-election and served as leader of the NDP until 1971. He continued to move people with his oratorical feats at universities, conventions, churches and synagogues that attracted huge crowds. He continued as his party's energy critic until his retirement in 1979.

He lived a quiet life with his wife and two daughters. His cheerfulness spilled over into his meetings with strangers and friends and did not diminish during his battle with cancer that ended his life in 1986.

Canada obviously remembers him fondly because in a 2004 Canada wide poll he was voted the Greatest Canadian. He was a great man in our midst.

Gaétan Dugas
Patient Zero in the AIDS Epidemic

Gaétan Dugas was born in Ancienne-Lorette, Québec on February 28, 1953. His first job was as a hairdresser but he landed his 'dream' job in the 70's when he became a flight attendant for Air Canada. He enjoyed flying overseas and was outgoing, flashy and he had no problem meeting people. He was strikingly attractive and often fell in love with breathtaking speed.

In 1980 his life was to change forever. He was diagnosed with a rare form of skin cancer. The doctors were finding the same disease with unusual frequency among homosexual men in San Francisco and New York. It became known as the 'gay disease.' It was even given the name GRID, meaning Gay Related Immune Deficiency. Others called it ACIDS, meaning Acquired Community Immune Deficiency Syndrome. We now call it AIDS, Acquired Immune Deficiency Syndrome.

He was most certainly the first Canadian to be diagnosed with it. American journalist Randy Shits reached the stunning conclusion in his research that Dugas was likely the first North American to contract the deadly disease. He passed it on to thousands of his homosexual lovers and became in doctor jargon, 'Patient Zero.'

It was medical researchers in 1980 and 81 that made a breakthrough in understanding the way AIDS was transmitted. Gaétan admitted to thousands of sexual partners and when hundreds of these men were tracked down it became clear that the AIDS virus might be transmitted sexually. It is ironic that through Gaétan's cooperation researchers saved many lives though he had unwittingly infected hundreds if not thousands of others himself.

Blood agencies and health authorities responded to this 'gay' disease with the speed of a snail. Prejudices against the homosexual life style stifled scientific inquiry and gay organizations felt defensive and were reluctant to become educated about the disease. Gaétan died March 30, 1984 in Québec City.

Ben Dunkelman
A Great Soldier Who Just Wanted to Go Home

David Dunkelman emigrated from Poland to Toronto and began a mass-produced men's clothing store called Tip Top Tailors. It became a huge success. David and his wife Rose had a son in 1913 they named Ben.

The family was very well off and grew up in the lap of luxury. There was some anti-Semitism in Toronto in those days and they were not allowed to join the Royal Canadian Yacht Club. It didn't bother Ben in the least for he had a naturally sunny and relaxed disposition.

His mother however was feisty. When they were excluded from Balfour Beach on Lake Simcoe the Dunkelman's purchased 30 acres of waterfront and turned it into a club for Jews. She named it for Sir Arthur Balfour, the British politician that paved the way for the creation of the State of Israel with the Balfour Declaration.

When Ben was seventeen he was sent to Palestine and worked on a *kibbutz*. When the Nazis rose to power in Germany he was brought back to Toronto to work in his father's factory. This did not make Ben happy.

When the Second World War broke out in the autumn of 1939 Ben saw a way of escaping the dull routine of the men's clothing business. It was also a way to demonstrate his pride in his country. He tried to join the Navy but was rejected. He found a place with the Second Battalion of the Queen's Own Rifles and was commissioned as an officer.

On D-day June 6th, 1944 Ben was with the Queen's Own in the second wave to hit Juno Beach. Mortars had become his specialty and here he could work his tragic magic. He would coordinate his team or teams to pummel a position launching a dozen to two dozen mortars into the air at once. The target position would be bombarded with mortars and it left no place for the targeted soldiers to hide. It was a very successful technique and he became know as Mr. Mortar of the Canadian Army.

Ben was particularly proud of their conquest in the zone between Caen and Falaise where Panzers and SS divisions were holed up. With his mortars he pinned down the Germans and 'Operation Totalize' killed or wounded an astounding 400,000 enemy. He wrote: "We crushed the whole damn army."

In 1945 his mortar crew was working in the mud of the Scheldt estuary clearing the way to the crucial Belgian port, Antwerp. Now a

Major Dunkelman picked up a discarded gun and rushed forward killing ten Germans with his pistol and bare hands. He was awarded the Distinguished Service Order.

After over three hundred days of combat from Normandy to the banks of the Rhine he was offered command of the Queen's Own. Though honoured, he turned it down and was happy to return home to his family.

He didn't stay there for long for he was soon off to the war in Palestine as second-in-command of the Jewish army. Ben developed a close relationship with the Israeli leader David Ben-Gurion who assigned him to open the road to Jerusalem. It was a brutal fight and it was eventually named Road of Valour.

The Israelis were outnumbered and out gunned but Dunkelman took the towns of Latrun, Tel Kissam and Shafa Amir. He deployed surprise attacks at night and made a stunning victory in Nazareth.

Tired and racked with malaria he rested and during the lull met a female corporal named Yael Lifshitz. They fell in love and got married. He had again shown his courage and inventiveness as he helped get the fledgling nation on its feet. The government offered him a position as commander but Dunkelman turned it down and returned home with his bride.

Ben died peacefully in 1997.

Early History

Columbus first gave the term "Indian" to the inhabitants of the New World in 1492 on the false assumption that he had landed in the vicinity of India. The largest group in Canada were the Algonquins but there were numerous other groups of natives spread over the land. The Indians called the natives in the far north Eskimos and the name they gave themselves was 'Inuit.'

The first visit by Europeans to North America was by the Vikings about 1000 A.D. Lief 'the Lucky' Erickson landed near L'anse aux Meadows, now in Newfoundland. In 1003 Gurdrid, the wife of Karlsefni, gave birth to the first European child born in America named Snorri. The Beothuk soon drove them out of the colony and America was left to the natives for almost another 500 years.

June 24, 1497 the 'Great Admiral', John Cabot landed in the vicinity of Newfoundland. He found fish plentiful in the waters and soon numerous fishing boats plied the waters of the Continental Shelf each summer hauling in fish and drying them on bawns along the shore.

Soon the French were also exploring the coast of North America. Jacques Cartier asked the natives what the name was of their land and was told that it was *kanata*. This word actually means a group of huts or a village in the native tongue. Never the less Cartier named our great country and discovered the mighty St. Lawrence River in 1534. He then took the Iroquois chief Donnacona back to France with him in 1535 and the chief died from smallpox in 1539. When their chief failed to return the Iroquois could not forgive the French and many others would die from this mysterious disease brought by the white man.

Much of Canada's early history is marked by massacres, slaughters, battles and wars. Natives fought the French and English as well as each other. The English and French fought each other. Indians fought each other. All in all the era was marked by hostilities between all the groups that inhabited the New World.

Samuel de Champlain came to Canada in 1603. He fired the first shot in North America at Ticonderoga July 29, 1609 killing three chiefs. The Iroquois-French Wars raged on until 1624. During this time the Jésuits went amongst the natives to convert them to Christianity. Many of the priests were martyred such as Brébeuf and Jogues.

In 1647 the French brought the first horses to Canada. In 1660 Adam Dollard des Ormeaux and 16 men intercepted 1000 Iroquois warriors at Long Sault and though they were massacred they saved Ville Marie, now known as Montreal from attack. In 1668 Pierre Radisson and

Chouart des Groselliers set out for Hudson Bay. Pierre was forced to turn back but Groselliers completed the journey in the *Nonsuch* and returned loaded with fine pelts. On May 2, 1670 the Hudson's Bay Company was established. The fur trade flourished as the European fashions brought a handsome price for pelts, which were made into felt for the beautiful feathered hats of the era.

In 1685 Pierre le Moyne d'Iberville captured three British forts around Hudson Bay. In 1688 he outfought three British war ships and captured one and in 1698 he sacked St. John's. In 1689 the Iroquois massacred 200 settlers at Lachine. As many as 950 drowned in 1711 when ships attached to the British fleet were preparing to attack Québec and sank on the rocks of Ile-aux-Oeufs.

In 1720 the French began construction of Louisbourg, named after the 'Sun King' Louis XIV. The British sieged the fort in 1745 and captured it after 40 days. The British again captured it in 1758 and destroyed it.

From 1756 to 1763 the Seven Years War raged on as the British and French fought to assert their colonial rule. September 13-14, 1759 was the date of the epic battle between the French and British on the Plains of Abraham. Both the British General Wolfe and French General Montcalm lost their lives in that battle but the British emerged as the decisive victor. In 1763 the Treaty of Paris ceded all of the conquered French territory to Britain except for the islands of St. Pierre and Miquélon. The Québec Act of 1774 guaranteed the French freedom of language, religion and legal rights.

During the American War of Independence 1775-1783 the British and many other men loyal to the crown fought the American forces. At the end of the war the British Loyalists fled from the U.S.A. and settled around the Bay of Fundy. Of course the Americans won their independence and wrote their Declaration of Independence. They thought that in time Canada would join them.

Although the Treaty of Paris ended the American War of Independence in 1783 there was still friction. In 1812 the British were at war with France and claimed the right to search American ships for cargoes bound for the enemy. In the process the British often forced American sailors on these ships to join the British navy. Resentment grew until June 1812 when the U.S. declared war on Britain. There were many notable battles on both American and Canadian soil. April 27, 1813 American General Pike captured York, now Toronto, and burned the public buildings. August 24 British General Ross occupied Washington and returned the favour by burning the White House. The war like the

Battle of Lundy's Lane was bloody but ended in a draw. December 24, 1814 the Treaty of Ghuet provided the release of prisoners, restoration of territory and arbitration of border disputes. Since this time no international wars or battles have been fought on Canadian soil. However in 1829 Nancy Shawnadithit, the last Beothuk native in Newfoundland, died making her tribe extinct.

Edmonton Commercial Grads
Greatest Team in Canada's Sporting History

The greatest team in Canada's sporting history was a little known womens' basketball team called the Edmonton Grads. The Grads were formed in 1915 with students and graduates of McDougall Commercial High School. J. Percy Page was the coach and he recruited solely from his 'farm system' at McDougall High. There were two exceptions to this rule Gladys Fry and Mae Brown. Both had been outstanding players on other Edmonton teams.

In 1923 the typewriter company, Underwood, sponsored the first North American Basketball Championship. The Edmonton Grads defeated all the teams to win the championship.

The following year the Grads traveled to Paris to take part in the Olympic Games. Unfortunately women's basketball did not become an official sport until the 1976 Olympics in Montreal. Nevertheless, the girls won all six of their exhibition games by a combined score of 360-47. In fact they beat the Paris team that had claimed to be world champions, by the score of 86-14. The Edmonton Grads were proclaimed world champions, a title they would hold until they disbanded in 1940.

Coach Page, had them practise twice a week and over their 25-year history he missed only 3 practices. Once was to skip a city championship curling team and twice to campaign for a seat in the Alberta legislature. Page demanded from his team the same sacrifices he made himself. He said, "You must play, think and dream basketball."

The Grads traveled to subsequent Olympic games and in Amsterdam in 1928 they won all nine of their games. They scored 664 points to their opponents' 100. So awesome was their international reputation that at the 1932 Los Angeles Olympics they could only find three other willing opponents, all of which they beat of course. At the 1936 Olympics the Grads won all their matches, including a 100-2 win over the London (England) Pioneers.

The Grads traveled some 125,000 miles over the years. Generally they doubled the other teams score. They even accepted challenges from men's teams and chalked up a seven-win and two-loss record. In one stretch the Grads won 147 consecutive games.

In their final season in 1940 the Grads made 38% of their shots from the floor and 58% from the foul line. One Grad, captain Maggie MacBurney, once sank 61 straight free throws, a world record at the time for men or women. MacBurney was not the only one who could shoot. There were the likes of Mae Brown, Babe Belanger, Winnie Martin,

Connie Smith and one of the most skilled of them all Noel MacDonald. She sat on the bench in her first season in 1933, but the 5' 10" MacDonald soon won the starting centre position. In 135 games she scored 1,875 points for a 13.9 points per game average, the best in the club's history. In 1980 Noel recounted her biggest thrill, a game where she was assigned to check the great American star Alberta Williams in a crucial Underwood Trophy match. Williams was a hook shot specialist and could sink a basket with either hand. She was also tall, five-eleven, very quick and powerful. That night Noel held Williams to a mere four points while scoring twenty herself.

When World War II broke out the Edmonton Grad team was disbanded when the Royal Canadian Air Force appropriated their playing facility. They had been world champions for an incredible 17 years from 1923-1940. When the team disbanded they were given the Underwood Trophy. No other team had won it. Their record stood at 502 wins and 20 losses. James Naismith who invented basketball in 1891 said, "There is no team I mention more frequently in talking about the game. My admiration is not only for your remarkable record of games won but also for your record of clean play, versatility in meeting teams at their own style and more especially for your unbroken record of good sportsmanship."

Percy Page went on to sit as a Conservative member of the Alberta legislature from 1952-59 and was the lieutenant governor of Alberta from 1959-66.

Bob Edwards
Editor Who Would Open Your Eyes

Robert Charles Edwards was born in Edinburgh, Scotland on September 24, 1864. He was orphaned at five and raised by aunts. He attended university in Glasgow where he graduated. He roamed Europe for a few years before heading to Idaho in 1892 with his brother Jack. He turned up in Calgary in 1894 and moved to Wetaskiwin, a small town south of Edmonton. He liked to drink and was employed by Jerry Boyce as a handyman and part-time bartender at the Wetaskiwin Hotel. When his brother died in 1897 Bob left the hotel and started a small weekly newspaper, the *Wetaskiwin Free Lance*. He said the purpose of the paper was simply to amuse.

This proved to be somewhat untrue for he was a social activist. He took on everyone from real estate agents and speculators to loan sharks and he used his humour as a very sharp sword to whittle that person down to size. He was just as likely to lampoon his own mistakes and drinking habits. When some churchwomen let it be known that the town would be better off without him he packed up and left. Jerry Boyce had become a good friend by this time and was buying and building hotels all over the Calgary area. Robert simply followed Boyce to his next purchase.

In 1899 he showed up in High River, southwest of Calgary and launched the *Eye Opener*. In the first issue he began his tirade against the hypocrisy of the churchgoers who are righteous on Sundays and absolute assholes the other six days of the week.

In 1904 he moved to Calgary, which at the time was a frontier town of only five or six thousand. Its boom was soon to come due to the Canadian Pacific Railway (CPR) station. The busiest corner in town was where the Alberta Hotel stood and this became Edward's watering hole. He became friends with Patty Nolan, a prominent lawyer, who loved a joke and a drink. They became conspirators when they launched the *Eye Opener* in the Sandstone City, so called because buildings were mandated to be built of non-flammable material for prairie grass fires had burned the wooden structures to the ground more than once.

The theme of a remittance man was a fairly regular staple in his newspaper. In reality the remittance man was usually the youngest son of a well to do family in England who was sent to Canada after he had knocked up too many bar maids around home. Every six months he would receive a remittance from his parents with the hope that he would not come home. He developed a character named Buzzard Chumley who wrote home with different schemes for getting more money out or his parents. Some of the schemes Edwards dreamed up were hilarious and Chumley became a favourite of the readers. He wrote, "Cheer the family up by assuring them that my poor half-breed wife is suffering from acute alcoholism and is not expected to live. Even as I write, an Indian medicine man is beating a tom-tom by her bedside in an adjoining tent to drive away the evil spirits, though I fear her system is too thoroughly impregnated with spirits to yield to such treatment...Love to mother and the girls. Drink my health at Christmas. I shall drink to your right now if the medicine man has not finished the jug."

He engaged a cartoonist named Forrester whom he encouraged to depict politicians as apes and hooligans. Edwards blasted everybody from the Premier of the province, Alexander Rutherford, to the federal minister of the interior Sir Clifford Sifton, to R.B Bennett the future Prime Minister of Canada. Bennett was a lawyer for the CPR and Edwards believed the CPR was the diabolical enemy of the people. When there was a train wreck he would put a big photo on the front page with the caption 'Another CPR Wreck' as if they happened all the time.

He did more thoughtful pieces like the 'Negro Question' and championed Mother Fullum, the Pig Lady, who fed her pigs from garbage collected from the Alberta Hotel and other restaurants. His real job was to irritate people and he was serious about it. It was how he tried to keep them honest.

The Liberal government in Ottawa was trying to make some headway in the west and decided the *Eye Opener* was their enemy. They launched a Liberal funded paper called the *Calgary Daily News* and the editor Daniel McGillcuddy set out to destroy Edwards. Edwards shot right back and lampooned Lord Strathcona, otherwise known as Donald Smith. He was the bearded figure who drove the last spike.

McGillcuddy published a vicious personal attack on Edwards just prior to an election. He called him a libeller, a drunkard, degenerate, 'tin horn' and welcher who writes smut and slander. Bob hit the bottle and the *Eye Opener* did not appear for weeks. Editors across the country came to his defence saying editors with independence and fearlessness like Mr. Edwards were sorely needed.

His lawyer friend Paddy Nolan took McGillcuddy to court and he was found guilty but the judge also scolded Edwards for his satirical editorials. Bob was fed up and left Calgary in 1909. He tried Toronto, then Port Arthur and then Winnipeg. By 1911 the *Calgary Daily* was out of business and friends convinced Edwards to return where he belonged. When his friend Paddy Nolan died in 1913 Bob was wrought with emotion and it was weeks before he could write about the loss of his good friend.

With the outbreak of World War I Edwards tried to enlist but he was too old and his drinking habits were legendary. Surprisingly he supported the Women's Christian Temperance Movement that was fighting for Prohibition. When the hotelkeepers tried to bribe him to their side they found that he could not be bought and got a good tongue-lashing as only Bob could do. The Prohibition Act passed July 1, 1916. He soon began to rethink the Prohibition issue as he saw no discernable effects and 'speakeasies' thrived. He campaigned for its repeal.

He also campaigned for votes for women. He thought they were thoughtful with good common sense unlike many men who wanted to keep them in a servitude role. A confirmed bachelor all his life he surprised every one when he married a young twenty year old named Kate Penman. He next ran and won a seat in the provincial legislature as a Conservative representative. He sat for only one session championing social justice issues then stepped down.

Edwards began to address more national issues advocating minimum wage, old age pensions, public hospitals, school texts with Canadian stories and he applauded social activists like Nellie McClung and Emily Murphy. By now the *Eye Opener* was being read from coast to coast and he had garnered a loyal following and was dearly loved.

November 20, 1922 the wire service flashed 'Bob Edwards is dead.' Those who hated him rejoiced, those who adored him mourned his passing but almost everyone had an opinion about this bigger than life character. The humorous, challenging, outrageous journalism he gave to the country almost died with him and was not revived for decades.

Empress of Ireland
Tragedy on the St. Lawrence River

The *Empress of Ireland* first sailed across the Atlantic on June 29, 1906. She would transport 186,848 passengers safely to their destinations. During this time many immigrants came to Canada attracted by the Minister of the Interior, Clifford Sifton's policy of populating western Canada with the offer of cheap land. Many people have fond memories of their voyage to the new land, the excitement, the hope and the promise of a brighter future.

In the winter of 1913 four big ocean liners the *Virginian, Scandinavian, Teutonic* and *Empress of Ireland* were berthed in the Halifax Harbour. In 1914 the *Empress* had completed four crossings before Henry George Kendall took command from Captain James Murray. As usual the ships pilot Adélard Bernier, brought the *Empress* up the St. Lawrence to the Breakwater in Québec City. She berthed at 3:15 P.M. on Friday May 22, 1914. Passengers and goods were unloaded and inspections were made.

Hugh Stanton, the Canadian Pacific Railroad's (CPR) Superintendent of Life-Saving Appliances, noted in the watertight door exercise that it took only 3 ½ to 4 minutes for all the doors to be closed. The ship was on an even keel without passengers and it all seemed so simple.

During the stop over a few men who shovelled coal, called the Black Gang, jumped ship or 'swallowed the anchor' as they said. Work as a stoker or trimmer was hard and the pay was poor so this was not unusual and they were simply replaced.

The preparations for departure had started the day before when fires were lit in the cold furnaces as the black gang got the steam up.

A CPR train called the 'Empress Special' delivered a contingent of Salvation Army personnel heading to an event in England. Also on board were 212 silver bars from the Nipissing Mine at Cobalt. They were worth almost $1 million and weighed five tons. At the last moment the ship's cat Emmy, ran down the gangplank and could not be coaxed back despite having a litter of kittens on board.

There were the usual last minute photographs, kisses and tender embraces.

The last hawser holding the *Empress* to the dock was cast off and at 4:27 P.M. May 28 the great ship slowly pulled away, her funnels belching black smoke as she headed out on a rising tide.

On the wharf a large, colourful crowd gathered and waved farewells, threw paper streamers, waved handkerchiefs, blew kisses, and shouted, "Bon voyage!" The Salvation Army band offered an impromptu concert playing *O Canada* and *Auld Lang Syne*. When they played *God Be with You Till We Meet Again* there was a long blast from the whistle. Soon the *Empress* swung around the point at Indian Cove and was lost to view.

Down in the galleys, butchers were cutting meat and the first loaves of bread were already being baked.

Aided by the current, the engines settled into a steady rhythm as she accelerates slowly to full speed, at just over 18 knots. She rides low in the water for her ballast tanks are full and the river is fairly fresh. It is a pleasant evening as the sunsets and dusk slowly gives way to night.

At nine the band played their last number Charles Gounod's *Funeral March of a Marionette*. Most nights no one would notice but like an omen it would be recalled in hindsight. It is a beautiful clear night and at 9:45 they passed a Norwegian collier loaded with coal named *Alden*. They pass port to port at a distance of ¾ of a mile.

Slowly the weather changed and they encountered two patches of fog. As convention would have it they slowed to a snail's pace not wanting to tempt fate as safety and caution are of the utmost importance. They are not entered in the logbook.

With the *Empress* now riding higher in the water due to the higher salinity of the water, they stop a mile north of Father Point gas buoy and a tug, the *CGS Eureka*, comes alongside to take off Pilot Bernier. The ship is stationary for a few minutes and at 1:20 A.M. the mighty engines rumble again. The crow's nest lookout sights and reports the Cock Point gas buoy.

At 1:38 A.M. spotter John Carroll sights masthead lights about six miles distance on the starboard side and strikes the 10-inch bell once.

He had seen the *Storstad* a collier loaded with coal so it sits low in the water. It is painted black and plods upstream at 8 ½ knots. She is 3,561 tons, is 452 feet long and 58.2 feet wide. She is sailing from Sydney bound for Montreal. She is designed to have great fore-and-aft strength to the hull to navigate through the pack ice of the St. Lawrence. Her chisel shape made her a potentially dangerous weapon.

They have visual contact at four miles and Kendall intends to pass starboard to starboard. Suddenly a bank of fog drifts off the land and visual contact is severed. They do not have radios or radar.

The *Empress* reverses her engines and slows to a stop as a cautionary measure. The *Storstad* does not stop but slows to 4 knots and the Chief Officer Alfred Toftenes changes course anticipating a port-to-port passing. He does not call Captain Thomas Anderson to the bridge as directed should they encounter fog. Each vessel sounds their foghorns in long piercing blasts.

Some passengers on the *Empress* are alarmed and rise from bed to investigate. This action would save some lives.

The captain of the *Storstad* Thomas Anderson finally scrambles to the bridge but arrives too late.

Captain Kendall sees the *Storstad*'s forward masthead light and both red and green sidelights less than one ship length off his starboard bow. He then knew the vessels were about to collide. Hoping to kick the starboard rear quarter out of the way, Kendall orders full speed ahead with a hard starboard turn.

At 1:55 A.M. the *Storstad*'s whistle blared, as she sliced into the *Empress* mid-ship right between the funnels. It punched a gaping hole below the waterline ploughing fourteen feet into the liner. The hole in the *Empress* is estimated to be 25 feet high and 14 feet wide. This allows 265 tons or 60,000 gallons of water per second to flood the *Empress*.

Captain Kendall orders Murphy to activate the ship's siren. The wireless operator sends out an SOS and their position. The ship's crew moved into mandatory action and secured all watertight doors, others headed for the lifeboats and still others aroused the passengers in first class. The ship sunk so fast that passengers in second and third class received no warning and those who escaped acted swiftly on their instincts.

Kendall used the bullhorn imploring the captain to keep engines full ahead hoping that the vessel will stay wedged into the gaping hole.

The *Storstad*'s bow was crushed back 14 feet which was forward of the first watertight bulkhead. She was in no danger of sinking.

Not so for the *Empress*, the impaled ship quickly fills with water that gushed even more as the *Storstad* swung around and slipped out of the hole she had created. Down below the crew are trying to close the doors but the *Empress* was listing so badly the doors cannot be closed try as they might.

Panicked people assembled on the upper promenade deck. The lifeboat davits made launching them difficult under normal circumstances. It was almost impossible with the 30-degree list. As they were launched some passengers in them were spilled into the icy waters. Some passengers on the port side were able to escape through portholes.

As the list became even more extreme women and children were no longer able to hang onto the handrail and they went catapulting across the deck into the void.

Captain Anderson backed the *Storstad* toward the listing *Empress* and hears shrieks from passengers in the water. He orders their lifeboats launched. Helplessly all watch as the *Empress* rolls to her starboard until both funnels hit the water simultaneously missing a lifeboat by inches. Another full lifeboat was not so lucky as falling objects squashed it. This propelled many more passengers into the water. A half a minute later there is an explosion that blasted more people from the ship as though they had been shot into the sea. Those that hit the water remember the cold instantly penetrating their bones.

Slowly the *Empress* rolled over until her keel was pointed skyward. There were many people who managed to stay with her even though the hull was very slippery. She never did roll completely over. The bow went first then the stern rose four feet out of the water and all that were still aboard were jumping for their lives. The *Empress* gave a final hiss and gurgle as the port propeller hung over the water then plunged into the inky depths. It had taken only 14 minutes for the *Empress* to sink.

People who were dragged under by the suction began to pop up all around the wreck site. Corpses bobbed up and down as those still alive struggled to stay afloat. There was an eerie light from flares of automatic lifebuoys that floated free from the vessel.

Lifeboat 3 saved Captain Kendall. He took command of it and began rescuing those in the water until he had 60 aboard. Still he searched throwing lifelines to people with frozen arms and clenched fists. They headed for the *Storstad* where they were unloaded. Kendall called for some men to man his boat. They threw sails and provisions over the side and headed out to rescue more survivors.

The *Eureka* arrived on the scene at 3:00 A.M. The *Lady Evelyn* steamed into the vast field of dead bodies and wreckage at 3:45.

Unlike the *Titanic* the *Empress of Ireland* sank so quickly that few of the sleeping passengers had time to abandon the ship. Crew members were under instruction to head to the lifeboats in any emergency. As a result more crew members survived than passengers. Of the 465 people who survived the disaster, 250 of them were members of the crew.

One hundred and seventy-five crew members were among the approximate 1,014 people who died that tragic night.

Captain Henry Kendall sent the heart-rending message: 'SHIP GONE.'

Reginald Fessenden
Greatest Wireless Inventor of His Age

Reginald was born at Milton-East, Canada East on October 6, 1866. His mother Clementina had three more sons and his father, Elisha, was a minister. He was a brilliant student at Trinity College and was granted a mathematics mastership at Bishop's College in Lennoxville, Québec. He learned French, Greek, Latin and Hebrew. At 18 he accepted a teaching position in Bermuda. On his first day on the island he met his future wife Helen May Trott. They would have a son they named Ken.

He was an avid reader and subscribed to *Scientific American*. He followed all of the inventions of Thomas Alva Edison, 'The Wizard of Menelo Park.' He eventually went to New York to meet the famous inventor and to seek employment. Edison was too busy to meet with Reginald and undaunted he remained on site. When an instrument tester walked off the job, the foreman offered the position to Fessenden. He gained further knowledge and experience and was soon the electrical 'trouble shooter.'

When word of the skilled work of Fessenden reached Edison he was brought to the New Jersey plant to assist Edison with experiments on generators and on developing rubber insulation for conducting wires. By 1890 he was elevated to the post of chief chemist. He developed new lead-in wires for light bulbs. This solved Mr. Westinghouse's problems enabling him to fulfill his contract to light the Columbian Exposition in Chicago.

Reginald went to England to observe the operation of the newly invented steam turbine designed by Charles Parsons. He saw great possibilities of applying steam turbines to power ships, which soon happened.

He was hired by Purdue University in Lafayette, Indiana, but left the facility at the end of the year to pursue his own passion. George Westinghouse asked him to come to Pittsburgh. He did with his wife Helen and their son Reginald Kennelly. He began researching electromagnetic waves that were pioneered by Henrich Hertz.

He developed and patented some of his own inventions like microphotography used in banks and businesses today.

Following an impressive demonstration of his improved telegraph system to the United States Weather Bureau, he was given a salary of $3,000 a year and furnished with a testing station and aerial masts at Cobb Island on the Potomac River. Officials were astounded when he transmitted signals without wires from Cobb Island to Arlington, Virginia, a distance of 50 miles.

He further challenged himself, toiling day and night, for he knew rather than dots and dashes he could transmit speech. On December 23, 1900, Fessenden said into his microphone, "One, two, three, four. Is it snowing where you are Mr. Thiessen? If so telegraph back and let me know."

Excited Fessenden wrote, "This afternoon here at Cobb Island, intelligible speech by electromagnetic waves has for the first time in world's history been transmitted." Marconi's transmission in Morse code from England to Signal Hill, Newfoundland, December 12, 1901 was almost a year away. The honour of taking the first steps in developing what we now universally call the 'radio' belongs to Reginald.

He was moved to Roanoke Island off the Carolina coast. When a bureau superior demanded a share of his patents, rather than submit, Fessenden complained to President Roosevelt but resigned when the letter he sent was returned.

Pittsburgh millionaires, Walker and Given agreed to finance a company, the National Electric Signalling Company, on the condition that Fessenden place his inventions in the name of the company. Soon two wireless stations were built at Brant Rock, Massachusetts equipped with 400-foot antenna towers and the latest equipment.

The towers performed so well that three more were built in New York, Philadelphia and Washington. He sent a message to Alexandria, Egypt and beat Marconi by transmitting Morse code in both directions across the Atlantic.

On December 24, 1906 Fessenden sent the message, "CQ...QC" in Morse code, alerting all ships at sea to expect an important transmission. All telegraphers assembled in the ship's radio shacks and heard the unimaginable, the sound of a human voice wishing them a Merry Christmas then '*Silent Night*' played on an Edison wax-cylinder phonograph.

Interestingly his financial backers were not interested in voice or music communication they just wanted dots and dashes. Just the same they seized his patents thinking they did not need him anymore. Fessenden sued. He turned to inventing gadgets in order to earn a living and to pay legal fees.

In 1912 after the sinking of the *Titanic* Fessenden stated he could bounce signals off icebergs by radio and measure the distance. His invention was the forerunner of radar. He patented an invention called the fathometer to measure the ocean depths. It could also be used to detect enemy submarines.

Fessenden held over five hundred patents. He invented the following: sonar, depth sounder, carbon tetrachloride, the beeper/pager, voice-scrambler, radio compass (known today as LORAN), tracer bullets, gyroscope and the automatic garage-door opener.

Finally in 1920 when interest in the radio reached a fever pitch he demanded a settlement of his long running lawsuit. He gained recognition for his pioneer work and was given an out of court settlement of $500,000 in 1928.

Not only did he invent but he was also the world's first broadcast producer.

He died in Bermuda on July 22, 1932 and is buried in St. Mark's Church Cemetery.

Imagined postscript: Fessenden to Alexander Graham Bell, "Fine device you have developed there Mr. Bell but I just know that you don't need all those wires between your devices. You can do it wirelessly."

Michael J. Fox
Small for his size BIG for his cause

Michael's mother Phyllis and dad Sergeant William Fox brought their young son into the world June 6, 1961 in Edmonton, Alberta. They were army brats and as a result were often uprooted and sent from one city to another. His older brother Steve and sisters Karen, Jackie and Kelli often lived in cramped quarters for the army considered families 'nonessential personnel' and were treated as such. Michael wondered how his dad could put up with that bullshit for 25 years. Sergeant Fox, though for the most part a loving father and husband, could be as volatile as Jackie Gleason on *The Honeymooners*. In a heartbeat he could go from "How sweet it is" to "One of these days Phyllis karpow right to the moon."

Michael had a special relationship with his grandmother he called Nana. She believed in him and said some day that he would make it 'big' and his name would not be Mike it would be Michael. Nana had a reputation, deservedly so, of being a clairvoyant.

Even as a young boy he wrote epic poems and liked to cartoon and sketch. At school he did well in the creative subjects, like writing, drawing and painting but those based on fixed rules like math and chemistry he literally flunked. In Richmond where the family had moved he helped form a band named Halex. It did very well and gave him some celebrity through his high school years. He also appeared in every school play sponsored by drama teacher Ross Jones.

Michael was recruited from high school and got a part in a long-running play at the Vancouver Arts Club in the Equity Theatre. He worked well into the night and slept through the first classes of the day. Here he was receiving solid reviews for his professional acting and flunking high school drama because of absences.

Though his dad wanted him to finish high school he saw Michael's predicament with a softer eye and finally agreed to drive him to Los Angeles for his adventure of making it big. He was immediately cast in a Disney feature called *Midnight Madness* and things looked promising. However by 1982 things did not look good, he was starving on macaroni and didn't have enough money for a month's rent. He had read for *Family Ties* but a month passed with no word. He was just about ready to call it quits when he was called back.

He felt like the luckiest guy on the planet and experienced both relief and joy at the opportunity. His time on the *Family Ties* set was pure bliss. He developed his talent and when the ratings exploded he was nearly guaranteed financial stability.

In 1985 with everything going his way he was cast as Marty McFly, a girl-chasing high school rock and roll musician in *Back to the Future*. He didn't have to act this was his life. Just the same, having both projects in production at the same time was exhausting. When *Back to the Future* became a hit Michael shot to super star status. He was on the cover of *People, GQ, Playgirl* and a host of other magazines.

Michael likened television to a miniaturized icon that becomes part of everybody's family. On the big screen twenty feet high one assumes the dimensions of a god. Everything now seemed to be part of the show and his private life was relegated to the past.

He relates a story of meeting Princess Diana stating she was more beautiful than you can imagine. He had a couple of beer and low and behold he was seated next to her for a viewing of his new movie. Royal protocol says that one does not rise before she does and just getting up and leaving was out of the question. Michael spent two of the most uncomfortable hours of his life before he could go to the bathroom.

An actor's burning desire is to spend as much time as possible pretending to be somebody else. This increases the uncertainty about who they really are. No matter the adulation, wealth, for some actors there is the gnawing fact and deep-seated belief that you are a phoney and a fake.

Ironically now that he was finally making money, companies gave him tons of free items hoping that he would endorse their product for free.

In 1986 he was mobbed at the Expo World's Fair in Vancouver and had to arrange for a private tour for him and his family. That same year he earned an Emmy for his role as leading actor in a comedy series.

About this time his character in *Family Ties*, Alex Keaton, got a girlfriend by the name of Tracy Pollan. She only appeared in seven episodes but her impact was seismic. Both were romantically linked to other people at the time.

In 1987 Michael and Tracy were reunited in *Bright Lights, Big City*. They were now both unattached and soon were dating and on July 16, 1988 they were married in a small ceremony. The tabloids were enraged and a host of helicopters hovered annoyingly all day long but they didn't get a single picture. They received quite a bit of bad press but Michael thought they had to draw a line.

Soon Tracy was pregnant and they had their son Sam. All too soon she was back to work and they were thousands of miles apart.

In 1990 his father died and this brought its own grief and heartache. It was also about this time that Michael woke up to a message in his left hand. It wasn't a memo, telegram or fax, in fact there wasn't anything in his hand at all. The trembling was the message. He had a spastic left lunatic pinkie. He would grab it and when he let it go like a cheap wind-up toy, it would whir back to life again. He was so frustrated at one point he wanted to amputate it. He didn't feel it was his - it was somebody else's pinkie - it was possessed. He was soon diagnosed with Parkinson's Disease (PD). He denied it for a long time for it rarely struck someone so young.

His illness and fast pace of life began to catch up to him. He led a life fuelled by fear made liveable by insulation, self-indulgence and isolation. So it came as a mixed blessing that he finally relinquished his careening life to a therapist named Joyce. His silence about the disease had cut his wife and family from his experiences. Michael's motto was: if you can't fix it, don't even mention it or think about it. This method clearly was not working. Joyce didn't let him retreat to his 'bubble.' She made him accountable to all. She said you confide in me and I listen and advise you. I bill you, you pay me. This is how the world lives, not in a bubble of agents and accountants. It came down to showing up for life and doing the work.

Michael finally took Tracy's advice and saw a neurologist. He was referred to Dr. Allan Ropper in Boston. And to really add flames to a hot situation he quit drinking cold turkey. Life was hell for a while but slowly ever so slowly things began to change.

In 1994 he was pleased to pass a five-part General Equivalency Diploma test and graduated.

February 15, 1995 they had twin daughters Aquinnah meaning 'beautiful colours by the sea' and Schuyler, a Dutch name meaning 'teacher of scholars'

Spin City made its debut in 1996.

In 1998 Michael was scheduled for surgery to tap into the thalamus, a small part of the brain that controls body movement. Though sedated, he needed to be conscious and all electrical equipment had to be turned off so they could pick up signals from his brain. They would rely on light from windows in the operating ward. Brain surgery leaves no room for error. The operation was a huge success. The only thing was, there was still a tremor only this time it was on his other side.

By now, keeping the disease a secret from the public was an almost impossible task.

Michael issued a story to *People* magazine about his affliction that hit the stands November 30, 1998. He also did a television interview and took Tracy and the kids to Connecticut for Thanksgiving to wait for the storm to subside. It didn't however; Michael had sparked a national conversation about Parkinson's Disease.

Barbara Walters interviewed him when he returned to New York. She asked Michael to demonstrate how difficult it was to put on his coat. Tracy intervened, fearing for Michael's dignity.

The best outcome of Michael's 'coming out' was the response from the P.D. community like a teacher who thanked him for being a 'public witness.' He felt, in their letters and emails, a kinship and the message that Parkinson patients have the stigma of being seen as a freak because of their trembling and other symptoms.

Michael was inundated with requests by Parkinson organizations. He was in the ideal position to really make a difference and many told him as much. He waited while he pulled off the heartfelt exit from *Spin City*. He received another Emmy in 2002 and thanked Tracy in his acceptance speech in a most touching manner.

He has been a strong advocate for PD and has been contacted by Muhammed Ali as well as other notable sufferers. They believe a cure is just around the corner.

Tracy and Michael had a fourth child Esmé Annabelle and he wrote a book *Lucky Man: A Memoir* published in 2002.

Michael is amazed at how many people say to him "you're in my prayers" and says that the power of prayer has risen on his list for it has affected his life in a positive way.

He joined Joan Samuelson, the founder and director of the Parkinson's Action Network, speaking at the Senate appropriations subcommittee to increase their funding. They have shaken the ground and it is amazing what is transpiring in this area of research. Michael has spoken on behalf of stem cell research. He founded the Michael J. Fox Foundation for Parkinson's research and now uses his celebrity currency, to promote the cause that now has his absolute attention.

Terry Fox
'Marathon of Hope' Runner

April 12, 1980 one of Canada's greatest heroes dipped his prosthetic leg into the icy water of St. John's Harbour and began his epic journey by running twelve and a half miles of his dream run across Canada for the Canadian Cancer Society. When he began, few people knew him but when he finished, he would be a national hero. This is the story of Terry Fox.

Betty and Rolly Fox gave birth to Terrance Stanley on July 28, 1958 in Winnipeg, Manitoba. He was the second oldest. He had two brothers, Fred and Darrel and a sister named Judith. In 1966 Rolly, a Canadian National Railway switchman, transferred to Surrey where Terry went to Mary Hill Junior High School. He loved athletics and tried out for the basketball team. He played only one minute in his grade eight year. That summer he played against Doug Alward but never won. By 1976 Terry could beat Doug 21-0 and was a starter for Port Coquitlam High School Ravens. He shared the Athlete of the Year award with Doug in grade twelve. His mother was annoyed when he belittled his academic abilities. He was an above average student who could get very good marks if he worked hard. He went to Simon Fraser University to play basketball and please his mother. Alex Devlin coached the team and though others were more talented no one could 'out-gut' him. It was March 1977 when Terry's world changed and he had to cope with the nightmare of cancer.

After banging his right knee in an automobile accident in November 1977, Terry found that it was not healing and continued to be bit sore. He did not mention it to the coach or his parents. It was not unusual for basketball players to have sore knees. Finally the pain was more than he could endure so he contacted their family physician Dr. Heffelfinger. Unable to get a quick appointment with the specialist his dad took him to the Royal Columbian Hospital in New Westminster on March 3, 1977. Within twenty minutes Dr. Michael Piper, an orthopaedic specialist felt sure Terry had an osteogenic sarcoma, a rare malignant tumour that develops most often among males 10-25. It usually begins in the knee and makes the bone soft and mushy. They would have to operate.

The night before the surgery Terri Flemming, his basketball coach at PoCo, gave Terry a recent issue of *Runner's World*. It included a story about an above-the-knee amputee, Dick Trauman, who ran in the New York Marathon. On March 9 Terry's right leg was amputated above the knee. He was thoroughly examined for other tumours and loose cells, which often are carried into the lungs by blood. The usual post-surgery follow-up was chemotherapy. Terry bounced back with an excellent attitude. When he lost his hair from the cancer-killing drugs, adriamycin and methotextate, he was embarrassed but bought an inexpensive wig. At the cancer clinic Terry saw mortally ill patients and the grim reminder that two-thirds of cancer victims die. On the last day of his treatment his nurse gave him a little cake, but the clinic had changed him.

In the summer of 1979 Rick Hansen asked Terry to play basketball for the Cablecars wheelchair team, which won 10 championships in 12 years. Terry joined and played on three championship teams. Once during a game, his wig was brushed off much to his embarrassment, but curly blond locks soon topped his head.

Throughout these months Terry had harboured a dream of running across Canada and in February 1979 he began training with his $2,000 plastic leg. He worked with his prothetist Ben Speicher on the development of a better running leg. He entered and finished last in the Prince George Labour Day Marathon and covered more than 3,000 miles in training. After he found sponsors, the Canadian Cancer Society gave the word to go. He recruited Doug Alward to accompany him and drive the motor home.

Terry began his marathon in St. John's, Newfoundland on April 12, 1980. Terry would rise at 4:30 or 5:00 and Doug would find the marker they set the day before and drive one mile ahead. Terry would run to the motor home and Doug would mark off one more mile. His objective was 26 miles a day - or a marathon a day. He ran across Newfoundland and met his parents for a brief visit in Halifax while running across Nova Scotia. He then ran across Prince Edward Island. He ran an all time high of 30 miles in one day in New Brunswick. On June 10 he entered Québec, which was in his words was, "a great disappointment." Cars forced him off the road and even hit a CBC camera crew destroying their equipment. He did see Gerard Côté, a four-time winner of the Boston Marathon and was featured on the front page of the French daily, *Le Soleil*.

He was glad to leave the language barriers of Québec for the tumultuous welcome Ontario gave him. Vern Kennedy wrote a song for him 'Run Terry Run', with all proceeds going to cancer. A grade five class from Odessa raised $15 and their teacher Brian Norris pledged to match them. *NBC's Real People* and hostess Sarah Purcell ran with Terry to do an interview. He met Governor General Ed Schreyer at Government House and Prime Minister Trudeau on Parliament Hill July 21. He made his best speech at Scarborough. Darrel Sittler ran with him to Nathan Phillips Square in Toronto and gave him his 1980 NHL All-star sweater. He threw the first pitch of a Blue Jay game, dined in the world's highest restaurant in the CN Tower and the restaurant's lights, which usually read 'Sparkles', read 'Terry Fox.' He met the mayor of Toronto, John Sewell and Pauline McGibbon, Canada's first woman lieutenant governor. Brad Barber of Mississauga put on a pair of kneepads and vowed to break the world record for crawling in Terry's honour. He raised $5,000 and crawled 11.5 miles but missed the record of 14 miles. Bobby Orr presented $25,000 from his sponsors Planters Peanuts. On Terry's birthday July 28 he ran 20 miles and celebrated in Gravenhurst. His last mile was filmed just outside Thunder Bay. He had a cough and suspected the worst, for he had symptoms early in the run such as nausea, dizziness and coughing. He felt the slight discomfort caused by these symptoms and the prosthesis rubbing his stump was inconsequential compared to the pain he saw others endure at the cancer clinic.

Terry had pushed himself 3,339 miles going 700 miles out of his way to promote the 'Marathon of Hope' but it was all over for him now. Dr. Michael Noble found malignant bone cells growing in Terry's lungs and reported he had a 10% chance of living. He had raised $1.7 million for the Canadian Cancer Society before he stopped running. Others took the cause to their heart and the result was a telethon.

John Denver, Elton John, Glenn Campbell, Anne Murray and Nana Mouskouri were but a few who performed on the CTV tribute to Terry. The huge tote board jumped $25,0000 per minute as people pledged. Many companies such as Imperial Oil, Shell, Coca-Cola and McDonald's pledged large sums. The final sum was the unbelievable total of $23,000,000.

Terry was on methotextate. His mouth and throat were sore with cankers, a condition known as mucositis. The tumours responded briefly but then the drug seemed to have no effect. Still he received such visitors as Gordon Lightfoot and Kenneth Taylor. Governor General Edward Richard Schreyer traveled to British Columbia to award Terry the Companion of the Order of Canada. He received the Order of Dogwood and was enshrined in the Canadian Sports Hall of Fame. A new drug called interferon was used to treat Terry but it was not successful. On June 28, 1981 he died.

Many people were heart broken at the news of the death of their brave young hero. With the maple leaf on his chest he had brought the people of Canada together as it had never been before. He made the world a finer place by his presence. He had sacrificed himself for a cause.

The memory of Terry Fox shall always shine bright for the unselfish courage and determination he exemplified.

By 2005 over $350,000,000 has been raised mainly in Canada though there are runs each fall in his name in countries all over the world.

Northrop Frye
Tower of Literary Power

Herman Northrop Frye was born in Sherbrooke, Québec on July 14, 1912. When he was only six his brother Howard died overseas in the Great War. The family business failed and the family moved to Moncton, New Brunswick. At fifteen Northrop read George Bernard Shaw. He was what you'd call a nerd with a great mop of yellow hair. He had a slight build and a pale complexion. At Victoria College someone said, "Good morning Butter-cup, does your mother know you're out?" He let loose a string of profanity that would turn a sailor's head and nobody ever called him that to his face again.

One student did give him a nickname, 'Feathertop' because of his mop of hair, her name was Helen Kemp, a gifted pianist like himself and a fine artist too. Soon he was editing the college literary magazine and making a mark on the debating team.

During summer break Helen wrote to him: "I will not improve my mind or do anything the least uplifting...I shall be very interested in seeing how your muse develops, Feathertop."

He responded: "You ask about my muse. I have a conception for a really good poem...what I put down is flat and dry as the Great Sahara."

Before long the professors at the college could see his wit and he wrote perceptive essays. His romantics' professor, Pelham Edgar told him, "I think you're the guy to write on Blake." Blake is a poet who has created some of the most powerful images in the history of English literature. Who has not heard:

>Tiger! tiger! burning bright...
>And what shoulder, and what art,
>Could twist the sinews of thy heart?
>And when thy heart began to beat,
>What dread hand? And what dread feet?...

Certainly fewer have encountered:

>To see a world in a grain of sand
>And a heaven in a wild flower
>Hold infinity in the palm of your hand
>And eternity in an hour

Though familiar with Blake, Northrop had not delved into his complicated mythic epics, the origins of the world and the titanic struggle of huge mythic figures with names such as Urizen and Orc.

Northrop found Blake to be a daunting writer.

Already a very religious man who was well on his way to joining the ministry Frye said, "The Bible to Blake was really the *Magna Carta* of the human imagination."

Again during their summer's parting Helen wrote and told him someone asked if she was in love with anybody. She wrote, "I did mention you, Norrie. Do you mind very much?"

He replied:

"You frighten me a little. Love may mean anything from a quiet friendship to an overwhelming passion. It may be anything from a purely sexual impulse to a declaration of honourable intentions based upon a close survey of the economic field. It acts like a tonic upon me to hear you say you love me...it does make me nervous to be carrying such a pulsating heart around in my pockets. I'm afraid it might drop out and break."

In 1936 he wrote:

"There are very few moments if any, when you are out of my mind. I think at least half of you must be inside me."

August 24, 1937 Reverend Arthur Cragg married Helen G. Kemp and Herman Northrop Frye in Emmanuel College Chapel. Soon Word War II raged but he was found to be medically unfit for military service and he threw himself into his book on Blake.

Despite becoming an ordained minister of the United Church of Canada he would condemn the way traditional churches allowed themselves to be used as political instruments to keep people in their places so that the powerful could rule comfortably.

In 1945 Frye finally finished *Fearful Symmetry*. The world of literary criticism had a new giant. The book was an argument for the power of myths and metaphor that challenged the conventional view of the nature of reality. Furthermore Northrop claimed, "Tyranny requires a priesthood and a God." He held that Shakespeare, Walt Disney, and Steven Spielberg are all doing their parts in a comprehensive world vision. They are adding to the same body of myths that begins with Greek mythology and the Bible.

Northrop delved deeper into his revolutionary thoughts by reading in Greek, Latin, Hebrew, Sanskrit, French, German, Italian and Spanish. In *Anatomy of Criticism*, 1957, he argued that criticism was not just saying whether a work was good or bad but identifying the myths and metaphors it contained within.

He would also write two provocative books on the Bible: *The Great Code* and *Words With Power*. He said, "Religion was not about what you're supposed to do to get into a place called Heaven, where there is nothing left to do. It is about love and liberty. Man has the power to create and imagine…love will set you free. Along with the Bible, Blake's work was Northrop's *Magna Carta* of the human imagination. God is everywhere including inside each and every person.

Eternal joy is a positive thing. A world where the lion lies down with the lamb is a world of stuffed lions. Love, however, is the door through which most of us enter the imaginative world. Mating and sex may be 'animal', but love and its imagination is part of our divine birthright."

Northrop was a great teacher and revelled in bringing joy to a young mind as he led them to the edge of discovery and saw them plunge over the edge. This was perhaps his greatest joy other than his beloved Helen who fell into the dark shadow of Alzheimer's disease tainting their last days together.

Frye died on January 23, 1991. Scholars still meet to discuss his work and debate his discourses with fascination and intrigue. He might smile if he knew the examination and deliberation of his work his towering wake departed.

Igor Gouzenko
Russian Defector's Revelations Starts Cold War

Igor Gouzenko was born in Rogachovo, Russia on January 26, 1919. He came to Canada in 1943 to work as a cipher clerk in the Russian embassy. His wife, Svetlana, soon followed him. Scheduled to return to Russia, he defected but it was not easy.

Close to midnight on September 5, 1945 Igor and his pregnant wife walked out of the Soviet embassy with a substantial sheaf of documents and went to the *Ottawa Journal*. It was a hot humid night. Igor beckoned Chester Frowde to leave his desk. Frowde led him to a room opposite the main office. Igor was short man with a tubby build and appeared as white as a sheet. The first words he spoke were, "It's war, it's war. It's Russia."

Frowde plied him with questions asking him where he was from, the nature of his complaint but he just stood there paralysed with fright and refused to answer any questions. The Belle Claire Hotel was next door and night after night drunks would come and bother the night team. Often they had to call the police. Frowde would later regret that this exceptional story slipped right through his fingers. Igor and his wife departed very late at night.

Svetlana could not comprehend what was happening. She said in Russia this kind of miss would result in the person not paying attention being shot.

The Gouzenkos were panicked when they returned to their apartment. They were afraid for their life and sought refuge with their neighbour Harold Main and his wife Mildred. Harold was an RCAF corporal at the time. They brought their son with them and that night men from the NKVD, the predecessor of the KGB, broke down their door

Gouzenko was afraid to go to the police because he didn't trust them. Though he was advised by many to contact the RCMP he went to the Crown Attorney's office where foreigners can become a naturalized citizens. About 2 P.M. Igor and his wife talked to Fernande Coulson who asked some questions and determined as Russians they couldn't apply for citizenship. Igor informed Mrs. Coulson they left last night and "Were not going back."

Fernande contacted the *Journal* and they couldn't do anything but knew something was in the wind. She called the RCMP and they sent a Mountie over but after investigating said there was nothing they could do and he left. By now Fernande was getting mad. She called Prime Minister

Mackenzie King's secretary Sam Gobeil and spoke to him. He said he would call her right back. A few minutes later Gobeil phoned back and told her to have nothing more to do with the man and to get rid of them. Coulson was getting shaky but was spitting mad at time. She phoned Inspector Leopold of the RCMP who said they couldn't help him. Coulson insisted that something be done for she feared for their lives. Leopold agreed to see him the next day at 9:30.

Fortunately the master spy Sir William Stephenson was in Ottawa at the time and when he heard of the defector he induced the RCMP to rescind the previous order and place the Gouzenkos under surveillance.

Soon the Gouzenkos were put under protective security and removed to a cottage at Otter Lake. Igor continued to be very suspicious and anxious. They got a Russian interpreter Mervyn Black to interrogate Igor. The officers who were assigned to guard the Gouzenko family were not enamoured by Igor who expected them to act as chambermaids, cooks and everything else. Bill Campbell helped them buy groceries. He said they wanted to buy everything in the store. They bought caviar and other expensive goods then didn't eat. Half of the stuff had to be returned and exchanged for other stuff. By the end he hated him.

RCMP officers Herb Spanton and George McClellan both thought of a great place to secret the Gouzenkos at the same time - Camp X. It was a major spy headquarters during World War II and would prove to be the ideal place as it was still a little known and retained the appearance of a farm with a barbed wire fence and cows across the road.

Though the place was remote the tension was high. Slightest noise had to be investigated. One night at 3 A.M. one of the officers investigated a noise. Here he was he said running around the place naked with his revolver. He smirked when it turned out to be a cow.

Igor felt that Johnny Leopold, who was an undercover officer for the RCMP, was a spy and he refused to have anything to do with him.

Late in the year Svetlana, who went by the name of Anna, delivered her baby at the hospital.

Among the major revelations by Gouzenko was that a senior scientist Allan Nunn was exposed as a spy who was privy to nuclear secrets. He worked at Chalk River where a nuclear reactor would be built a year later. Almost as important was that Fred Rose, a Member of Parliament, was an agent. He also fingered Kathleen Willsher in the British High Commission, Alger Hiss a secretary for the U.S. Secretary of State and a senior civil servant in the American treasury named Harry Dexter. He revealed much more but these top the list.

Prior to the Gouzenko defection Canada had two people working on counter-intelligence in Ottawa. Canada had to ask the British for some agents to come over and assist in the debriefing of Gouzenko.

A Royal Commission was set up and the hearings began on the seventh flour of the Justice Building on February 6. Gouzenko began to give evidence on February 13. At 6 A.M on February 14 twelve people were arrested simultaneously. There had been some discussion about making the arrests during the night but it was stopped because they felt they shouldn't act like the Russians. February 20 the Russians in Moscow owned up to their actions.

During this time officers were alarmed by Igor's personal habits. He preferred to eat with his fingers and had to be trained to use knives and forks. When they went out to eat the Gouzenko's would order two or three extra plates of food. All the dishes often could not sit on the table at once. The way he spoke and acted brought attention to him. He was still in harms was for undoubtedly if they could have found him he would have been shot on the spot. That is the way the Russians took care of business at that time.

The first trials began in June of 1946 and stretched into 1949 because Sam Carr was not caught until then. Igor refused to testify until the received the finest camera in the world. Despite misgivings many people had about Igor's character he was an ideal witness. He was clean-cut and acting out of conviction. He was solid about his statements and never retracted anything. He wouldn't bend and they couldn't shake him down. He was quick to answer question and seemed to have an instinct for what to say and how to confine his remarks to what he could support. The smart lawyers soon knew they should not press him for he always had some extra ammunition in his pack. He prepared in advance. He anticipated questions and if they weren't asked he want to know why and saw that they were asked. He was brilliant in this area and he liked to be in the spot light.

Igor was given some very nice clothes but to him they were just clothes. He was so intense that he looked like he had been pulled though a knothole. They had to pull him together and straighten him out before he went on the stand.

One lawyer tried to question his thinking by asking why he didn't go to the Mounted Police. He replied, "Because they were federal police and I was afraid of them. I thought they had sold out to the Russians."

The lawyer responded with a scoff and said, "Do you really believe the Mounted Police could be sold out to the Russians?"

Gouzenko said, "Why not? A Member of Parliament (did)." The defence was shattered and a titter went thought the courtroom.

The espionage ring in North America he disclose were intent on getting information for the Russians on how to make a nuclear bomb that resulted in the expulsion of Soviet 'diplomats' and the conviction of 11 Canadians. He furnished evidence of a high-level spy rings in Britain and the United States.

He was given another identity and received his Canadian citizenship. He appeared in the media with a bag over his head giving him a comical appearance. He wrote *This Was My Choice* 1954 and *The Fall of a Titan*. He died in Toronto, Ontario on June 25, 1982.

Nancy Greene
'Tiger' on the Hill

Mr. and Mrs. Greene began their life together in Rossland, British Columbia. Mr. Greene was an engineer and was posted to Ottawa during the war. It was here that Nancy was born May 11, 1943. She has an older sister Elizabeth and four younger siblings, Judy, John, Ken and Ricky. After the war the family returned to Rossland and the whole family skied at Red Mountain, one of the premier ski mountains in North America at the time. It was here that Nancy learned to ski.

Nancy skied for fun and was not interested in ski racing but her sister Liz was on the Rossland Senior High School ski team. All that changed in 1958 when the Canadian Junior Championships were held at Red Mountain. Nancy felt the excitement and felt in her heart that she could beat some of the competitors. She decided to race and surprised everyone including herself when she placed third, of course her sister Liz won.

By 1960 she was on the Olympic ski team and participated in the Squaw Valley Olympics. She was euphoric as she walked around the Olympic Village. The athletes were treated like kings and queens. She heard languages spoken from around the world and got autographs from the stars of the day. By her own admission she was hopeless at the slalom but made the team on the strength of her giant slalom. In that event she finished 26th, five seconds behind the winner. Still the highlight of the entire event was when Anne Heggveit won the gold medal in the giant slalom and the Canadian national anthem was played. There wasn't a dry eye in the entire place. When Nancy returned to school she wrote an essay about the Olympics.

At the end of the 1961 season Nancy broke her leg and had to spend the summer in a cast. As a result she began to weight train. In 1962 she won her first victory winning the Toni Make Memorial race in Austria. It would be years until she won again.

In 1963 when the Canadian Amateur Ski Association (CASA) decided that competitors who could afford to pay their own expenses would again be allowed to compete for the Canadian National Team in Europe. A number of skiers decided this was unfair and they began their own program. They trained in Kimberley, B.C. and were labelled renegades by CASA. The team competed on the North American circuit. Nancy won the downhill at Aspen with the help of an American coach Tome Corcoran. The following weekend she placed second in the slalom and downhill at Vail.

At the Innsbruck Olympic Games Nancy finished seventh in the downhill, fifteenth in the giant slalom and sixteenth in the slalom. It was a disappointing Olympic showing for not only Greene but the entire team. The only gold medal won by Canada that year was the four-man bobsled team of Doug Anakin, Peter Kirby, John and Victor Emery.

In 1967 in order to win the World Cup, Nancy had to win the slalom and two giant slalom races at Jackson Hole, Wyoming, the last event of the year. She won the first one on Friday and had a tense moment on Saturday's run when she went through a gate backwards but it did not slow her down as she won anyway.

All she had to do was win Sunday's race. She did not sleep well Saturday night. She had to wait at the starting gate because the girl in front of her fell and the gates had to be reset. A calm came over her and she felt relaxed and eager. When she raced though the part where all the other girls crashed, she glided through it and finished with a time of 44.51 giving her a combined time of 90.67.

Now she had to wait for the French girls Marielle Goitschel and Annie Famose to make their last run. Waiting was the hardest part of the whole competition. When Marielle's time was posted at 44.35 Nancy's heart dropped but the officials quickly changed her time because they had mistakenly reversed the last two digits and her actual time was 44.53 seconds giving her a total of 90.74. Nancy had won by 7/100ths of a second and claimed her first World Cup. There was a party that night but Nancy was kept busy with a constant stream of friends and acquaintances bringing their congratulations. Her phone rang off the hook and telegrams poured in.

Nancy hoped to get a fast start in the 1968 season but lack of snow in Canada and Europe hampered all the skiers that year. At Oberstaufen she finished third in the giant slalom and slalom. At Grindelwald it was snowing heavily and she won the giant slalom but missed a gate and was disqualified in the slalom. At Bad Gastein she lost concentration, whirled through the air and crashed into the bushes spraining her ankle. With the Olympics two weeks away she went into water therapy. The week before the games she tested it at Saint Gervais. She drew the #1 starting position, a disadvantage in the downhill, especially since it was snowing heavily. She skied and placed 25th.

During the opening Olympic ceremonies Nancy carried the Canadian flag. She felt confident about her chances. Unfortunately she had trouble with her wax that got contaminated with mud inside the starting hut and had a miserable run and placed 10th in the downhill. Olga Pall of Austria won the race.

She was distraught and cried over the worst disappointment of her career. She skied that afternoon with reckless abandon. She fell and crashed all over the place and didn't care if she hurt herself.

The next race was the slalom that she had not done well in. She was pessimistic going into the event. After the first run she was in fifth place, with American Judy Nagle in first. Nancy had a solid second run and many of the front-runners skied poorly or fell. Nancy won the silver medal behind Marielle Goitschel who took the gold. Nancy's confidence was boosted and she prepared for the giant slalom. She studied the run memorizing every bump, gate, turn and snowflake. She took off from the starting gate and never looked back.

As Nancy crossed the finish line Bob Swan and Bill McKay from the men's ski team rushed out and hoisted her on their shoulders and that set the tone for the celebration. She won the gold medal by almost three seconds with Annie Famose taking the silver and Fernande Bochatay taking the bronze.

She went to press conferences, then went to the hockey arena for the presentations and she heard the national anthem played in her honour. She watched a hockey game and went out to dinner where she finally reached her parents, who were overjoyed. She forgot to reverse the charges and the sixty-five dollars for the call emptied her wallet, but not the joy in her heart.

Following the Games, Nancy scored nine straight international victories beating the best consistently. When she returned to Canada 1,500 people awaited her arrival. She rode in a parade through the Ottawa streets, was received by Governor General Roland Michner, had a ticker-tape parade in Toronto and a wild procession in Vancouver.

Far ahead in World Cup points for the year, Nancy was excited as one of the final events of the year was the du Maurier Cup to be run on her home turf Red Mountain. She was nervous as crowds of people came to see her and furthermore she had announced her intention to retire. She fell disqualifying herself in the downhill but came back and won the giant slalom. Nancy's greatest delight was when the great French skier, Jean Claude Killy, breezed into town, ate dinner at her parents' house, won the slalom and then breezed out as swiftly as he breezed in. There was a banquet in the Cominco gymnasium in Trail followed by a dance with a real band. For Nancy it was one of the greatest race days of her life.

She competed in Heavenly Valley where she logged her last race, finishing second in the slalom and fifth in the giant slalom. She won the World Cup competition for the second straight year. It was a memorable sun drenched day when Nancy and Jean Claude hoisted their respective trophies above their heads.

She served as the national ski team coach until 1973 and was instrumental in the early development of Whistler-Blackcomb Resort with her husband Al Raine. They have twin boys.

Wayne Gretzky
The Great One

Walter Gretzky married Phyllis Hockin and on January 26, 1961 Wayne was born in Brantford, Ontario. He was the first of five children. He has one sister, Kim and brothers Keith, Glen and Brent in that order. In 1963 Wayne got his first skates and was bundled up to skate on the near by Nith River. His father carefully whittled a hockey stick small enough for the toddler to grasp. During the Saturday *Hockey Night in Canada* game, Wayne would shoot a sock ball at his Grandma who would be knitting in her favourite rocker. She would toss the sock back to him and he would shoot until the commercial was over and settle back into watching the game until the next commercial. Wayne constantly wanted to skate and in the winter of 1965 Walter flooded the back yard for the first time so he would not have to transport Wayne to the rink all the time. This became an annual occurrence, for Wayne was born to skate. Wayne would skate until supper and then go skate until he was called in for bed. He would even bribe the neighbourhood kids with a nickel to stay longer so he wouldn't have to go in. In 1967-68 Wayne joined his first organized hockey team coached by Dick Martin. It was a major novice team and the other boys were up to ten years old. Wayne managed to score one goal that year.

In his second season Wayne scored 27 goals and in his third he scored 104 goals plus 63 assists in 62 games. In 1970-71 he scored 196 goals and 120 assists in 76 games and he was starting to be noticed. The next year he scored 378 goals in 82 games. As a major pee wee in 1972-73 he dropped to 105 goals but the next year he bagged 192. In his last season of minor hockey, 1974-75 he scored 90 goals.

Wayne was getting a great deal of publicity for his scoring feats. In fact in 1971 at the Hespeler Olympic Tournament Wayne scored 50 goals in nine games. In 1972 the *Canadian Magazine* ran a two-page spread on Wayne titled: 'Wayne Gretzky has 300 Bubble Gum Cards and a Future You Wouldn't Believe.'

Over the years Wayne had created a lot of publicity for himself but also had to put up with a lot of criticism. He was called a puck hog and his coach was accused of favouritism by other parents who thought he got too much ice time. Wherever he went he filled rinks with spectators who came to see him play. The only cheers he got occurred if he was heavily checked. The irony of it is that minor hockey groups outside of Brantford made oodles of money from game admittance fees, but in Brantford, the people just wouldn't come out to the games. The hardest place to impress people is in your own backyard.

The last straw came February 2, 1975 when it was Brantford Day at Maple Leaf Gardens in Toronto. When Wayne skated out on to the ice the Brantford people booed him. It was a hard thing for a fourteen year old to take. Wayne was unhappy and needed a change.

Wayne pestered his parents to let him go to Toronto to join the Metropolitan Toronto Hockey League. Finally his parents relented and allowed him to become the legal guardian of Bill Cornish so he could play in Toronto. Bill thought that it would be a 'piece of cake.' However it took a court case, six months of bickering and enough turmoil to cause ulcers, for the move to Toronto to be accomplished. He had to play junior "B" rather than in his age group which was bantam. He missed the first two months of the schedule but managed to score 27 goals and got 33 assists for 60 points and was named the league's rookie-of-the-year.

In the 1976-77 season Wayne began it with an atypical type of mono and had a very slow start. He needed lots of rest and was given a tonic crammed full of vitamins. He didn't feel quite right until Christmas and by that time he seemed to be out of the scoring race. His team, the Senecas, won the league title and Wayne finished fourth in scoring with 36 goals and 36 assists for 72 points. He also added 75 points in 23 playoff games. He began a weight-training program and in fifteen months he'd gone from 5' 1" and 89 pounds to 5' 8" and 130.

In the 1977-78 season Wayne moved up to junior 'A' and was drafted by the Soo Greyhounds. The club had an initiation rite for rookies. They had to streak through the park. They were picked up by the police and put in the slammer. Soon all the cops were laughing and the coach Muzz McPherson appeared splitting a gut with the rest of the veterans on the team.

Wayne, with 70 goals and 112 assists for 182 points, ended up second in scoring behind Bobby Smith who had 192 points. It was here that Wayne picked up the famous #99. He always wore the #9 but returning veteran Brian Gaualazzi had his number so Muzz suggested he wear two 9's. It was not a good year as the team finished fourth and it would be Wayne's last year as an amateur.

It was Nelson Skalbania, who owned the Indianapolis Racers, who signed Wayne to his first contract. It was for four years of hockey for $825,000. His salary went from $25 per week with Soo to about $3,000 a week and he was in the World Hockey Association. His career as a Racer can be summed up this way - 8 games, 3 goals, 3 assists for a total of 6 points and no penalties. Incidentally he scored the first two goals of his pro career against the Oilers. Mr. Skalbania traded Wayne to Peter Pocklington of the Oilers and he shifted without missing a game. He played the full 80 games that season and wound up with 46 goals, 64 assists and 110 points. He was third in scoring and was the WHA rookie-of-the-year for the 1978-79 season.

Wayne had not been in Edmonton for more than 2 weeks when Peter told Wayne's agent Gus that he wanted to sign Wayne to a twenty-one year contract that would make No. 99 an Oiler until 1999. On his eighteenth birthday Wayne signed the contract for $280,000 per year plus a $100,000 bonus.

In 1979-80 the Oilers were one of the new 'expansion' clubs in the NHL. In his rookie NHL season Wayne ended the up with 137 points, tied with Marcel Dionne of the LA Kings. Dionne won the Art Ross Trophy because it was decided that in the event of a tie the player with the most goals would win the title and Dionne had scored 53, two more than Wayne. Wayne was ineligible for the Calder Trophy as the rookie-of-the-year because he had already played a full season with a major professional hockey league. Interestingly enough Peter Stastny holds the record for the most assists (70) and most points (109) by a rookie in a single season, set in 1980-81 after playing for the Czechoslovakian national team. A year earlier Wayne had 86 assists and 137 points in his first NHL year, but he wasn't considered a rookie.

At any rate Wayne did win the Lady Byng Trophy as 'the player judged to have exhibited the best type of sportsmanship and gentlemanly conduct combined with a high standard of playing ability' and the Hart Trophy as 'the player judged to be the most valuable to his team.' Unfortunately the Oilers lost in the playoffs to the Philadelphia Flyers in three straight.

In 1980-81 Wayne won the Art Ross Trophy with 55 goals, 109 assists for 164 points. The Oilers were hot in the playoffs against the Montreal Canadians and blew them away in three straight. However in the quarter final round the Oilers lost to the Islanders 4 games to 2 and another season was over. Wayne won the Hart Trophy again.

In the 1981-82 season Wayne blew all the NHL records to bits. He scored 92 goals and 120 assists for a total of 212 points. His nearest competitor was the Islander's Mike Bossy with 147 points, 65 behind Wayne, the widest winning margin in league history. He scored 50 goals in 39 games to demolish 'Rocket' Richard's record of 50 in 50. He won the Hart Trophy for the third straight year but mysteriously the Oilers lost 3 games to 2 to the Los Angeles Kings in the first round of the playoffs. It seemed the Oilers could fill stadiums and score points during the season but couldn't cut it in the playoffs.

In the 1982-83 season Wayne again won the Art Ross Trophy with 71 goals, 125 assists (another league record) for 196 points. This time the Oilers made it to the finals in the Stanley Cup against the Islanders but lost in 4 straight games. Wayne set playoff records for assists, 26 and points 38 but they were still stuck with the fact that they couldn't win the big one.

Of course Wayne and the Oilers went on to win the Stanley Cup in 1984 and 85 as well as in 1987 and 88. He tied the knot with *Playboy* centrefold Janet Jones on July 16, 1988 and to Canada's horror Peter Pocklington traded him August 9, 1988 to the L.A. Kings.

Gretzky felt like he had been sold out and Edmontonians were outraged at Pocklington. However he made hockey a hit in Los Angeles.

In 1991 Canada won the Canada Cup defeating team U.S.A. in the final, winning two straight games and Gretzky tallied 4 goals and 8 assists.

As time marched on his new owner Bruce McNall ran out of money and Wayne grew tired of the corporate instability that under cut the quality of the team. He asked to be traded and in 1996 he was dealt to the St. Louis Blues and played with Brett Hull. In the off-season he was not retained so he joined Mark Messier in New York with the Rangers where he spent his last three seasons.

Wayne was crushed by the Team Canada loss in the 1996 World Cup and that the team came away without a medal in the 1998 Nagano Olympics. Never the less Gretzky celebrated the Olympics with his team-mates.

The Great One played his last game in 1999 and held the secret until the last game when he announced his retirement. He didn't want a great deal of fan fare so he did it his way.

The one honour Wayne missed the most was winning an Olympic medal but he was the executive director of the Canadian gold-medal-winning team at the 2002 Olympics. He is currently the part owner of the NHL Phoenix Coyotes. Wayne's mother Phyllis died in 2005 and the country grieved with him.

Halifax Explosion

The natives called it Chebucto, or 'big', and the French explorers called it *Baie Saine*, or 'Safe Harbour.' Halifax Harbour is roughly the shape of an hourglass, with one end broken off towards the sea. The inner harbour is a landlocked sheet of water, 20 miles in circumference, known as Bedford Basin. The hourglass waist is called the Narrows; then comes the main harbour.

December 6th, 1917 was a beautiful day. The air was still and warm. The sun was a ball of fire as in the season of Indian summer. There was no snow on the ground. Shortly before nine o'clock a French ship, the *Mont Blanc*, was proceeding up the harbour at a rate of six knots, towards the Narrows. It was a cargo steamer of 2,250 tons loaded at Gravesend, New York with high explosives. It was loaded to the gunnels and ready for the convoy that would take it to its destination. Her cargo consisted of chiefly picric acid, 2,250 tons, 61 tons of gun cotton and 225 tons of T.N.T. It also carried a deck loaded with drums of benzene. Its value was three million dollars. Such a cargo was, of course, extremely dangerous, but in wartime, when explosives are vital every cubic foot of shipping capacity is invaluable. Dangers must be risked.

A Belgian relief ship, the *Imo*, left her anchorage in Bedford Basin and proceeded towards the Narrows. In congested shipping lanes the *Mont Blanc* signalled according to established rules of the waterway that she would keep to the right. Suddenly the *Mont Blanc* turned out of her course and moved directly across the bow of the *Imo*. The *Imo*, which cut her engines, drifted its stem into the starboard bow of the *Mont Blanc* crushing the plating in to a depth of ten feet. It was not a violent collision and almost immediately the ships separated. It was seventeen minutes to nine.

Almost at once the *Mont Blanc* was observed to be on fire. Soon black smoke rose into the still air, shot with flashes of fierce red flames. Everyone stopped to gaze at the spectacle. The crew of the *Mont Blanc* were seen rowing lifeboats frantically to the shore. Through the smoke observers saw bursts of flames, evidently the barrels of benzene igniting. It was like the first of July.

The fire raged between decks until suddenly at 9:06 the whole twenty-six hundred tons of cargo converted in a split second into a hemisphere of intensely hot gas, which shot into the air for a cubic mile. Captain Campbell, on a ship outside the harbour, shot the angle with his sextant and calculated the height of the smoke and fire to be about two miles. The *Mont Blanc* was blown to bits. A spray of metallic fragments were hurled in all directions and rivets showered like shrapnel. One gun was found three and a half miles away near Albro Lake. Part of the anchor was found near the Exhibition Building. The *Imo* was stripped of her superstructure by the blast and thrown across the channel and beached on the Dartmouth shore.

The explosion hurled a tidal wave to the shore, which destroyed life and ruined property. The harbour district housed the poorer families and their houses were two or three story structures. The compression wave from the explosion blew them down. Many were buried in the wreckage of their houses. That was not the worst, for every house had wood stoves that were upset. Soon each individual house was on fire. The beautiful morning turned into a horror. Men and women were bleeding, half conscious or worse still uninjured but imprisoned in the wreckage, the flames sweeping nearer. The pity of it all, to see people perish before your eyes, unable to help, it was heart wrenching. To see their faces and hear their words and being forced away by the flames. For ten minutes after the blast a black rain fell from the sky. All morning a silvery column of smoke rose.

The streets filled with men, women and children, their faces streaming with blood from head wounds dealt by flying glass. Faces chalk white with terror. Faces streaked red and blackened by the rain. The dead, dying and severely injured lay about the streets. A man lay torn open his entrails exposed. A woman naked walked unconscious bathed in blood with her left breast severed and held in her hand. The scene can be faintly imagined but words cannot describe the horror as 1,600 to 2,000 people died and so many more were maimed.

The next morning a blizzard struck. It is hard to imagine the pain, suffering and death as Halifax had suffered the largest man made explosion ever. It would take an atomic bomb to exceed the destruction unleashed on that fateful day in Halifax.

Rick Hansen
'Man in Motion'

The story of this great modern day Canadian hero started on August 26, 1957 when Rick Hansen was born in Port Alberni, British Columbia. He was a good student who enjoyed sports. Life was progressing beautifully until the summer of 1973. Before the world knew about Terry Fox, young 15-year-old Rick was riding in the back of a pickup truck with his friend Don Alder. They were hitching hiking home to Williams Lake after a fishing trip. Suddenly the truck swerved out of control and rolled over. Doug was thrown free but Rick was not so lucky. The accident severed his spinal cord leaving him permanently paralysed below the waist. At that fateful moment his life was suddenly changed.

Rick set himself on a series of goals. In 1976 he graduated from high school in Williams Lake. He went on to the University of British Columbia where he completed a degree in physical education, the first disabled person in the university's history to do so. At the same time he was establishing his credentials as a world champion wheelchair athlete. He won national titles in wheelchair volleyball and basketball. He encouraged Terry Fox to join the Cablecars wheelchair basketball team that won 10 championships in 12 years. He entered 19 international marathons including the Boston Marathon in 1982. He crossed the finish line in one hour, forty-eight minutes and twenty-two seconds, knocking more than six minutes off the course record. He won the race but no one knew his name for he was an unofficial entry and had no number. Officially he did not win the race because the winner cannot use a mechanical device. Rick had the idea of wheeling around the world a year after the accident and he was inspired by Terry Fox to make his dream a reality.

In 1984 Rick contacted Timothy Frick, a physical education teacher at Selkirk College in Castlegar who had coached Rick in wheelchair sports since 1977. It was a tough sell and after four months of trying to raise funds for the trip he had $50,0000, most of that from a B.C. Provincial grant. March 21, 1985 when he rolled out of Vancouver's Oakridge shopping mall there was little pomp and even less money as all that Hansen could glean from the crowd of 300 was a $100 personal donation from Mayor Michael Harcourt. As the tour left the mall and drove under an overpass the roof rack on top of the motor home was scraped off. Such was the inauspicious beginning.

Initially the tour consisted of Don Alder, Timothy Frick and Hansen's cousin Lee Gibson. Funds from the United States and many other countries were just enough to keep the tour rolling. Two weeks into the tour Rick sustained severe physical injuries to his wrist and shoulders. Thank goodness they were able to get physiotherapist Amanda Reid to quit her job at G.F. Strong Rehabilitation Centre and join the tour. Romance blossomed and July 1986 in North Carolina Rick popped the question to the attractive brunette. She accepted but for much of the tour they kept their engagement under wraps.

He wheeled through 34 countries. He was ignored in much of Europe. In China he was allowed by officials to climb the Great Wall. It was one of the steepest inclines he had to face and it took all his strength. In New Zealand he and his crew relaxed and chartered a fishing boat for a days excursion. Though originally denied access to Russia they finally were permitted to bring the spirit of the tour there. He passed through Israel in a time of war. He was thrilled to reach the half way point in Melbourne, Australia. Still Rick points out it was not a holiday. He wheeled 80 km three out of four days, pushed himself over five mountain ranges and four continents in temperatures ranging from subtropical to sub-zero. He used five wheel chairs, was robbed four times, went through 80 pairs of gloves and had 100 flat tires.

Throughout his journey he spoke of the need to show more understanding toward the disabled. Fund-raising was not his main goal. Still, when he reached Cape Spear, Newfoundland on August 25, 1986 he had raised only $174,000. The Canadian part of the tour was the best planned as he traced the steps of the two men who inspired him, Terry Fox and Steve Fonyo. He had a special four-wheel-drive wheelchair for icy conditions and special clothing for sub-zero temperatures he expected to face. However Canada was much nicer to Rick than he could ever have hoped. The winter weather was for the most part mild and Canadians threw their financial support behind the tour. Prime Minister Brian Mulroney gave $1 million and Alberta and British Columbia promised to match the public funds. All across Canada, Canadians came out to see Rick and donate to his cause.

Hansen's goal was to wheel the equivalent of the circumference of the earth. Some 40,073 kilometres. May 22, 1987 he wheeled back into Oakridge Mall to a hero's welcome. May 23 the tour ended with a lot of glitz and some sobering words from Rick at B.C. Place. The message was the same as it had always been. "Show some respect for the disabled. They are still people who must cope with their disability. The least we could do is encourage them." Oh by the way, it was announced that the tour did reach its projected fund-raising goal of $10,000,000 to start a legacy for the disabled. Rick, we salute you for your 'dream', well done.

A sub note to this story, Amanda and Rick got married October 10, 1987. *Vancouver Province* sports reporter, Jim Taylor, helped Rick write his autobiography. Incidentally Jim has a daughter who was involved in a ski accident that left her a quadriplegic.

It should be noted that 33 countries of the world donated less than $180,000 to the 'Man in Motion' World Tour. With total revenues exceeding $10 million Canada contributed over $9.8 million of the total revenue. Canadians should be congratulated for their humanitarian efforts in supporting not only Rick Hansen but also Terry Fox and Steve Fonyo. Canada you have a big heart.

Rick established the Rick Hansen Institute that he administers from the $24 million Legacy Fund that has grown to over $107 million. He campaigns to give full medal status to wheelchair athletes in the Olympic games and a school Life skills program. Rick is a mentor who champions many causes and loves his three daughters Emma, Alana and Rebecca to death.

Hillcrest
Canada's Worst Mine Disaster

There is nowhere else in Canada that has seen as much drama, heroism and terror as the small valley that encompasses the towns of Frank, Bellevue and Hillcrest, Alberta. Frank, 165 miles southwest of Calgary, suffered a massive landslide April 29, 1903 when 70,000,000 tons of rock broke from the face of Turtle Mountain and killed 76 people. December 10, 1910 an explosion in a mine at Bellevue killed 30 men and as devastating as these events were they pale compared to the Hillcrest mine disaster.

The mine had been closed for two days due to over production and though it was Friday, a workday was scheduled. The day before the pit committee, comprised of Frank Pearsons, president of the miners' union, George Pounder and James Gurtson, found the mine in satisfactory condition. The fire boss, Daniel Briscoe's duty was to inspect the mine and he reported gas in several sections of the mine but found plenty of moisture and reported the ventilation was good. He sent word to the miners to be ready for work. At 7:00 A.M. June 19, 1914 workers arrived at the mine prepared to work.

Some like William Dodd, the oldest miner at 63, decided not to work that day. A youthful line of men tramped through the timekeeper's office. The oldest was Robert Muir, 54 and the youngest was Alex Petrie only 17. Most of the men were in their late 20's or early 30's and many were related by blood or marriage. John B. McKinnon who hailed form Cape Breton was known as 'Sampson of the Pass.' He stood 6' 4" and was reputed to be the strongest miner in Western Canada. The previous week he had picked up a 30-foot piece of railway track and lifted the 480-pound rail over his head for the amusement of his friends.

As they passed through the office, each of the 229 men deposited one brass identification tag with timekeeper Robert Hood and placed the second in their pocket. Because of the reported presence of gas Mine Superintendent James S. Quigley entered the mines first. He worked on the air flow with a giant fan on Level 1 and a second giant fan that drew the air out. It was the responsibility of the bratticemen to control the flow of air with brattices or screens. Soon men were dispersed to all parts of the mine. In the inky blackness of the mine their solitary Wolf Safety Lamps illuminated their way.

At 9:00 A.M. eight more miners pass through the lamp house and picked up their lamps and brass checks and headed to the timekeeper's office. Hood passed 6 of them but detected the odour of liquor on the breaths of the remaining two and he refused to let them pass. There is no argument and the two made their way back to the Miner's Hall to continue drinking.

With 235 men now in the mine Hood picks up the two brass checks of the men he had not allowed to work and hangs them on the board inflating the number to 237.

Suddenly there is an explosion at 9:30 A.M., or as one survivor reports three separate blasts that are so close together they seem to be one. The oxygen was burned out of the air leaving deadly carbon dioxide called black damp or after damp. It causes unconsciousness and death from prolonged exposure.

Three men stagger from the mouth of Mine #2. An immediate call for help is sent out to the town Blairmore as well as to the police. Men groped for the entrance relying on their intimate knowledge of the mine. Bill Guthrow caught his boot in the switch of a mine track and could not free himself. John Moorehouse stopped to help him and they used Bill's pocket knife to cut the boot off.

By now a frantic crowd of women and children had gathered. Only 18 men emerged into the sunlight. David Murray scrutinized the coal blackened faces and saw none of his three sons were among them. He wheeled and re-entered the mine pushing the constables aside who tried to bar his way. He was never seen alive again.

The oxygen masks had not yet arrived and the first crews entered the mine without them. By 10:00 A.M. oxygen masks arrived. An emergency tent hospital was erected and manned by Dr. William Todd.

By 11:30 thirty-seven men had escaped or had been brought out unconscious and were alive. As the horror deepened it was apparent there was little hope for the 198 men assumed to be still in the grips of the mine.

Robert Hood reduced the number to 196 when he remembered the two men he had refused entrance. Seven men were found with signs of life but were otherwise unconscious. They were rushed to the surface and revived.

Miracles ceased by noon. There were few men alive who had intimate knowledge of the mine system never the less, many men ventured into the depths only to find miners badly burned and disfigured so badly they couldn't be identified. They were not immediately removed lest the sight unnerve the survivors and the crowd of widows and children. As the crowd thinned the grim task of removing the dead progressed. The corpses were taken to the wash-house.

Fortunately Inspector Junget assessed the situation and placed a bottle of whiskey on a shelf. Miraculously the bottle never seemed to run dry.

At 11:30 P.M. a fire was found in the mine and was quickly suppressed. Throughout the day men had braved the possibility of another explosion but this did not deter them from their mission. By midnight it was evident that no other survivors would be found.

Bodies were washed and wrapped in a shroud and taken to the Miners' Hall and laid out for identification and burial by relatives. When the hall was filled George Cruickshank's General Store was requisitioned.

Another fire was found at 3:00 A.M. and was finally under control by dawn. By noon on Saturday, 162 bodies had been exhumed from the mine. Progress was slower as the rescuers were weary from lack of sleep. Now the only remains were fragments of bodies.

On Sunday many bodies were placed in three huge graves. For two weeks funerals marked the passing days. All but 2 bodies had been recovered within a week.

Corporals Meade and Grant and Constable Hancock worked at the grim task for a week with little sleep faced with a very grim task. They were each awarded a sum of $50.00 for their courageous work.

On July 7 the body of Joseph Oakley was found and identified by his brass tag. The only miner unaccounted for was Sidney Bainbridge. One hundred and eighty nine men had died on that fateful day.

Francis Aspinall, the District Inspector of Mines, stated that in his opinion the mine was both gaseous and dusty. A spark had ignited the explosive mixture. Perhaps it was a pick or a rock fall as hypothesized by survivor Harry White. The safety committee of the Hillcrest mine union was scorned for not having enough safety apparatus on hand in case of an accident.

September 19, 1926 another blast rocked the mine at 10:20 P.M. Two men, Frank Lote and Fred Jones, had been inspecting it. Both men died but the cause could only have been a rock fall. Never the less the mine was not closed until December 1, 1949 when dynamite sealed the mine forever.

Judith Jasmin
Television Pioneer Who Covered the 'Quiet' Revolution

Judith Jasmin was born in Terrebonne, Québec on July 10, 1916 into a family with strong political and social values. Her mother was, what would now be considered a feminist. At the time the French in Québec were comparatively poor and backward. The education system was abysmal. The Roman Catholic Church dominated the political and social standards at the time. As evidence, Québec women didn't get to vote provincially until 1940, seventeen years after they were given the right federally.

In 1921 the family moved to Paris. Amédée wanted to expose his two little girls to an environment rich in human imagination unlike the stifling convent school of Québec. They returned in 1927.

When the stock market crashed in October 1929 Judith realized her family was poor. She returned to Paris for two more years of education, then returned and went to a college for girls and finally received her degree.

She worked at a bookstore and listened to the radio. She joined a theatre group and took to acting with a natural gift for the stage. In 1939 she auditioned for a radio drama series *La Pension Veldor* and got a starring role. She fell in love with a theatrical impresario named Paul Maugé but he was married and refused to get divorced. At the time getting a divorce required an official act of the Senate of Canada. It was a long, difficult and expensive procedure. To be with a married man was scandalous in Québec at the time and after twelve years Judith called it quits.

While cutting her journalistic teeth in radio she met René Lévesque. Though younger, he had more experience having been a war correspondent through World War II. They took their equipment, as primitive as it was, to the streets of Québec. With the arrival of Radio-Canada's first French-language television station in 1952 they made the move into the new media. Judith Jasmin became a household word in Québec as night after night she made sense out of the chaos of poverty, revolution and global transformation.

Initially her relationship with René, a married man, was strictly professional but after a year and a half he allowed his marriage to dissolve. Judith later wrote, "It was as if we had loved each other in another life." She now traveled the world with the man she loved and their personal chemistry made them a powerful team. She was deliberate, thoughtful and a demon for preparation. Lévesque was always an improviser and would show up with fifteen seconds to spare. His pockets bulging with notes, he simply stood there and spoke to the viewers. Occasionally he would dig a crumpled note out to refresh his memory. They were such a contrast.

Suddenly four years later René just up and left. There was no explanation or opportunity for an emotional plea. Judith's life was shattered. In 1954 she left the country and reported around the world. She returned a year later. She wrote in her diary: "I am more connected to you than ever…six years of loving an unattainable man…the thought of suicide has subtly been taking shape."

With the help of a therapist she survived and found healing in her work. While in war torn, poverty-stricken Haiti she fell in love with a tall, handsome black man named Jo Chetelain. He was not married and wanted to keep it that way. Hoping she would see more of Jo she decided to take her chances as a freelance writer and returned to Paris. They were together off and on for seven years. There was little work and Radio-Canada paid her a disgraceful pittance for her reports. Still she delivered an international perspective on her favourite issues of justice and liberty.

Those issues would draw her back to Québec as the long, simmering movement brought the *Révolution Tranquille* in the 1960's.

There were even a few clergy whose views gave Québecers enough pride to pursue justice and liberty. She interviewed Father Jean-Paul Desbiens who anonymously published *Les Insolences* a book on Québec and the church. His views were so outrageous at the time he signed it 'Frère Untel', Brother So-and-So. Some fellow journalists were outraged that she gave her support to the cause casting out objective journalism. She did support an independent Québec, as did many journalists at Radio-Canada. It is a tribute to their professionalism that their views did not contaminate the news service.

In 1963 Judith was distraught when *Front de Libération du Québec* blew up a couple of mailboxes. She wrote from Algeria to *Le Devoir*, a separatist sympathizer:

"Here, in this land bathed in the blood of a million victims of the war of liberation, I think about those of you who have adopted some of the combat methods employed by Algerian patriots. At the core, both are issues of independence. But the context here is very different. In the history of the conquest of Algeria in the 19th century there are countless pillages, rapes and massacres. What exists in our Québec rebellion to compare in scale with the martyrs of Algeria? Aspiring heroes of Québec's independence, lay down your arsenal of violence. The work we must accomplish at home is more difficult than you imagine."

Judith did miss having a husband and family despite her successful career. She remained a strong and independent woman even when she lost a breast to cancer. Jean LeTarte, who had been her cameraman in some of the hottest spots, says she was always more courageous than he. The cancer would eventually take her life as it spread to her bones.

She had been a pioneer, the first woman to be made an official foreign correspondent. Her broadcasts were deep and thoughtful and news editors came to expect meaningful stories from her so it hurt her deeply when Radio-Canada management decreed she was not to do live reports or commentary any more. She was instrumental in putting the CBC on the map. Toward the end of her life, when she was ill, she was treated shabbily. They did not try to treat her with dignity and respect prior to her death October 20, 1972. Just the same she deserves a great deal of credit for her contribution to the amazingly peaceful revolution that took place.

In one of her last interviews she was asked what her life as a reporter had meant to her. She said, "It was marvellous; it was the kind of life you'd expect to pay for the privilege of having."

Harold Johns
Cobalt-60 for Cancer Patients

Harold Johns was born in Chengtu, China on July 4, 1915 to missionaries. Mounting turmoil in China forced the family back to Canada. Harold earned a doctorate in physics from McMasters University in 1939. He taught at the University of Alberta then at the University of Saskatchewan. At the time the Saskatchewan government was Canada's leader in progressive reform. It had established North America's first government sponsored cancer clinic in 1931. It was a leading authority on the treatment of cancerous tumours using radiation beams.

Johns persuaded his superiors to fund his research on finding another source of radiation. Premier Tommy Douglas personally approved the expensive research. The key to the research was cobalt-60. The world's source for this radioactive element was the nuclear reactor at Chalk River, Ontario. Johns convinced scientists there to prepare small quantities of the cobalt-60 for his experiments. At the same time he set to work designing and building a treatment machine. When he was finished, the results were spectacular. His machine was much cheaper and vastly more powerful than anything else in existence. The first patient was treated in 1951 with, as the media dubbed it, the 'cobalt bomb.'

Harold concentrated on the appropriate doses of radiation for specific cancers developing a vast body of research. Today more than 3000 'cobalt bomb' machines are in operation in over seventy countries. Most of the machines are Canadian made. More than 7 million patients have been treated. Cobalt-60 is not a cure but it buys time and can give a new life to patients that once had no hope.

Pauline Johnson
Quill of Her People

A young English woman Emily Howells, was visiting her bother-in-law in Canada and met and fell in love with the Mohawk chief George Johnson. Both families were opposed to their union but neither was dissuaded and the two were married. George was prosperous and gave his bride a fine house as a wedding gift. It was called Chiefswood and is just a few miles from Brantford. Pauline Johnson was born there March 10, 1861.

She grew up in two cultures, her father's Mohawk culture and her mother's English traditions. Under her grandfather Smoke's tutelage she learned to handle the subtle, elegant birch bark canoe. She also relished her grandfather's stories of her people.

Her father was so prominent she met a number of distinguished people who came as guests to their house. It had two entrances, one for the river travellers and another facing the road that brought visitors from town. She met young Prince Arthur, Duke of Connaught, whose mother was Queen Victoria. The prince gave the Johnson's a gift of a fine red blanket.

Alexander Graham Bell was another visitor and Pauline's father helped string telegraph wires for Bell's experiment and was present for the first long distance telephone call from Brantford to Paris, Ontario.

Though she could understand a number of native languages it was in English that she found her voice. She wrote poetry from a young age and it would become her medium. She also had a great stage presence that she honed at the Brantford Amateur Theatre where she was in a number of plays.

Her father protected his beloved private forest but white people would come and steal wood. As a result he was beaten and almost died. He was also opposed to the selling of whiskey and was twice attacked by the peddlers resulting in ill health until he died.

With this background she would turn her early love of storytelling and verse into a life and livelihood. When her father died they had to rent out Chiefswood and took a small place in town. Pauline tried to make some money as a freelance journalist and found that the editors and readers of the *Brantford Examiner* seemed to enjoy what she had to say. In 1892 Frank Yeight invited Pauline to recite her work at a gathering of young Liberals in a Toronto club. She recited, "A Cry from an Indian Wife"

They but forget we Indians owned the land

> From ocean unto ocean, that they stand
> Upon a soil that centuries a-gone
> Was our sole kingdom and our right alone.
> They never think how they would feel today
> If some great nation came from far away
> Wresting their country from the hapless brave
> Giving what they gave us, but wars and graves.

She began to give performances pouring out her Mohawk soul. Audiences were taken, swept with her proud beauty and performances that left tongues wagging. She dressed in buckskin and wampum and carried the famous vice regal red blanket wrapped around her shoulders. As her status grew, so did her delivery. She would sweep into town with props, costumes, and poetry and stories to lull and shock. Her voice was thrilling. She would first appear on stage in an evening gown, presenting herself as her mother would wish - aristocratic, educated, sophisticated and articulate. She would give them the contained lady-like lyric poems first.

Later in the bill she would come out and she would be the complete opposite with her hair unbound, wearing a buckskin dress with daring exposure of her arms and ankles. She would have her father's hunting knife and a bear-claw necklace. She then recited the really blood-curdling, violent poems.

> A thrust above the heart, well-aimed and deep
> Plunged to the very heart in blood and blade
> While vengeance, gloating, yells "The debt is paid!"

She wowed audiences in Toronto and Montreal, then headed to London, England and once again put her arrow to the heart. She said, "Suppose we came to England as a powerful people. Suppose you gave us welcome to English soil, worshipped us as Gods, as we worshiped you white people. And suppose we encroached upon your homeland, and drove you back and back then said, "We will present you with a few acres of your own dear land." What would you think of it all?"

Her audiences would nod wisely and sadly and think, yes we have done wrong. But isn't it nice that she does not hate us for it because of course though she may be Mohawk she is also one of us.

She marched into Bodley Head a publishing house for poetry and talked them into publishing her collection of poems *White Wampum* in 1894. When she returned to Canada she was aglow with her British success. She toured to packed venues wherever she went. She traveled by railway across Canada to places like Moose Jaw and Banff and she also performed in mining and lumber towns. People would come from miles around to see her perform. It wasn't unusual for people to travel 50 or even 100 miles by horse, carriage or on foot.

She didn't disappoint the rough men and ladies of the night as she gave them a taste of her own lusty, blood-pumping drama. When she walked on stage she owned the house.

In 1897 she moved to Winnipeg and became engaged to a banker, Charles Drayton. It did not last. Some of us might find her work contrite and others down right offensive but this pretty princess with the mighty quill really said it like it is:

> You have killed him. But you shall not dare
> To touch him now he's dead
> You have cursed and called him 'cattle thief'
> Though you robbed him first of bread-
> Robbed him and my people
> Look there at that shrunken face,
> Staved with the hollow hunger
> We owe you and your race
> What have you left us of land?
> What have you left us of game?
> What have you brought but evil
> And curses since you came?

In 1906 she returned to Britain again but it wasn't the same. In 1909 she stopped travelling and moved to Vancouver to be with her friend Joe Mathais an Elder of the Squamish tribe. She wrote some of his stories down in her style and with the Chief's permission sent them off to the *Vancouver Province*, which serialized them. They were assembled into a book, *Legends of Vancouver* and the first edition sold out. When she published it under *Flint and Feather* it was also an instant success. She needed the money because she was diagnosed with breast cancer. The rest of her days were spent in hospital and it was costly before the public health system existed.

Prince Arthur, Duke of Connaught, was later appointed Governor General of Canada and in 1912 came to the poet's side. She dedicated *Flint and Feather* to him. She died soon after in 1913 and her ashes were spread in Stanley Park overlooking the ocean. A small marker with a carved profile in stone marks the site.

Ruby Keeler
Innocent Blue Eyed Bombshell

Like so many Irish immigrants Ralph and Nellie Keeler came to America but ended up living in a tiny house in Dartmouth. They had a son William and then along came Ruby on August 25, 1909; two years later came her sister Geurtrude. Her father was a butcher and it was not an easy life.

Not surprisingly they decided to try their luck south of the border. They moved to a rundown cold water tenement on the east side of Manhattan. The family then had three more daughters, Helen, Anna May and Margie. They never had enough money and only barely enough to eat. Everybody helped in their own way.

Their Irish love of music at home was an important part of the environment for the young Keeler family. Ruby showed a natural gift for it. She had a smooth rhythm and one of the nun's that taught her at St. Catherine of Sienna's Catholic School, persuaded the Keeler's to enrol Ruby in Jack Blue's School of Rhythm and Tap.

Blue thought the slim adolescent kid with the amazing blue eyes and smooth tap-dancing style could make it in the chorus line for *Rosie O'Grady* on Broadway. She auditioned and was soon bringing home more money than her father. It opened in the Liberty Theatre on December 22nd, 1922.

With Prohibition in full swing it was the speakeasies that changed Ruby's life. When Nils Grunland saw her, he offered her a regular spot at his nightclub The El Fey. A mere teenager, Ruby had an air of innocence although she looked older in her makeup.

She ran into Johnny 'Irish' Costello, an Italian gangster. He was a lieutenant for Owney 'The Killer' Madden. He was smitten with her and soon Broadway producers found her more roles in musicals.

By seventeen she was Costello's girl and was protected. However the black face himself, Al Jolson, saw her in Chicago and was taken by her. He had to follow her closely for she was usually accompanied but he finally got his chance in Los Angeles where she had a brief unescorted engagement.

Jolson knew he was living dangerously and Ruby was initially terrified, but when he turned on his full power and charm, Al got what he wanted and they secretly became engaged. When Costello found out instead of assassinating the great man he acted in Ruby's best interest. He made sure Jolson knew if he ever harmed Ruby his life was in mortal danger. They married September 21, 1928, Jolson was forty-five.

Jolson's career had peaked and Ruby's was just picking up steam. She starred in Ziegfield's *Whoopee,* dancing with James Cagney and the next year she was in a Gershwin musical, *Showgirl.* She appeared in her first film *42nd Street* in 1933. Producers were calling all the time and Jolson hated it. Unable to conceive they adopted Al Jr., 'Sonny', in May 1935. He was fittingly half Irish, half Jewish, which seemed to fit. However it did not save the marriage. Ruby asked for nothing but her son and left. They were divorced officially in 1939. She did *Sweetheart of the Campus* in 1941 and met John Lowe on a blind date. He was handsome, wealthy with a solid character and a generous disposition. Though saddened that they could not have children they married but to their joy and surprise Ruby was soon pregnant and had two daughters and a son.

Movies were still an important part of their life but they were home movies now. They clowned by the swimming pool and she was always the #1 car-pool driver. There was little to remind her children of her past. However when they went to her birthplace the children were surprised at all the fuss over their mother at the border. Ruby was front row centre at swim meets and yo-yo contests. She was always there for her kids. There was only a little hint of her unusual past when she did a little soft shoe from the sink to the refrigerator. Her children would laugh and comment about her dancing prowess but they could not do it.

They had no idea that she was famous. Her daughter Theresa said "Every once in a while she would make a television appearance like Jackie Gleason for instance. Honestly, we thought that probably everybody's mother did that once in a while. Isn't that remarkable?"

Death began to mark her life as it had her career. Her father had died just after Theresa was born and in 1964 her mother died. About the same time her husband was diagnosed with cancer and he succumbed to the disease in 1969. Tragedy was all about, Kennedy, Vietnam, Kent State and Ruby seemed to be inconsolable.

Harry Rigby, a producer wanted his two idols, Busby Berkeley and Ruby Keeler to get involved in their old 1925 musical, *No No Nanette.* Ruby flatly refused but her children and friend Madelyn Jones said what do you have to lose?

She auditioned and when they opened in Boston, John Lowe, Jr., now in his fifties said, "And to be the son of that…not just part of it, but to have that be my mom, was probably the proudest thing I have ever experienced in my life." She brought the house down, then on they went to New York and sell out time. She brought the 'Big Apple' to its feet and her daughter Kathleen says she went back time and again saying, "My heart would pound…I was nervous for her and I knew she was nervous…you'd hear murmurs as she came down the stairs…she'd start with the soft-shoe, then everyone relaxed…it was a wonderful, wonderful moment."

She was sixty-one and back in the spotlight again. But Ruby knew what was truly important in her life. Four years after the greatest comeback in the history of the Broadway stage she fell with a massive aneurysm. She was unable to walk but she fought back and learned to walk again and even started dancing again albeit with a cane. The end came at her Rancho Mirage in California with all her children around. John Jr. said it was "Okay to go" and so she did into the Broadway and Hollywood book of legends.

Frances Kelsey
Thalidomide Heroine

She was born Frances Oldham in Cobble Hill, British Columbia on June 24, 1914. She earned her Bachelor of Science and Master of Science degrees from McGill by 1935. By 1938 she had earned her Ph.D. from the University of Chicago. She taught at the university where she met her husband Dr. Fremont Kelsey. They married and had two daughters. She worked as an editorial associate for the American Medical Association before teaching pharmacology at the University of South Dakota.

In 1960 Dr. Frances Kelsey joined the U.S. Food and Drug Administration (FDA). One of her very first assignments regarded the approval of the drug thalidomide for use as a sleeping pill.

She and her husband did not like the way routine pharmacological tests were done. She delayed approval while the manufacturers tried everything they could to change her judgement or discredit her decision in this regard.

Kelsey maintained the company did not have results from well-designed, well-executed studies on the effects of the drug. Dr. Joseph Murray, the manufacturer's representative repeatedly called and made personal visits to Kelsey. He complained to her superiors that she was unreasonably fussy and was delaying the drug's approval unnecessarily.

When the side effect of thalidomide was clearly evident it was with drawn November 26, 1961.

Only 17 thalidomide babies were born in the States thanks to doctors who made the decision for their patients. They distributed samples of Kevadon that were given to them by representatives of the Richardson-Merrell pharmaceutical company.

It was nothing compared to Germany where 3,500-5,000 were affected or Great Britain that suffered 1,000 deformed births. There were even more in her country of birth, Canada, with about 115.

August 7, 1962 President John F. Kennedy awarded the Distinguished Federal Civil Service award to Dr. Kelsey for her tenacity in holding her ground under the onslaught of corporate greed. It continues to be a problem for those poor children afflicted with life altering deformities who did not receive nearly enough compensation for the tragedy.

William Lyon Mackenzie King
The Commonwealth's Longest Standing Prime Minister

On December 17, 1874 William Lyon Mackenzie King was born in Berlin, Ontario. His mother was the daughter of William Lyon Mackenzie, the leader of a group of Reformers in Upper Canada and one of the instigators of the Rebellion of 1837.

'Billy' came from a political background with his father active in the Liberal party. In 1891 he enrolled in the University of Toronto. He thought of becoming a lawyer but became interested in social work. As a tribute to his ability as a student he was granted a fellowship to the University of Chicago. When he arrived in 1896, instead of living in the university residence he made his home at Hull House, a settlement in the slum section of the city.

On his return to Toronto he decided to investigate working conditions in some factories. He arranged to write a series of articles on his findings for the *Mail and Empire* newspaper.

He found the conditions shocking. Women and girls had been working excessive hours, under unwholesome conditions and receiving payment for actual work performed at a rate of three or four cents per hour.

By this time King had decided to become a university professor. He went to Harvard University to continue his studies in social and political science. There he was given a travelling fellowship to study in Great Britain, France, Germany and Italy. While abroad he was offered a position at Harvard. Shortly thereafter he received a cablegram from Sir William Mulock inviting him to return to Canada to organize a Department of Labour and to edit a government publication called *Labour Gazette*. He decided in favour of teaching and wired his decision. Mulock wired another cablegram and he changed his mind. At the age of twenty-five he was the Deputy Minister of Labour.

In the next few years he got some excellent training in conflict mediation. He was largely responsible for an important piece of labour legislation, the Industrial Disputes Investigation Act. He would not be happy as a civil servant so in 1908 he resigned his position and ran for Parliament in the riding of North Waterloo where he had spent his boyhood. Shortly after he was elected, Prime Minister Wilfred Laurier took him under his wing and made him Canada's first full-time Minister of Labour. In the general election of 1911 King lost his seat in Parliament, as did many of his colleagues. King increased his reputation by becoming Director of Research for the Rockefeller Foundation in the U.S.

In 1919 the Liberals met to elect a successor to Laurier. Laurier had said some years earlier, "Young Mr. King has the best brains in the country." Apparently the party agreed and he became their leader. In 1921 the Liberal party defeated Arthur Meighen and King found himself the prime minister of Canada.

Canada was still subordinate to Great Britain in many respects, when King resigned in 1948 Canada was a nation. In 1923 he insisted on Canada's right to make and sign her own treaties with other countries. Three years later the famous Balfour Declaration was made which affirmed that Canada and other Dominions were equal in status with the United Kingdom.

The King government was defeated by Richard B. Bennett in 1930. King led the opposition during the depression and was elected again in 1935.

On September 1, 1939 Germany invaded Poland. Two days later Great Britain and France declared war on Germany. In view of her status as an independent nation, King let Parliament decide the matter. When Parliament convened on September 10th war was declared. King played a pivotal role negotiating between Churchill and Roosevelt. Through his diplomacy the Lend-lease Agreement was reached and he was present at a number of secret diplomatic meetings between the two great men.

Near the close of his public life, King was invited to London to attend the wedding of H.R.H. Princess Elizabeth in 1947. At the time King George invested him with the Order of Merit, the first Canadian to receive this special honour.

On April 20, 1948 William Lyon Mackenzie King resigned, having been in the office for 7,825 days. He holds the world longevity record for elected leader of a nation. On July 22, 1950 King died never having married.

Klondike Gold Rush

In midsummer 1896, Robert Henderson had staked a claim on Gold Bottom Creek where he had panned about eight cents' worth of gold, considered a good prospect. Shortly there after three men, George Carmack and native relatives 'Skookum' Jim and 'Tagish' Charley encountered Henderson on his claim. George said, "What are the chances to locate up here? Everything staked?"

Henderson glared at the two natives and uttered the phrase that cost him a fortune, "There is a chance for you, George, but I don't want any damn Indians staking on this creek."

Gold lay scattered for the full length of the great Yukon River. The river and time had ground down the veins of gold that streaked the mountain. Gold as fine as dust was carried by the water but it did not reach the sea, for its specific gravity was nineteen times that of water. It sank when it reached the more leisurely river and was caught in sand-bars at the mouths of the tributary streams. Coarser gold moved a lesser distance and was trapped in the crevices of bedrock where nothing could dislodge it. Over the eons a deepening blanket of muck concealed it. In the Klondike Valley gold lay more thickly than any other creek, or river in the world.

Carmack was less interested in gold than logs, which he hoped to chop down along Rabbit Creek and float them down to the mill at Fortymile for twenty-five dollars a thousand feet. They proceeded to Rabbit Creek promising Henderson they would tell him if they found gold. They began to dip their pans into the black sand, which showed a tiny streak of colour. They trudged on stopping to pan and finding minute pieces of gold, they wondered whether or not to stake. They came to a fork in the frothing creek. At that instant they were standing on the richest ground in the world. Below their feet was millions of dollars worth of gold.

It was August 16, the eve of a memorable day that is still celebrated as a festive holiday. Who found the nugget that turned the world on its ear is blurred. At any rate the gold was lying there thick between the flaky slabs of rock like cheese in a sandwich. A single pan would yield a quarter of an ounce, or about four dollars' worth. A ten-cent pan had always meant good prospects, this was indeed an incredible find.

They collected enough coarse gold to fill an empty Winchester shotgun shell and let out a whoop while performing a celebration dance. The following morning the trio staked their claim. This done and with no further thought of Robert Henderson, they set off. As was the creed of the day the three men told each man they met of their find. Each man that encountered the emerging trio was given the opportunity of a lifetime. George sent 'Skookum' Jim back to guard the claim while he and 'Tagish' Charley went straight to Bill McPhee's Saloon at Fortymile. After a couple of whiskeys, the non-drinking, 'Lying' George broke the news to the crowded saloon and convinced one and all with his cartridge full of gold. The seasoned prospectors could tell where the gold came from just by looking at it and they could tell that this gold was undeniably foreign. By morning Fortymile was a dead mining camp, empty of boats and men. All were heading for the Klondike.

The strike was barely five days old when a miners' meeting hastily convened on a hillside, decided to give Rabbit Creek the more romantic title of 'Bonanza.' Already the valley was the scene of frenzied confusion. At the Klondike's mouth boats piled up on the beach day and night, arriving as if by magic from the silent forests of the Yukon Valley. They acted like madmen in their desire to stake and by the end of August all of Bonanza Creek had been staked.

The old-timers were sceptical of Bonanza. The valley was too wide, they said, the willows did not lean the proper way and the water did not taste right. The men who staked claims saw the Klondike as a last chance. Many sold their claims in the first week, believing them to be worthless. In that first winter two thirds of the richest properties could have been bought for a song.

Nobody knew it that first winter, of course, but this was the richest placer creek in the world. From where the first claims were staked they were numbered up and downstream and every claim from 1 to 40 was worth at least half a million and some were worth three times that amount.

In that winter enormous fortunes changed hands as easily as a package of cigarettes and poor men became rich and then poor again without realizing it. Al Thayer and Winfield Oler staked out 29 and, believing it worthless looked for a sucker on whom to unload it. They found it in Charley Anderson who was drunk in a saloon. When Anderson woke up next morning he found he had bought an untried claim for every last cent he had, $800. He went to the police but they could not help because his signature was on the title. It was several months before 'the Lucky Swede' found out his claim was worth a million dollars.

Mining in the sub-Arctic is unique because the permanently frozen ground must be thawed before the bedrock can be reached. It is the bedrock, ten, twenty and even fifty feet below the surface that contains the gold. It was laborious. Prospectors lit fires to burn overnight to thaw the earth below and in the morning they would remove the ashes. The shaft sides remained frozen and by this method they tunnelled, choked and wheezed in their smoky dungeons until they reached the 'pay streak.'

Thousands flocked to the gold fields but few were able to cash in. One of the few that did was a young lad who carried in a grinding wheel. He would sharpen picks, shovels and anything the prospectors had for an ounce of gold. He left with gold worth over $1,000,000.

It did not take long for the prospectors to sluice the claims of their riches. After that huge dredging machines appeared and they dragged up the last remnant of the world's greatest gold find. Dawson became Canada's most famous ghost town and is now a tourist destination spot, however there are still some adventurous souls that go to that location in hopes of finding a small fortune. Gold can still be found but the dredges did a good job and it is very unlikely that a fortune remains in the riverbed but elsewhere...

Albert Lacombe
Prairie Missionary

The son of a farmer, Albert Lacombe was born near the village of St. Sulpice, Québec on February 28, 1827. By the age of fourteen he could do a man's work on the farm but having heard accounts of the work of such 'heroes of the Cross' as Brébeuf and Lalément, he decided to become a missionary to the native tribes. A parish priest in St. Sulpice took an interest in the lad and arranged for his education. This was completed in Montreal.

As soon as he was ordained to the priesthood he set out for the west. Just to reach the west in those days required months of travel by ox-cart over winding trails. He eventually reached Pembina where he spent a couple of years learning the ways of the experienced missionaries. In 1852 he joined the Hudson's Bay Company flotilla of boats and went west with the annual shipment of supplies and mail destined for the trading posts on the North Saskatchewan River. He stayed in Fort Edmonton which was his centre of activity for the rest of the century. Although just a small village in those days, Edmonton was fast becoming a busy trading centre. The population was 150, almost all of whom were Hudson Bay employees. They collected furs from a vast area populated by Métis and Cree. Within the stockade Lacombe was given a building, which served as living-quarters and chapel. Here he began holding services for people in the community and for the voyageurs that passed that way. Finding no school he began one in the log chapel. It was the first one established in the West beyond Manitoba.

After a few years Lacombe moved his headquarters fifty miles northwest to Lac Ste. Anne where there was a settlement of Crees and Métis. His first problem was to learn the Cree language. Fortunately a Highland piper named Colin Fraser, had accompanied George Simpson, Governor of the Hudson's Bay Company and he had married a Cree woman. They settled with her tribe. Colin was the teacher Lacombe needed. In the evenings he would have his lessons and when they were over he would write down the words he had learned and the rules of grammar that governed their use. Later he developed this into a dictionary of the Cree language. The missionary was well loved and had considerable success in winning them to his religion. They gave him a name that meant 'Noble Soul.'

Once a year another tribe came to the fort to trade for the white man's goods. They were the Blackfoot. They came in large bands and were heavily armed. The fort took on a military air as cannons in the bastion of the palisade were loaded for action and men with loaded muskets were stationed in the sentinel's gallery. The Blackfoot were not allowed inside the fort to trade. It was done through a grate in the gate.

In 1857 scarlet fever broke out among the Blackfoot and their children were dying like flies. They sent for Father Lacombe to come to their aid. The Cree, suspicious of the Blackfoot, pleaded with him not to go but go he did. He visited the sick giving what help he could. Soon his scant supply of medicine was gone. Then he contracted the fever himself and his faithful half-breed guide and servant, Alexis, nursed him back to health. Out of gratitude the Blackfoot gave Lacombe the name, 'The Man with the Good Heart.' Though both tribes were bitter enemies they now both regarded the missionary as their friend.

On December 4, 1865 Lacombe was sleeping in the tent of Chief Natous of the Blackfoot tribe when the Cree made a vicious attack. Bullets whizzed through the tent and Lacombe rushed out, cross in hand, and in a powerful voice commanded the Cree to stop and withdraw. He couldn't be heard so he busied himself caring for the wounded and dying. A bullet grazed his forehead, but he continued to work. The battle continued through the night into the next day. One of the Blackfoot got close enough to shout to the enemy, "You have wounded your Blackrobe, dogs!" When that message was passed among the Cree they ceased firing and withdrew hastily.

Father Lacombe was given an assignment that particularly pleased him. He was made a roving missionary of the plains. He constructed a house tent of fifty tanned buffalo skins to celebrate the Mass. Two horses transported his mobile church as he tried to keep in touch with the tribes as they wandered. Lacombe and his faithful accomplice Alexis faced severe hardships, were often caught in blizzards and were in constant danger from starvation. On one occasion they had to stand for hours in a river to escape a forest fire and snow to their waist was not uncommon.

The respect he had among the natives of the western plains was soon to be tested and demonstrated. When the railway pushed into Blackfoot territory, they proceeded to tear up the tracks and a serious situation was developing. Lacombe hurried to the scene and gave his word to the Blackfoot that they would be compensated for any land taken by the railroad. The railroad tracklayers were given peaceful passage. The Canadian Pacific Railroad honoured Lacombe with a banquet in his honour and a lifetime railway pass.

When the Riel Rebellion broke out in 1885 most of the western tribes refused to join the outbreak and it was due in large part to Lacombe's intervention.

Lacombe was to provide more service to the government. In 1898 when gold was found along the Klondike River in the Yukon a commission was organized to go north to arrange a treaty with the natives of the area. Lacombe, then seventy-two years of age, felt he would be a handicap so he refused to go. The government persisted and on May 29th the party set out from Edmonton in heavy stage wagons with eleven North-West Mounted Police. The mission succeeded and Lacombe's health improved. When he died in 1916 he had witnessed the settlement of the West. Thanks to his contributions the change was a comparatively peaceful one.

Sam Langford
The Boston Tar Baby

Pound for pound they say he was the greatest boxer who ever lived. Sam Langford was born in Weymouth Falls, Nova Scotia on March 4th, 1880 or 1886. He was only 5' 6" and began boxing weighing only 132 pounds. His best boxing weight was 172.

In 1906 Jack Johnson, a Negro boxer like himself, met Langford in the ring. Langford weighted 151 pounds and Johnson 186. The fight went 15 brutal rounds in Boston. Johnson won the decision. Later when Johnson defeated another Canadian Tommy Burns in Australia in 1908 to become the Heavyweight Boxing Champion of the World, Langford asked for a shot at the title. Johnson refused to fight the brawler saying there was not enough money in it as they were both black and would not attract a large enough gate.

Langford boxed frequently in Boson and became highly regarded and loved. He was soon sporting the name 'The Boston Tar Baby.'

In 1908 Sam fought a fireman named Jim Flynn who was 210 pounds and was six foot one. Langford jostled Flynn toward the ropes above the ringside seat of the sportswriter H.M. Walker. Walker had written that Flynn should not mix it up with clowns like Langford. Sam grinned saying, "Here comes your champion" as he knocked Flynn into the writer's lap. Flynn climbed back in the ring and Langford broke his nose in the second round and broke his jaw in the third. Langford put him away with a right upper cut that left Flynn unconscious for 20 minutes. Sam was lucky he didn't kill the American.

Langford had a broad flat nose, thick heavy lips, flashy white teeth with one gold tooth, a cauliflower ear and short crisp curly hair that looked like a skullcap. He fought in a crouch and was therefore a difficult target to hit. He could punch like he had a bomb in both hands.

In 1910 he took on a brute named Dewey who weighed 205 pounds and stood six foot two. The bout was in Cheyenne, Wyoming where the trains were irregular. His manager Joe Woodman discovered the train left a half hour after the fight was scheduled to start. Sam knocked out Dewey at one minute 42 seconds into the first round and they caught the train.

Stanley Ketchell, the middleweight champion of the world, agreed to a non-title bout in Philadelphia on April 27, 1910. Langford went easy on Stanley and only blocked his shots for the last few rounds of the six-round bout. He hoped it would give him a shot at the title. Unfortunately Ketchell was shot and killed six months later.

Sam was so good that some fighters extracted a promise that he would carry them for some time before nailing them with a TKO. It didn't look good to go down in the first few rounds.

Georges Carpentier, the light-heavyweight champion of the world, also refused to fight Langford. In fact in his entire career, The Boston Tar Baby never was given a shot at any title. It seems a shame that such a fine fighter could be denied a title shot given his skill and stature in the boxing community. It was blatant discrimination that skilled boxers were denied title shots for years as the white boxing establishment tried to keep the crown on a white champion who would then refuse to fight competent black contenders.

On June 19, 1917 Langford, overweight, at 181 pounds faced Fred Fulton, a towering 215-pound brute. In the sixth round Sam went down for the third time as he took a dreadful beating. When the seventh round bell sounded Sam just sat on his stool and didn't answer the bell. Tears trickled down his face and his eye was swollen shut. The fight was called and Sam never did regain the sight in his eye. He should have retired but he didn't.

In 1920 Langford twice knocked out another Negro named George Godfrey who stood six foot three and weighted 240 pounds. He stopped boxing in 1923 after three fights in Mexico City. He fought one last exhibition fight in San Antonio in 1929.

The Tar Baby just disappeared. Years later a boxing writer Al Laney found him in Harlem. He was totally blind and broke. Laney began a fund that enabled Langford to return to Boston where he lived with his sister. When his sister died Mrs. Grace Wilkins, who ran a forlorn rest home, agreed to look after Sam, which she did until his dying day despite the fact that the fund had run out. She asked Sam what he would do if he could do anything in the world.

Sam replied, "Missus, I've been everywhere I wanted to go, I've seen everything I wanted to see, and I guess I've eaten just about everything there is to eat. Now I just want to sit here in my room and not cause you any trouble."

Sam Langford died January 12, 1956.

Marie de La Tour
Heroine of Acadia

François Marie Jacqueline was an actress in France and was the toast of the aristocratic Parisian stage door set. In 1640, feeling her age at thirty-eight, she accepted a marriage proposal by proxy and sailed over the seas to marry Charles Saint-Étienne de La Tour. They live at Fort Sainte-Marie at the mouth of the Saint John River. She sailed into a bitter feud between La Tour and his neighbour across the Bay of Fundy, Charles de Menou Sieur d'Aulnay.

Amid raids, reprisal raids, ambushes, blockades, pursuits, midnight escapes and desperate appeals from both sides to Versailles for help. None was forth coming. Marie sought aid in England and chartered a ship captained by Bayley. He drew her annoyance by leisurely making passage up the St. Lawrence trading with the natives. Entering the Bay of Fundy they were halted by d'Aulnay's patrol and Bayley asserted he knew nothing about Madam La Tour and sailed on to Boston. When they arrived she stormed ashore raging and sued the captain for violating his charter. An English colonial jury awarded her 2,000 pounds sterling. She chartered three New England vessels provisioned them with food and armaments and boldly penetrated the blockade sailing into St. John Harbour to a rousing welcome from her husband and son. The battles raged on and on. The costs were high with more than 30 of d'Aulnay's men dying and many more injured. La Tour's forces must have been similarly affected and finding new recruits was essential.

During one of the lulls in the feud in the depth of winter Charles left home to get supplies in Boston and find support for his struggle. He left Marie behind with about forty-five men to defend the fort. When d'Aulnay intercepted a ship carrying supplies and men he found a note that said a large force would be arriving soon. It was signed by La Tour. d'Aulnay, perhaps fearing the odds might shift, attacked the garrison in force. He had several hundred men and a warship, the *Grand Cardinal*s. Late in the afternoon of April 16, 1645 on the fourth day of the bitter fight, d'Aulnay withdrew his forces beyond the range of the artillery. Glad for the respite Marie ordered her men to rest. She left a 47-year-old Swiss man, Hans Vandre, to keep watch.

An hour before sundown d'Aulnay attacked. Vandre passively watched as they surged ahead. Vandre's motives were unclear, but they were surely betrayed as the troops poured over shattered sections of the fort wall Marie's defenders gathered their weapons and rushed to meet them. Marie led the charge but they were hopelessly outnumbered 4 to 1.

Still they fought on for hours until d'Aulnay roared, "We've beaten you! Surrender and I'll spare all your men."

Reluctantly Marie nodded and laid down her sword in defeat. One by one her men surrendered.

D'Aulnay suddenly flew into a rage cursing Madam and shocked her by swearing he would hang every last man who had fought against him. Starting with Marie he took a thick rope, made a noose and placed it around her neck. Tears came to her eyes as one by one her soldiers were similarly placed with nooses about their necks. Marie pleaded for their lives for she would gladly give hers for theirs. She watched in horror as one by one her men were strung up in a slow agonizing strangulation because they were not dropped for that would have meant a quicker cleaner death. d'Aulnay forced her to watch them dangle and struggle until their cries and movements stopped. It tore her heart out.

Only Vandre and the women there including Marie were spared. He took her to Port Royal and threw her into a dungeon where she died three weeks later of a broken heart and spirit.

Wilfred Laurier
Follow My White Plume

Wilfred Laurier was born to poor parents at St. Lon, in the County of L'Assomption, Québec on November 20, 1841. His ancestors had farmed in Canada for generations. It was his father who first suspected that his son was a boy of outstanding ability and felt that an important career was possible for him. With this in mind Wilfred was sent to attend school in New Glasgow when he was eleven. It was here that he learned to speak English with a slight Scottish accent. He also learned to understand and appreciate people from a different culture and religion. Sandy Maclean, one of Wilfred's teachers, loved to quote English poetry to his pupils. It was here that Laurier gained his love for the great writers of English. From New Glasgow he went to L'Assomption College, about 30 kilometres from his home. He did not take part in the athletic activities of the school but he did become the leading debater.

At age twenty he went to Montreal to study law. He entered the law office of Rodolph Laflamme and took the law course at McGill University. He was a brilliant student and when he graduated, he was chosen to deliver the farewell speech.

He began to practise law in Montreal but poor health forced him to leave the city and he moved to a new community called Arthabaskaville. Rural life left him considerable time to study the lives and speeches of Abraham Lincoln and other great orators. In 1871 a provincial election was held in Québec and he was chosen as the Liberal candidate for his county. Though ill through much of the campaign, his friends rallied to his support and he was easily elected.

During the next years his rise to power and recognition was rapid. In 1874 he was elected to the House of Commons and three years later became a Cabinet Minister in the government of the Honourable Alexander Mackenzie. This was short lived for the Conservatives under Macdonald were swept into office again and it would be eighteen years before the Liberals won. In 1885 he was elected leader of the national Liberal Party and was the chief critic of the government for the next nine years.

On June 23, 1896, Laurier was elected to the position of Prime Minister. The following year, 1897, marked the Diamond Jubilee of Queen Victoria's accession to the throne and Laurier went to London to represent Canada. There he was the centre of a great deal of interest for he was the first person of French ancestry to represent a major country in the British Dominion. His striking appearance and his exceptional oratory skills won hearts everywhere. Before he left the Queen knighted him. He also visited France and his public speaking did much to promote friendship between Britain, France and Canada. He stated in one of his public speeches, "We are faithful to the great nation that gave us life (France); we are faithful to the great nation that gave us liberty (Britain)."

In 1899 Laurier sent troops to fight in the Boer War in South Africa. He knew that Canada needed people to fill up the unoccupied areas of farmland. He placed Clifford Sifton in charge of the Department of the Interior in his cabinet and a vigorous immigration policy was adopted. Between 1897 and 1914 three million settlers came to Canada. In 1905 two new provinces were christened, Saskatchewan and Alberta.

In 1911 Laurier's long term in office, fifteen continuous years, came to an end. Well on in years now he offered to resign but his offer was declined. He continued as a Member of Parliament until his death on February 17, 1919. On the morning of the funeral common folk came from miles around to pay their respect to their dead leader who by his courtesy, chivalry and outstanding achievement had endeared himself to all. Over the years many Canadians had 'followed his white plume", now they could no longer and they wept.

Tom Longboat
'Greatest Distance Runner of All'

Tom Longboat was born of Onandaga blood on the Six Nations Reserve, Ontario on July 4, 1887. His native name was *Cogwagee*, which means 'Everything' but he went by his English name. He practiced on the reserve and won the five-mile race at the Caledon Fair, May 24, 1906. He took a ribbing at the Hamilton round-the-bay race that year. He was wearing a droopy cotton bathing suit and cheap sneakers. His stride was over six feet long and after testing the favourite the experienced English marathoner John Marsh he cut loose and left Marsh as if he was standing still. Tom won by three minutes. He trained for the Boston Marathon and entered the race in 1907. At noon 104 competitors started the race. He completed the course in the record time of 2:24.24. The record was not broken until the course was made easier.

He competed in the 1908 Olympics in London, England though there were questions about his amateur status. From the start of the race at Windsor Castle, Longboat took the lead and set a scorching pace. By the ninth mile he had dropped to fourth. Inside the stadium an official disqualified the fainting Dorando Pietri by helping him across the finish line thereby giving the race to Johnny Hayes of the United States. Longboat did not complete the race due to heat exhaustion.

Professional long distance running became the rage for a short time. Longboat, Pietri and Hays ran a rematch at Madison Square Gardens, Dorando won. On December 15 he ran for a share of the gate receipts at Madison Square Garden against Dorando and Pietri. Dorando collapsed on the last half mile. Longboat won and took the prize.

On February 5, 1909 he squared off against Alfie Shrubb in the 'race of the century.' Shrubb took the early lead and stretched it to 2/3 of a mile. Longboat reeled him in and during the twenty-fourth mile Tom spurted past him and Shrubb collapsed. In 1912 he set a new record for fifteen miles. He was sentenced for public drunkenness in Toronto and his drinking became his undoing.

He served overseas in the Great War and was falsely reported killed and his wife remarried. He wound up working on a Toronto garbage wagon in 1927 and died back on the Six Nations Reserve on January 9, 1949.

Elijah McCoy
'The Real McCoy'

Elijah McCoy was born in Colchester, Ontario on May 2, 1844 (though there are sources that claim other dates). He was the son of former slaves who had fled from Kentucky. (see Underground Railway) Elijah's father George, enlisted with the British army and served during the Rebellion of 1837. For his loyal service he received 160 acres of farmland and raised a family of twelve there. At an early age Elijah showed a mechanical interest and would often take items apart and put them together. His mother, the former Miss Mildred 'Emillia' Goins and his father sent him to be educated in Scotland as a mechanical engineer. He returned to Canada but was unable to find work so he went to the States at the end of the Civil War and settled in Ypslianti, Michigan.

Still unable to find work as an engineer, he was hired as a fireman/oilman on the Michigan Central Railroad. He was responsible for shovelling coal into the fires to produce steam that powered the locomotive. As the oilman he was responsible for ensuring the train was lubricated. Every few miles the train had to stop and he would walk alongside the train applying oil to the bearings and axles.

He married Ann Elizabeth Stewart however she passed away four years later.

He experimented with a cup that would regulate the flow of oil onto moving parts of the train axel that needed it. On July 12, 1872 he took out his first of many patents, this one for a lubricator device. The cup was such a success that orders poured in from railroad companies from all over the country and even abroad.

His invention revolutionized the industrial machine industry for his device allowed the machines to remain running while they were lubricated. He established his own firm and took out a total of 57 patents. His lubricating devices became very popular. Other inventors tried to sell their own versions of the device but most companies wanted the authentic device and requested the 'real McCoy.' This helped popularize the expression that came to mean the *real thing* or superior workmanship.

Elijah also invented an ironing board and a lawn sprinkler.

Elijah married Mary Delaney in 1873 and they settled in Detroit, Michigan and were happily married for 50 years.

Over time the device was adjusted and modified in order to apply it to different types of machinery. Versions of his invention were adapted to steam engines, oil-drilling rigs, mining equipment, naval vessels and factory equipment.

In 1916 he created a graphite lubricator and in 1920 established the Elijah McCoy Manufacturing Company. In 1922 Elijah and Mary were involved in a serious automobile accident. Mary would die from her injuries and Elijah's health suffered until his death.

He died October 10, 1929 in Eloise, Michigan. In 1975 the city of Detroit celebrated Elijah McCoy Day by placing a historic marker at the site of his home.

Sir John A. Macdonald
Canada's First Prime Minister

John Andrew Macdonald was born in Glasgow, Scotland on January 10, 1815. His father Hugh Macdonald operated a small manufacturing plant in Glasgow but after the Napoleonic Wars in Europe there was no sale for his products. He had to close his business and on a summer day in 1820 Hugh and his family headed for the New World. John attended grammar school until the age of fifteen, when he had to drop out to help support his mother and sister. Despite his lack of schooling he soon became a successful lawyer and statesman, a skilled debater and a clever public speaker. In 1836 he opened a law practice in Kingston. He was however destined to do his greatest work in politics, not law.

During his early years, John A., as he was affectionately known, had shown his loyalty to the government and the British Empire by joining the militia during the Rebellion of 1837. His unit was sent to Toronto but he did not see any fighting.

In 1844 he was elected to represent Kingston in the legislature of the combined provinces of Canada. In 1848 he was made a cabinet minister and in 1854 he became the Prime Minister. There were no political parties as we have today. Macdonald was able to bring about the union of three groups, the Conservatives and Reformers of Canada West and the Liberals of Canada East. The coalition was named the Liberal-Conservative Party. Soon it was simply called the Conservative Party.

Although Macdonald was not among the first to suggest the idea of Confederation, he was crucial to its overall, long-term success. In 1864 he took his party into the Great Coalition, a union with his rival political party, which was Liberal under the leadership of George Brown. That summer he traveled to Charlottetown for a conference on Confederation and in October of the same year, Québec City hosted a conference on Confederation. At this meeting Confederation was agreed upon and Seventy-Two Resolutions were drawn up which were the terms on which the provinces agreed to unite. Macdonald was particularly skilled in bringing people together with opposing views and finding some basis on which they could agree.

Macdonald was one of the delegates sent to London in 1866 to get the consent of the British government. The Seventy-Two Resolutions drawn up at the Québec Conference became the British North America Act, which passed unanimously in the British Parliament and became law on July 1, 1867 the day Canada was officially born.

As a tribute, Macdonald was knighted Commander of Bath. Sir John A. Macdonald became the first Prime Minister of the new country he helped create. Ontario, Québec, New Brunswick and Nova Scotia had joined confederation but Macdonald had an incredible amount of work to do to coax the remaining provinces into the fold.

Macdonald knew it was a race against the Americans to the Pacific. He sent two emissaries to London in 1868 to arrange to take over the West. The British were favourable and the following year the Hudson's Bay Company agreed to surrender its charter and handed over the land to the Canadian government. In one stroke a vast empire of over two and a half million square miles was added to the fledgling country.

There was trouble ahead and he had to cope with the Red River Rebellion of 1869 led by Louis Riel. (see Louis Riel) Troops were sent and the rebellion quelled. In 1870 the Red River Valley was organized into Canada's first new province - Manitoba.

John A. coaxed British Columbia into joining Confederation in 1871 with the promise of a railway to be built to the Pacific coast within ten years. Prince Edward Island joined Confederation in 1873 and Macdonald was nearer to his dream of a country stretching from sea to sea.

The most pressing problem he faced following Confederation was the building of the transcontinental railway. A start had been made on the railroad but in 1873 his government was defeated in a general election due to the 'Pacific Scandal.' Macdonald was accused of receiving illicit funds from Donald Smith of the Canadian Pacific Railway (CPR).

In the west lawlessness developed as whiskey traders from the south preyed upon the native tribes. In 1874 John A. introduced a bill in parliament, which set up the North-West Mounted Police. That summer about 300 men arrived on the prairies in their scarlet uniforms. After the Great Trek they soon had the situation under control.

In 1878 Macdonald was elected again despite the scandal and took up the railway problem with renewed vigour. It was an enormous task to build the railway through the Rocky Mountains and the rugged stretch of country north of Lake Superior. Time after time the CPR came back for more money and it took all the faith and persuasive powers that Macdonald could muster to induce Parliament to approve the funds. It looked like the final stages of the railway would not be completed due to financial problems. However help came from an unexpected source. In 1885 Louis Riel staged yet another rebellion. Troops were shipped by rail to quell the insurrection and the importance of this transportation system became evident to all concerned. On November 7, 1885 the 'last spike' was driven at Craigellachie, B.C. and the great project was completed. Nine days later Louis Riel was hung in Regina.

Macdonald felt his work was done. He would have liked to retire but his party wanted him to stay. He was elected again in 1887 and again in 1891 under the slogan 'the old flag, the old policy, the old leader.' This last campaign was more than he could take and after a few months he suffered a paralysing stroke. He got increasingly worse and on July 6th, 1891 he died.

Though he is remembered for the famous phrase, "A British subject I was born, a British subject I will die," Canadians remember him as the founder of their country and their first Prime Minister. He remained at the helm for nineteen years, built the transcontinental railway and is rightly considered 'The Father of Our Country.'

Angus Mckay
Farmer with a Mission

In June 1882 Angus Mackay and three neighbours from Whitby, Ontario arrived in the district of Indian Head. They had traveled by way of the newly built Canadian Pacific Railway taking it to the end of the line at Oak Lake. Land was selling for $2 an acre and they each bought a section hoping to make a fortune growing wheat on the rich, black loam.

By seeding time in 1883, Mackay had broken eighteen acres of virgin prairie. He sowed Red Fife wheat, the standard variety in the West, which was introduced to North America by David Fife. That year Angus harvested forty bushels to the acre. In high spirits the four neighbours that summer broke five hundred acres of new land.

In 1884 they seeded Red Fife again and it shot up. By September, long, heavy heads hung on the tall stems but the kernels had not ripened. When September 7th came they decided they couldn't risk danger any longer. The next day they decided to start the harvest. That night frost struck and the bumper crop was reduced to a scant yield of chicken feed. Angus realized that a faster maturing wheat variety was needed for the Canadian prairies and this would become one of his chief pursuits.

In 1885 before work on the land could begin, Louis Riel and his followers had risen in revolt along the Saskatchewan River. Angus's neighbours and their best horses went to haul supplies for the government forces. Angus was left with only a couple of horses unfit for the trek to Batoché and Edmonton. He seeded as much land as he could but was forced to leave half of it idle. When weeds grew Mackay harrowed the uncropped land regularly throughout the summer. It was the first summer fallowing done in the West and in the process an important principle was discovered. The summer-fallowed land would yield thirty-five bushels to the acre in 1886 when all around crops lay in ruin due to drought.

Mackay was quick to grasp the significance of what he had observed. The secret of farming in dry country was to conserve the rainfall during one season for growing in the next.

About this time the Canadian government was establishing experimental farms. Due to Mackay's success in growing wheat during a drought, he was offered the position of Superintendent. He accepted and established a farm at Indian Head.

Angus continued to summer-fallow but conducted experiments to determine how the fields could be prepared to conserve the greatest amount of water. He ploughed some in the spring and some in the fall.

Another he sowed with a drill without ploughing. Farmers came from near and far to see for themselves and profit from what they saw. Soon the region took on the checkerboard pattern of gold and black patches.

Mackay missed the trees on the bald prairies so he planted 23,000 trees of all varieties the first season on the farm. The Experimental Farm became a show place.

Dr. William Saunders (see Saunders), the man in charge of the experimental government farms, found varieties of wheat that would mature faster than Red Fife but they all produced flour inferior to the Canadian wheat. He began to cross Red Fife with other varieties from around the world and produced new varieties called Preston, Chelsea, Gatineau and Marquis.

In 1907 Saunders sent Angus several bags of what he regarded as his best varieties. Mackay carefully sowed and tended them to find out what they would do under prairie conditions. It so happened that it was one of the worst years for growing and the wheat was slow to mature. On September 11th the temperature fell to well below freezing. The crop lay ruined the next morning when he inspected the damage. All the little patches were drooping and frozen except one, which stood erect and unharmed. Marquis, a cross between the Red Fife and Hard Calcutta was far enough advanced to withstand the frost. Within a few years Marquis became the dominant variety of wheat used throughout the West.

Angus McKay died at Indian Head, Saskatchewan on June 10, 1931.

Alexander Mackenzie
from Canada by land July 22, 1793

Alexander Mackenzie was born on the island of Lewis in the Outer Hebrides, Scotland in 1764. His father Kenneth had fought on the side of the King of England that culminated in a slaughter at the Battle of Culloden in 1746. The Gaelic nation was crushed in what would now be called ethnic cleansing. The Mackenzie family prospered and Alexander was given an excellent education. However in 1774 his mother Isabella died and the economy worsened so Kenneth took the young lad to the New World.

The American Revolution was brewing. His father enlisted with the British Army and sent Alexander up to Montreal to attend school. In 1779 Alexander joined the fur-trading firm of Finlay and Gregory. In 1784 he became a partner and supervised the post at Île-la-Crosse from 1785-87. When the company merged with the North West Co. he was assigned to a post on the Athabasca River under the command of Peter Pond.

He learned the value of the birch bark canoe in his travels to his post. It was easily repaired with materials you could find growing near by. The oily, waterproof bark of the silver birch was sewn together with spruce roots. White cedar was used for the ribs and paddles. Spruce gum was boiled with fat to make the seams waterproof.

It was undoubtedly in the wilds that he learned to use and load the musket. You had to be careful loading through the muzzle of the long barrel, measuring the black gunpowder and packing it carefully with the ramrod. Too vigorous a push could detonate the mixture and turn the ram into a projectile. Next came wadding, paper or a piece of rag followed by a bullet, which could be a single round ball or a spoon of small buckshot. Beyond forty feet the musket was useless and one shot was all you got for it took about two minutes to reload.

Alexander went out of his way to befriend the natives showing respect and courtesy. In 1789 Alexander took over command and decided to find the Pacific. He took one freight canoe, three smaller ones and a guide named Nestabeck, a Chipewyan leader. Along the way he befriended the Dene tribe and some joined his party. When they reached the coast and looked out on the Arctic Ocean he called it 'The River of Disappointment' because it did not discharge into the Pacific. It is now called the Mackenzie River of course.

He made it back in time to miss the river freeze and met Philip Turner, a surveyor for the Hudson's Bay Company. Turner showed

Mackenzie an instrument called a chronometer that aided a traveller in calculating their exact location. Mackenzie returned to London to get one of those devices and returned in 1793 to try once more. He wintered at Fort Fork on the Peace River. In May he headed west from the Peace watershed to the Fraser but was advised to journey overland as the river was too dangerous. He soon reached the Bella Coola River that took him to the Pacific. He mixed some red vermilion in melted grease and inscribed Alexander Mackenzie from Canada by land, the twenty-second of July, Seventeen Ninety Three on a good sized bolder that is still there with a plaque on it. Another great chapter had been written in Canadian history.

Willie McKnight
Bright Light McKnight

Willie McKnight was born in Edmonton, Alberta on November 18, 1918. Willie loved speed and earned free plane rides by saving up cigarette cards. When British recruiters showed up looking for young men to train as pilots McKnight jumped at the opportunity. The fact that he was on the verge of being expelled from college may have been a factor.

He was posted to Little Risington, near Gloucester where he trained. They flew the Avro Anson. While in training a big band led by Ted Heath was playing at the village dance hall. McKnight was on duty but he took off and arrived at the dance with his girlfriend on his arm. He encountered the commanding officer and was reprimanded but luckily was not kicked out of the Royal Air Force (RAF).

At first McKnight was put on a Bristol Blenheim bomber that he described candidly saying, "It's just like flying a bloody truck and makes me feel like a taxi driver with all those people on board."

In November 1939 he was posted to Church Fenton in Yorkshire as a Pilot Officer in the newly formed all-Canadian 242nd Squadron. His instructor Flight Lieutenant Donald Miller described him as a natural born flyer. Within hours McKnight was flying the Hurricane as if he had been there forever.

March 23, 1940 the 242 Squadron was fully operational and was posted to RAF Martson May 13. The next day McKnight and Robert Grassick were sent to Vitry, France to reinforce the 615th Squadron and Willie was truly at war.

May 18 McKnight logged his first kill, a Messerschmitt Me-109, near Cambrai. May 26 he was posted back to the 242nd Squadron who were reassigned to Biggin Hill. They saw action over Dunkirk. May 28 McKnight claimed his second Me-109 and on the 29th he downed two more 109's and a Dornier Do-17. Two days later he claimed two Me-110s and damaged a 109 and the next day downed two Ju-87s. In only 17 days of fighting he had destroyed nine enemy planes and damaged two more. He was awarded the Distinguished Flying Cross for his efforts.

With losses mounting the 242nd Squadron took on new recruits and lost its all-Canadian standing. The rookies recognized McKnight's name for he was the talk of every RAF mess hall. The Squadron was posted back to France. There was total chaos with the chain of command rapidly collapsing in the face of the German onslaught. The Squadron

Leader F.M. 'Papa' Gobiel was ill and unable to effectively command the unit. Many looked to young 'Willie' for support and leadership.

Things got so bad that it was every man for himself. One Hurricane that was abandoned on the airfield revealed an engine sump full of holes. One of the men went into the bushes and came back with a handful of branches he whittled down and hammered into the holes. He filled the engine with oil and fuelled it up. With a prayer the pilot took off and somehow landed in Kent with the last of the oil leaking from the makeshift plugs.

The Squadron had taken heavy punishment in France with nine dying, three wounded and three taken prisoner. McKnight collapsed from exhaustion and ended up in hospital but he did not stay for long.

When Willie returned to the 242nd Squadron they had a new leader, a pilot that had no legs named Douglas Bader. He had a very powerful personality and would go on to become a legend for his fearless combat style. Both men took an instant liking to one another and they fought with uncommon bravery during the Battle of Britain where McKnight won a second Distinguished Flying Cross (DFC). With sixteen and a half victories to his credit McKnight was killed in action January 12, 1941. He was Canada's fifth leading ace of World War II.

Alan McLeod
Courage on the Wing

Alan Arnett McLeod was born in Stonewall, Manitoba on April 20, 1899. In his youth he was fascinated by the new era of flight. He tried to enlist when he was fifteen but he was considered too young to get into the action of World War I. Authorities insisted he wait until he was eighteen.

By June 4, 1917 he was taking flying instructions at Long Branch, near Toronto, Ontario and flew solo five days later. He was a qualified pilot by the end of July and in September he was sent overseas. Once more authorities would not allow him to go to the front lines because he was so young. He was posted to a home defence squadron. McLeod was frustrated and finally found a sympathetic general who arranged for young Alan McLeod to go to the front lines in France. He was only 18.

In December 1917 he was posted to a Corps Squadron equipped with the Armstrong-Whitworth bomber-reconnaissance machines. These aircraft were cumbersome, however McLeod was a natural pilot with exceptional nerve and an incurably sunny disposition. He flew the Armstrong-Whitworth as if it were a fast, manoeuvrable Scout. Time and again he flew into impossible situations and time and again he came out laughing.

During a dangerous German offensive in March of 1918, McLeod's squadron was in the air every minute that the weather was fit enough to fight against the rolling tide of the German army.

On March 26 McLeod and his observer, Lieutenant A. W. Hammond made three bombing raids. The next day they were ordered to take off at nine A.M. on a special raid. Despite their fatigue they took off at the appointed time under wretched weather conditions. The planes were soon separated in the overcast. After searching for some time they found another British aerodrome where they touched down. They had lunch while the crew repaired their tailskid that had been damaged when they landed. Once the repairs were made they took off again. They decided to undertake the mission single-handedly.

They flew to Bray, behind enemy lines and picked out a German battery as a target for their bombs. As they were about to attack they were engaged by a Fokker triplane. McLeod swung the heavy machine to give Hammond a good shot at the German aircraft and with three short bursts the Fokker went down in flames.

At that moment the clouds parted and seven more Fokker triplanes, members of Richthofen's squadron, attacked them. Handling his machine with customary coolness McLeod gave Hammond a shot at the first triplane that had flown into point blank range. Bullets broke the fuselage of the Fokker in two right behind the pilot's seat and the wreck fell in flames.

Now disaster struck. One of the other triplanes flew underneath their aircraft and raked it from stem to stern. McLeod and Hammond were wounded and the engine burst into flames. McLeod kept his cool and put the heavy plane into a sideslip to keep the fire from the cockpit. They commenced a slow glide towards the British lines from a height of 2,000 feet. They had not gone far when the entire floor of the aircraft fell out and the observer's stool with it. Hammond climbed out on the edge of the rear cockpit and perched there. McLeod stepped out of the cockpit and stood on the lower wing and steadied himself by hanging onto a strut with his left hand. He reached into the cockpit and flew the machine with his right.

One of the Fokkers closed in to watch the stricken aircraft crash. Though he had been hit several times and one of his arms was useless, Hammond managed to shoot it down. Another one came in to attack and Hammond's gun jammed. The Fokker fired several bursts and they were both hit again. As they approached the ground Hammond straddled the tail of the plane and McLeod pulled the machine out of its sideslip and flattened out for a crash landing. They landed in a shell hole and McLeod was thrown clear. The wreck began to burn fiercely and the bombs and ammunition began to explode. Hammond with six wounds was helpless. McLeod with five wounds leaped into action and proceeded to drag Hammond clear of the explosions. Bullets whined about them as they had landed in No-Man's Land in the middle of a battle between the Allied and German trenches. While dragging his companion clear of the wreck McLeod was hit once more and finally collapsed from loss of blood.

Troops, amazed by the heroic feat they had just observed, rushed from the trenches and rescued the two men. They could not be moved until darkness. At eight o'clock they were carried to the support trenches, their wounds were dressed and they were given morphine for their pain. They were carried three miles by stretcher-bearers to a dressing-station and then moved by ambulance to Amiens. McLeod was taken back to a hospital in England and Hammond stayed in France. Though both men were severely injured they both recovered from their wounds. McLeod was awarded the Victoria Cross and Hammond was awarded a bar to the Military Cross he had won some months earlier.

By September McLeod was well enough to go to a special ceremony at Buckingham Palace to receive his award from the King personally. Shortly after he sailed for Canada though his health was still poor. When he reached Stonewall he improved rapidly. Unfortunately when recovery seemed certain he was struck down by virulent influenza. It was sweeping the world and caused more deaths than the war. Alan McLeod died in the Winnipeg Hospital on November 6, 1918 just five days before the Armistice was signed.

Maskepetoon
Tongue of Peace

The name of a great Cree chief was almost lost to history but through the effort of Reverend John McDougall and shreds of verbal history collected by Grant MacEwan it was saved. Maskepetoon, (written Maskipitoon by MacEwan) meant 'One Whose Arm Was Broken.'

In his youth he displayed unusual courage. Without flinching, he faced the Sun Dance, a ceremony where thongs are skewered through the breast muscle and tied to a central post. Grinning at the pain he strained until the flesh broke free to release him. He was strong and brave. He could be savage and cruel when gathering scalps and stealing horses. He displayed all the qualities that won him the admiration of his people. He was born to be chief.

The brave warrior soon became chief of the Cree. Many things in their culture disturbed him. Although he had once blindly accepted tribal customs, he now felt they should stand the test of reason. He became convinced that killing and stealing each other's horses and women was wrong. It simply bred more violence and evil. He dared to ask why the tribes could not adopt a policy of good will. He sought his father's advice and together they withdrew to the solitude of the hills. There the truth was more likely to be seen where the spirits hover much more closely to man. Surrounded by nature, with calm days and clear nights - it was perfect for meditation. Nearing the end of their sojourn his father produced four black and four white feathers.

"Son," he said, "the destiny of our people is in your hands." As he stabbed the feathers into the ground he said, "These black feathers represented Dishonesty, Hatred, Cruelty and War. The white feathers represent Honesty, Friendliness, Sympathy and Peace." With a sweep of his hand he said, "Son, it is your choice."

Without hesitation Maskepetoon scooped up the black feathers and hurled them into the fire symbolically cleansing all past sins. He took the white feathers back to his wife and had her fashion a dazzling white headdress. From that day forth the way of Maskepetoon was the way of peace. His people could not understand the change but his record of bravery was already unquestionable. His devotion to the new and better way of life would be severely tested in the days ahead.

'The War Eagles of the Plains', the Blackfoot, offered the most severe tests. When the Blackfoot stole their horses and took their scalps he remained steadfast and made no reprisals. The supreme test happened when a raiding party murdered his father. Still he did not retaliate.

Sometime later the young brave that murdered his father was brought before him. Maskepetoon said to the young brave, "You killed my father; you killed a good man. Once I would have sought your life as revenge; but I have found a better way. I will spare your life but I will ask you to think of the foolishness of killing each other. Will you help foster new feeling between our two tribes? Will you return to your Blackfoot tribe and tell them that we can live in happiness without killing each other?"

"Never have I heard such a thing," said the brave. "My people will ask, 'who is this young chief, so brave and yet so good?' He stands alone."

The Apostle of Peace ventured south to invite a discussion with the 'War Eagles.' A Blackfoot war party intercepted Maskepetoon and his followers. They were hopelessly outnumbered and his followers deserted him. The bloodthirsty horde came in for the kill but found only the brave Cree chief unarmed and alone. One of the party recognized the man they had heard about. His courage and new teaching caused a curiosity. The lone peace missionary invited them to send an envoy to discuss peace. A conference attended by Reverend John McDougall was successful as the leaders smoked the Pipe of Peace. The leader of the Blackfoot war party that encountered Maskepetoon alone declared him the 'Bravest Chief of All.'

This Cree chief in life as in death, had quite a lot in common with the Asiatic Indian, Mohandas Ghandi. His adherence to the principle of non-violence and his death at the hands of a Blackfoot assassin named Swan in April 1869, left a legacy to which Canadians should point to with pride. In a country now recognized for our world peace efforts let us not forget Maskepetoon, the first native Canadian peace missionary and martyr.

Métis

In 1869 the Hudson's Bay Company sold Rupert's Land to the British government for £300,000. Though this territory consisted of millions of hectares of land, not many people lived there. There were some wandering native tribes in the area and a few Hudson's Bay Company men at lonely, scattered trading posts. About 12,000 settlers lived in the Red River colony near Fort Garry. Most of the people living there were known as Métis. Métis were mixed-blood people - neither white nor Indian. When white men came to North America they would often marry a native woman. Occasionally a native married a white woman. The children of these marriages were known as Métis. They developed a whole new way of living. It was a mixture of the white ways and native.

In the early days the Métis were the backbone of the fur trade. They were the middlemen between the tribes and the Europeans. From their mothers they learned the native language and from their fathers they learned French or English. They could act as translators for both sides in the fur trade. The Métis were in an excellent position for they bought furs from the various tribes who could not speak English or French. They could then sell these furs to agents of the Hudson's Bay Company, most of whom could not understand the different native languages.

The Métis took customs of both worlds. In dress they used animal hides as the natives did, but made them in the style of the white man's clothes. They loved to dance. They added the fast footwork of the native dances and combined it with 'reels' and 'square dances' and the result was the Red River Jig.

Many Métis earned their living hauling goods in carts for the trading companies. They developed the Red River cart, which was a sturdy, two-wheeled vehicle. It was made entirely of wood and held together by wooden pegs and strips of rawhide. The height of the wheels, about two metres, prevented tipping. Old-timers recall the carts' shrieking noise eminating from the ungreased wooden axles. It sounded like a 'thousand fingernails being drawn across a chalkboard.'

The natives who lived on the vast western plains passed on to the Métis their skill as horsemen. This meant the Métis were excellent buffalo hunters and spent part of each year hunting. The rest of their time was spent farming small plots of land like their white ancestors. They made pemmican, consisting mainly of buffalo meat, that they sold to the fur traders who carried it on their long trips, for it was nourishing, light and easy to carry.

Unfortunately the government dealt unjustly with this group of people. Unlike the full-blooded natives who were given reservations, the Métis were swept aside and as a result the Riel Rebellion of 1885 took place. Louis Riel, a Métis, led a large contingent of his people and joined forces with the likes of Poundmaker but the rebellion was soon quelled thanks to the delivery of troops by the railway line. Riel was hung and became the stuff of folklore and debate. Many now see him as a hero. His people still walk among us unsung and unheralded.

Mount Logan
'Canada's Highest Mountain'

Following Pierre Trudeau's death in 2000, Prime Minister Jean Crétien suggested that the name of Canada's highest mountain be changed from Mount Logan to Mount Trudeau. It was only fifteen years ago that I discovered the name of Canada's highest mountain. This caused debate and controversy and in the end the mountain kept its original name.

I have surveyed hundreds of Canadians about our highest mountain and have found that less than 1% of us know our highest peak. Like many Canadians I thought it was Mount Robson but alas this peak is only the highest in the Rocky Mountain Range. It is not even the highest in British Columbia. It is Mount Fairweather in the Coastal Range close to the Alaska Panhandle at 4,664 metres high while Mount Robson is only 3,954 metres high.

Perhaps the best thing to come out of this episode by our Prime Minister has been that now perhaps more of us now know the name of our highest mountain. Mount Logan is in the Yukon and soars 5,595 metres above sea level. It was named after William E. Logan. In 1842 he became the first director of the Geological Survey of Canada. Mr. Logan was well known in his day. He made the first geological maps of Canada when there were few maps of Canada at all. He traveled across Canada in 1863 and produced an atlas in 1865. He was a man of great integrity and honesty.

Emily Ferguson Murphy
Janey Canuck

Emily Murphy was born in Cookstown, Ontario on March 14, 1868. This gifted lady was not content to be a parson's wife, mother and housekeeper; all roles she fulfilled admirably. She was one of the famous five Canadian super-women instrumental in obtaining Women's Rights in 1929. Her contemporary suffragettes - Nellie McClung, Henrietta Edwards, Louis McKinney and Irene Parlby felt that Mrs. Murphy deserved the lion's share of the credit for setting the precedent for women to sit in the Canadian Senate.

When ill health forced her husband to leave the ministry, she took up writing. Janey Canuck, her pen name, provided an income to support her family. They moved from her hometown to Manitoba, stayed briefly and finally settled in Edmonton. She was a very prolific writer, producing *Janey Canuck Abroad, Janey Canuck in the West, Open Trail, Seeds of the Pine, The Black Candle, Our Little Canadian Cousins of the North West* and *Bishop Bompas*.

Shortly after arriving in Edmonton in 1907 Emily and her daughters were soon well known citizens. Emily supported her husbands' speculation in lumber, real estate and coal mining. Articles she sold to national newspapers and magazines generated additional income.

In 1916 she was appointed Magistrate of the Juvenile Court in Edmonton, a first in all of the British Empire and an action applauded by suffragettes everywhere. As a magistrate, her approach toward 'wayward' women was motherly and many young women were given unsolicited advice on future planning and morals, often at her family's dinner table.

In her dual capacity as a magistrate and president of the Federation of the Woman's Institute, she petitioned Prime Minister William Lyon Mackenzie King to appoint a woman to the Canadian Senate. According to the British North America Act only 'persons' could be appointed to such a position. After a week of deliberation it was decided in the Canadian parliament that women were not persons and therefore could not become part of the Senate. Undaunted, Emily took their request to the Privy Council of England where Lord Stankey, after a day's deliberation, on October 28, 1929 enacted the necessary legislation to grant women the right to be 'persons.' She asked Lord Stankey to give that to her in writing. Emily returned to Canada jubilant and said to Mackenzie King, "Put this in your pipe and smoke it" as she stuffed the note into his hand. For their accomplishment, the Senate recognized

Alberta's Famous Five with a plaque in the Senate lobby. For some obscure reason none of them was ever appointed to the Senate.

Mrs. Murphy was known as a cheerful positive individual who chose her endeavours wisely and unselfishly. She did not go unheralded and King George V decorated her with the Lady of Grace of the Order of St. John of Jerusalem. Another of her causes was a campaign to prevent the importing of narcotics into Canada and she used the National Council of Women as a platform to outline methods of prevention. Her book, *The Black Candle*, published in 1922, details the evils of drugs. In 1924 she was appointed as the Canadian government's representative to the League of Nations Conference on narcotics in Geneva.

Emily Ferguson can well be described as an outstanding Canadian achiever. The country mourned her sudden death on October 27, 1933 at the age of 65. The City of Edmonton named a popular park in her honour and there is a plaque from the government of Canada that's inscribed:

'Emily Ferguson Murphy, 'Janey Canuck', a crusader for social reform and equal status for women, she devoted herself to these causes with unremitting energy...'

Northern Dancer
The Little Horse that Could

Nearctic set a record over six furlongs at Woodbine in 1958 and won the Michigan Mile in Detroit breaking the course record and winning $40,000. Edward Plunket Taylor or 'EP' as he liked to be called, saw a young filly named Natalma and he used $30,000 of his purse to purchase her. She had started seven races and won three of them but earned only $16,000. As a three year old in 1960 she broke a bone in her knee at Kentucky Oaks bringing her racing days to an end. Nearctic and Natalma were bred and in May 1961, Northern Dancer was born.

EP had put Dancer up on the blocks with some of his other horses but his small stature and $25,000 price tag, saw him passed over in the yearling sale. Under the eye of trainer Horatio Luro he developed into a game little horse with a tremendous desire to win. Cracked heels delayed his racing days but in August 1963 he won his first race at Fort Erie by seven lengths with Ron Turcotte aboard. Soon he had five wins in seven starts. In New York Dancer caught everybody's eye when he defeated Burpers, the winner of the $140,000 Coronation Futurity by eight lengths. It was on to the Rumsen Stake but Señor Luro had noticed a quarter-crack on the inside left fore foot but he let him race anyway. Dancer won the mile and one-eighth in an amazing time of 1:47.8.

The colt's hoof had to be repaired and Luro heard of a blacksmith named Bill Bane in California who had invented the 'Bane patch.' It cost $1,000 to bring Bane to New York and it took him a day to repair Dancer's hoof but it was probably the best $1,000 EP ever spent.

In 1964 the three-year-old Northern Dancer won the $100,000 Flamingo Stakes. He then raced in the Florida Derby and was ridden by Willie Shoemaker who was unimpressed with the little colt. Bill Hartack was brought in to ride Dancer in the Blue Grass Stakes and won convincingly.

At the Kentucky Derby in May, Dancer, with Shoemaker aboard, beat Hill Rise in a neck-to-neck thriller, winning an all-time record of two minutes flat. He won the Belmont Stakes and was poised to become the first Canadian horse to win the Triple Crown. The mile and one-half Preakness was too much for him and he finished third behind Quadrangle and Roman Brother.

EP brought Dancer back to Canada to compete in the Queens Plate at Woodbine where he swept to a seven-length victory. It was his last race. He was retired to stud and had won a total of $580,000.

In 1970 Northern Dancer was the leading sire in the world. He sired: Northfield, True North, One for All, Minsky, Laurie's Dancer and the magnificent Nijimsky who sold for $84,000. Nijimsky went on to win the Epsom Derby, the Irish Derby, King George VI and Queen Elizabeth Stakes.

Dancer was syndicated for $2.4 million. There are four Canadian horsemen in the syndicate insuring future progeny will be Canadian and carry our colours on race courses around the world.

Sir William Osler
Teacher of Doctors

On July 12, 1849 William Osler was born the eighth child in a family of nine just north of Toronto at Bond Head. When William was nine years old his father was transferred to the town of Dundas, Ontario to serve as the reverend. William attended the grammar school for the next few years then transferred to a boarding school in Barrie. He was a good student but was chiefly noted for his boyish pranks.

It was said that a group of students in the boarding school took a dislike to the housekeeper. The students decided to get their revenge for what they regarded as a series of offences on her part. When they got their chance they locked her in her room, which was over one of the classrooms. They proceeded to give her a generous dose of smoke. A mixture of mustard, molasses and pepper was put in the stove in the classroom and the fumes let to rise into her room through the stovepipe hole. The angry matron, coughing and gasping stuffed the hole but the boys poked the rags out with sticks. Her shouts eventually reached the headmaster who came to her rescue. The boys got the usual caning. Apparently the ringleader was William Osler, then about sixteen years old.

A profound change came over the young Osler when he attended Trinity College School in Weston. Two men, Reverend W.A. Johnson, the headmaster, and Dr. James Bovell who taught at the Medical College had a tremendous influence upon William. Both men were interested in natural history and spent weekends on exploration trips through the Humber River Valley to gather specimens of plant and animal life. They brought these home to study under the microscope. Often they took some students with them and when it was Osler's turn he showed such keen interest and skill with the microscope he became a regular member of the party.

In 1867 he entered Trinity College in Toronto to become a minister like his father but after a year he transferred into the medical course. He studied with new interest and enthusiasm. Bovell continued to have a great influence upon William while he attended medical school. However in 1870 he transferred to McGill University in Montreal where there were better opportunities. When he graduated he was awarded a special prize for an essay, which was submitted with fifty-three microscope illustrations. He went on to London, Berlin and Vienna to continue his studies. In 1874 he returned to Dundas to relieve the local doctor. Later that year he accepted the position of professor at the

Institute of Medicine at McGill University. From that point on his chief interest was to teach students to become doctors. He was a very popular teacher. He took students with him to the hospital and taught them the symptoms and treatment of diseases at the bedside of patients. This was a radically new idea. Students found this a welcome change from merely listening to lectures.

After ten years at McGill he accepted an invitation to become Professor of Clinical Medicine at the University of Pennsylvania. When John Hopkins died and left seven million dollars to establish a university and medical school, they looked for the most capable person to head the Department of Medicine. William Osler, only thirty-nine, was appointed to the position. He succeeded in building up one of the finest centres of medical teaching in the world. He used to say, "Remember the practise of medicine is not a trade or an art or a business. It is a calling into which you must carry both head and heart." He practised the principles he taught. He did not get married until he was forty-two. He married the widow of Dr. Samuel Gross in 1891 and wrote *The Principle and Practise of Medicine* in 1892. In 1895 a son was born to the Oslers and they named him Revere in honour of his mother's maiden name, which was Grace Revere, a descendant of the American patriot Paul.

William made important contributions to the knowledge of typhoid fever, pneumonia and malaria. In 1905 Edward VII asked him to become the Regis (Royal) Professor of Medicine at Oxford University and Osler accepted. In 1911 he was knighted and during World War I he helped organize the medical profession. August 29, 1917 Revere was killed in battle. Sad of heart William went on with his work as usual. He saw the war's end, was stricken with pneumonia and died December 29, 1919.

Mona Parsons
Canadian/Dutch Resistance Fighter

On February 14, 1901 Mona Louise Parsons was born in Middleton, Nova Scotia. Her father, Norval, owned Elliott Home Furnishings on Commercial Street. She was the youngest child and had two brothers, Ross and Quinn. The family was prosperous, but on January 26, 1911, downtown Middleton burned to the ground along with their store. Fortunately Norval had insurance and he moved the family to Wolfville and became a stockbroker. All the men in the family went off to the Great War. All would survive. Mona, a tall, lithe, elegant young lady had a bewitchingly sultry voice and decided to study voice and drama.

In the 20's she decided to make her move to New York to take a chance on a stage career. She got a mediocre job as a chorus girl in Ziegfield Follies. They were splashy, naughty, expensive and popular. The *Volstead Act* banned alcohol but that didn't stop the flow of booze as speakeasies flourished. She had a look that stopped men in their tracks. She liked the glamour, attention, lively dates and fantastic parties but she wanted more.

Mona returned home in 1930, because her mother Mary had suffered a stroke, unfortunately she suffered a second stroke and died. At the dawn of the Great Depression she decided she needed to do something that was more reliable, so she trained to be a nurse in a Jersey City medical centre. When she was done she went to Manhattan and a clinic on Park Avenue. She was among medical professionals with an upscale clientele.

Her brother Ross informed her about a wealthy Dutchman named Willem Leonhardt who was travelling to North America to develop outlets for his family's plumbing business. He was coming to New York and needed someone to show him around. At first Mona did not respond to the millionaire's charm but in the end the relationship blossomed and then developed rapidly.

When Willem returned with an 'American film star' in tow his family were less than excited. Mona had to start from scratch first learning the Dutch language, not the easiest of Germanic languages to learn.

Soon the initially suspicious Leonhardt family was won over by her charm as was Willem's best friend Piet Houtapell and his wife Pam. Willem and Mona married in 1937 and took a six-month honeymoon. They soon became part of the Amsterdam upper crust. They had fast cars, yachts and danced in glamorous ballrooms. They found some land an hour from downtown and built a house they called *Ingleside*. Willem had a pale oak August Förster grand piano built just for her. She would play the favourite tunes of her guests and preside over the gatherings like a queen.

The second Great War was moving in on them and in May 1940 the German *blitzkrieg* devoured Holland in only five days. For the first few months life carried on as usual. The Battle of Britain was in full swing as the teenage pilots in Spitfires and Hurricanes put up a brilliant defence, but late in 1941, the change was all too evident. Rigid rationing was introduced and there was a nine o'clock curfew. A resistance movement was organized, arrests were frequent as were executions and disappearances.

As Britain retaliated against Germany, wounded bomber crews would run out of luck and were forced to bail out over land rather than into the frigid North Sea. Many Dutch citizens took them in and the Leonhardt house became a refuge for these pilots. Farmers would hide aircrews in dikes or windmills before they were brought to the Leonhardt house. The airmen were then transported to Leiden along the coast and ferried by fishing boat to waiting British submarines.

It was a great adventure for the Leonhardt's as they faced the risk of death pulling off the impossible under the noses of the hated enemy. They were happy to actually be doing something. Unfortunately one of the conspirators in Leiden was in fact a Nazi informant.

Their safe house had only been used four times when two allied airmen, Richard Pape and William Moir stayed for an unprecedented six days. They were unable to move them because of the increasingly tight net of Nazi intelligence. When they finally moved the fugitive airmen to Leiden the Nazis made their move. One of the resistance fighters, Dirk Brouwer, was arrested and shot. Willem and Mona knew that if they fled it would be evidence of their guilt and if they stayed they would be sitting ducks.

They decided Mona would stay at *Ingleside* while Willem, a well-known fishing enthusiast, was on a fishing trip. Mona if questioned, would plead ignorance as to his expected return.

Soon two Gestapo agents appeared at her door. She invited them in, offered them drinks, but they were not fooled. She was soon in Weteringschane Prison in Amsterdam awaiting trail. They held her as bait to catch Willem. It took three months but they caught him on December 21, 1941.

The next day she was taken before a military court. It was held at the Carleton Hotel in the ballroom where she had often danced the night away. Though they did not convict women, she was, and when the judge said the phrases *Todestraffe* and *Exxekutionskommando* she knew enough German to know it meant 'death sentence' and 'firing squad.' She blanched by remained cool and erect before giving a courteous bow to the court.

She walked with dignity between her escorts. The judge must have been a man of character for he crossed the courtroom and stopped the escorts. He complimented her and recommended that she appeal. He said he would forward the appeal to the highest-ranking officer in Holland with a recommendation for clemency.

She was sent to Krefeld in the German Rhineland, the first of many prisons and was put to knitting socks for soldiers. In each sock she concealed a knot that would produce a painful blister on each sole. They found her out and she was moved to Vechta in northern Germany and put in solitary confinement. Soon she was put to work again, this time cleaning the kitchen. Here she met twenty-two year old Baroness Wendelien van Boetzelaer who was an incorrigible escape artist. Mona smuggled potatoes to the young woman and soon they became allies. They were housed in the top floors where the solitary cells were not heated. The two women pleaded for some warm clothes to help them survive the winter of '44. Fortunately the governess took sufficient pity and responded to their plea.

An airfield and rail yards flanked the prison and in the early months of 1945 Vechta was bombed. The men's prison was blown to fragments. The two friends fortunately were down on the ground floor that day. The head of the prison ordered the inmates out into the yard in case the building was targeted. The German women threw themselves on the ground but Mona and Wendelien took each other's hand and just walked out while the bombs distracted the guards.

It was 160 kilometres to the Dutch border. They made eighteen kilometres the first day with nothing to eat and drank water out of the ditches. They slept in a barn that night and bundled themselves in straw to keep warm. The next day they boldly walked up to the farmhouse. Wendelien did all the talking. Mona feigned that she was mentally disabled. She played the role so well the farmer felt sorry for her. Mona and Wendelein did chores in exchange for food and they were soon able to move on. As they got closer to the Dutch border they found people they felt they could trust. At a small border town they confided in the mayor. He gave them identification papers and they were billeted separately. They didn't see each other again until after the war.

The first troops across the border in that sector were Poles. Right behind them came the Canadians. The soldiers were careful about the German civilians trying to cross the border. Some were used as decoys and were armed with booby-trap bombs or weapons they could use to kill senior officers if they got close enough. Mona was picked up walking out of Germany and despite her fluent English and exhausted appearance they were not taking any chances.

After being questioned many times she was finally interrogated by a soldier who followed this line of inquiry:

"Where are you from?"

"I'm a Canadian," said Mona.

"If you are a Canadian where are your from?"

"My name is Mona Parsons and I come from a tiny little village in Nova Scotia called Wolfville."

The man almost dropped the box he was holding as he exclaimed, "Dear God! My name is Clarence Leonard, I'm from Halifax, and you've just encountered the North Nova Scotia Highlanders!"

The unit surgeon was Kelly MacLean and Mona had acted on the Acadia stage with him. There were other friends from those days: Captains Vincent White and Ralph Shaw as well as a childhood chum, Major General Harry Foster. Mona told her amazing story and got a ride home to *Ingleside*. She had a good long rest among friends but there was no sign of Willem.

He was alive but after three years of brutal prison conditions, starvation and an inherited kidney disease, he was not well. When his concentration camp was liberated he was put in hospital for ten weeks during which time he was able to get word to Mona. When he returned home they traveled between bouts of hospitalization and immobility. Mona had always suffered from lung problems and now she had bronchitis that became increasingly more serious. Willem sent her to the Birchel Benner Clinic in Switzerland for rest in 1953. He became permanently bedridden and Mona returned to find Piet's wife Pam had taken over as his caregiver. When Willem died in 1956 she discovered he had left one-quarter of his estate to Pam, they had been carrying on a secret affair for years. Willem's son from his first marriage, not even his natural son, sued for the rest. When the battle was done, little was left of the estate and Mona took her beloved August Förster piano back to Canada.

She ran into Major General Harry Foster, who had retired and they chatted about their extraordinary encounter and soon the affection grew and in 1959 they were married. He was diagnosed with cancer and died five years later. Mona went back to Wolfville and became an amiable eccentric. She died in 1976.

Discovered in her personal effects were two certificates of commendation for her allied war effort. One signed by British Air Chief Marshall Lord Arthur Tedder. The second bears the signature of the Supreme Commander of the Allied forces in Europe, Dwight D. Eisenhower. Her picture is still proudly displayed on the wall of Branch 74 of the Royal Canadian Legion in Wolfville. They say, "She was a brave and beautiful lady."

Lester B. Pearson
Winner of the Nobel Peace Prize

Lester Bowles Pearson was born in Newtonbrook, Ontario on April 23, 1897. The son of a clergyman, he played baseball and hockey with great skill. He began his studies at the University of Toronto but was quick to enlist when the Great War erupted. He served with a hospital unit in the Balkans then transferred to the Royal Flying Corps. After the war ended he completed his degree in Toronto and then went on to Oxford. He says his most notable success in Europe was playing hockey where he was called 'Herr Zigzag.' When he returned he had a new nickname, 'Mike', which stuck with him for the rest of his life. August 22, 1925 he married Maryon Moody.

After teaching history at the University of Toronto he wrote the examinations for External Affairs and joined the department in 1928. In 1935 he was sent to London as Canada's High Commissioner. He had a front-row seat to the unfolding war. He was profoundly affected by it and thereafter would attach great importance to collective defence in the face of dictatorships and aggression.

In 1942 he was assigned to Washington. When the war ended Pearson was Canada's ambassador who attended the founding conference of the United Nations (U.N.) in San Francisco in 1945. Shortly there after, he became the Ambassador to the United States. Working with Prime Minister Louis St. Laurent he helped Canada emerge as the leader of the middle powers and helped create the North Atlantic Treaty Organization in 1949.

He was a member of the Canadian delegation to the U.N. from 1948-57. He was also the president of the 7th U.N. General Assembly in 1952-53.

Egyptian President Gamal Nasser imported arms from the Soviet Block and helped arm Arab terrorists, or *fedayeen*. They attacked Israel violating the armistice agreement. However it was Israel that was condemned for their counter attack. Nasser blockaded the Straits of Tiran and nationalized the Suez Canal. In the ensuing war that started October 29, 1956 the Israeli forces defeated the Egyptians in less than 100 hours. Pressure from the United States caused Prime Minister David Ben-Gurion of Israel to withdraw his troops.

Mike solved the crisis by getting all sides to agree to the creation of a neutral U.N. force to maintain the peace in the region. Peacekeepers sat between the two factions on the blistering Sinai Desert to protect the peace. For his efforts Pearson was awarded the Nobel Peace Prize on February 15, 1957.

He won the leadership of the Liberal Party in 1958. The party lost the election so Pearson spent five years as leader of the opposition. His party was victorious in the next election though they won only 129 seats, four short of a majority. He became Prime Minister April 22, 1963. With a minority government it was amazing what his cabinet achieved. He instituted national Medicare, the Canada Pension Plan, veterans' allowances, extended family allowances and provided interest free loans to young Canadians to go to university.

He also introduced the national labour code with a minimum age of 16, an 8-hour workday, a 40-hour workweek, two weeks vacation and minimum wage of $1.25 per hour. In 1965 he signed the Canada-United States Automotive Agreement or Auto Pact. It created thousands of jobs and unemployment fell to an all time low.

He overhauled the immigration policy making it the first race-free policy and opened Canada's doors to the world. He set up a Royal Commission on Bilingualism and Biculturalism.

One of his more contentious moves was to replace Canada's flag with the new red and white Maple Leaf flag making it Canada's first official flag in its nearly 100-year history. It was unveiled February 15, 1965.

At Montreal's Expo '67 French President Charles de Gaulle made his infamous "Vive le Québec libre," speech.

Pearson responded by insisting, "Canadians do not need to be liberated." He was livid that de Gaulle would insult a country that had done so much to liberate his country during World War II.

Mike passed the torch on to Pierre Elliott Trudeau and retired from politics on April 19, 1968. He taught and headed a major study arguing the case for greater aid to developing countries. The secretary of the committee said Pearson drew out the best in them. That is a comment that could aptly describe Pearson's entire career.

Pearson died on December 27, 1972 following a battle with cancer.

In a 2003 survey of leading historians, political scientists, economists, government officials and other leading figures, he was voted Canada's best Prime Minister by a landslide. Furthermore in a Canada wide pole in 2004 he was voted the 6th Greatest Canadian.

Oscar Peterson
Jazz Giant on the Keyboard

Daniel Peterson was a sailor in the merchant marine who was born in St. Croix in the Virgin Islands. When he decided to settle in Canada he went to Montreal where he met Kathleen Olivia John who was a domestic worker. Daniel landed a job with the Canadian Pacific Railway (CPR) as a sleeping-car porter. It was a demanding and often demeaning job. Ninety percent of the black people in the city worked for the railway. In 1920 Montreal was a city that lacked public health or public sanitation services and blacks were a minority. Despite this they married and had children in the city that was considered to be one of the most dangerous in the civilized world for children.

Oscar Emmanuel Peterson was born on August 15, 1925. His father loved music and encouraged all his children, Daisy, Charles, Fred and May to play not one but two instruments.

Oscar's first music teacher was Daisy. She found Oscar had perfect pitch when one day he called out the names of the notes she had just played from across the room. She figured out Oscar wasn't reading the music and was playing by ear. She refused to play a piece before Oscar played it first. This forced him to learn to read music. When their dad traveled for his job they were assigned music he expected them to master while he was away. He could be gone for a week or even two. They had to sign a book indicating that they knew the piece. His brothers and sisters feared for their brother knowing that he hadn't even practised once. If they didn't know the piece when dad returned they were disciplined. Oscar would listen to the others play and on the last day he might go to the piano and practice it once. Poor Daisy received the most reprimands but Oscar never had to worry.

Montreal was the budding jazz capital of Canada. Oscar showed early signs of improvisation, one of the most important features of jazz music. His father wasn't pleased with the idea for he felt it was for uneducated, ignorant people. He wanted his children to play classical music. Olive, Oscar's mother, was religious and soft-spoken. In her own way she had a great influence in all her children's lives, especially Oscar's.

When Oscar was only seven he became ill with tuberculosis (TB). He was placed in the Children's Memorial Hospital for it was easily spread and rest was the best cure. After thirteen months Oscar was able to return home. His brother Fred wasn't so lucky, he died from the disease in 1934, he was only fifteen.

His first formal teacher was Lou Hooper, who had been part of the Montreal jazz scene in the 1920's. He could see great potential in Oscar but it was his next teacher, Paul Alexander de Markey, who had a greater influence. Paul was considered one of the finest classical pianists in Canada at the time. By studying his teacher, Oscar was soon exhibiting flashy, lightning-quick runs up and down the keyboard.

When he was fourteen, his sister Daisy pushed him into entering a nationwide amateur radio contest sponsored by the Canadian Broadcasting Corporation (CBC). There was no television back then but many listened to the radio. Oscar won the semi-finals then won the finals in Toronto. He hit the public spotlight and has been there ever since.

He was heard regularly on the radio right across Canada. There was still much hard work ahead and many obstacles to overcome for he was black and living in a world full of prejudice.

Montreal High School had an excellent academic program as well as outstanding school bands. Maynard Ferguson played trumpet, brother Percy the sax, Jiro 'Butch' Watanbe trombone and Hal Gaylor played the bass. Along with Oscar they would all have successful jazz careers. Thanks to Olive's intervention, Daniel's objections to the school jazz band were overruled and Oscar was allowed to join.

Oscar listened to early piano masters, James P. Johnson, Thomas 'Fats' Waller, Ferdinand 'Jelly Roll' Morton and Teddy Wilson. He played boogie-woogie through his teens and into his twenties and you can hear it on his first records. He also listened to the masters of stride piano that required more nimble finger and handwork.

When his father thought Oscar was getting too big for his britches he brought home Art Tatum's *Tiger Rag*. He says he gave up the piano for two months and at first did not believe it was only one piano and not two. He was awestruck and some of his arrogance was lost.

Tatum was such a legend that Fat Waller introduced him with the accolade, "Ladies and gentlemen. I play the piano but god is in the house tonight."

Daniel bought the family a radio after saving for months. Late at night Oscar would sneak down stairs and turn it on with the volume set so low he had to press his ear against the speaker to hear it. He was treated to live broadcasts of the great swing bands of the era like Count Basie, Jimmie Lunceford, Chuck Webb and Duke Ellington.

In the 40's Oscar began hanging out on the corner on Mountain Street and St. Antoine where the black jazz clubs were and was pleased when they asked him to 'sit in.' He knew his parents prized education but he decided he wanted to pursue a career in music. His father surprised him when he said, "I can't let you leave high school to be a jazz piano player. If you want to be the best, I'll let you go. But you have to be the best, there is no second best."

Perhaps this is why Oscar was so competitive and never stood by and let another player challenge him without answering the call.

Harold 'Steep' Wade took the 'kid' under his wing and introduced him into the fire of live jazz performances in the smoky St. Antoine Club. Word of the teenage sensation spread and the Johnny Holmes Orchestra, the best-known big band in Montreal, invited him to audition. He passed and Holmes became a friend, adviser and teacher. He worked on getting him to support the band and not dominate it.

Oscar practiced endlessly and practiced playing two different rhythms; melodies and beats with each hand making them work independently. He could achieve some dramatic effects because of his drive and dedication.

He'd been noticing a gal named Lillie Fraser whose father was also a porter for the CPR. August 15, 1943 they got engaged and the next year they got married.

These might have been trouble free years except for one thing, Oscar was black and the rest of the band was white. Not that the other band members minded, in fact they would come to really appreciate his talent but some of their venues did not. In 1945 the orchestra was booked in the Ritz-Carlton Hotel and the manager called Holmes and said he didn't want that 'nigger' in his hotel.

Holmes stuck by Oscar and said he would cancel the engagement and inform the newspapers about the hotel's racist policy. The manager backed down and Oscar played.

One CBC announcer Rusty Davis referred to him as a 'coloured boy', which offended him greatly for he felt it showed a lack of respect and was a form of racism. The jazz musicians like Count Basie, Mezz Mezzrow and Dizziy Gillepie said things like, "Never heard the ivories played that way by a youngster before."

One day he called Hugh Joseph of RCA Victor in Canada on his mother's advice and asked for a record contract. He got it and the first tune he recorded was *'I Got Rhythm'* by George Gershwin. It was on a 78 revolutions per minute (rpm) record. In 1945 he recorded eight songs mainly in the boogie-woogie style.

Holmes began letting Oscar play with the bass player and drummer for the last fifteen minutes of every dance. The rest of the band sat it out and he would be playing say *'Body and Soul'* and someone would call out another tune like *'In the Mood'* and he would incorporate that right away into *'Body and Soul.'* He was amazing. The band idolized him and was his greatest audience.

They received an offer to play nightly at the Alberta Lounge. It was one of the best gigs in town and on Wednesdays the radio station CJAD broadcast live for fifteen minutes. The band played there for two years. Right across the street was the Windsor Train Station, which was owned by the CPR. Oscar could look out the window and was reminded what might have awaited him if he had not become a musician.

Norman Granz came to love jazz and wanted to be part of the scene. In 1944 he put on a Sunday concert called Jazz at the Philharmonic Auditorium (JAPT) in Los Angeles. It was a great success and he scheduled monthly JAPT concerts. He took some of the musician both black and white and toured the West Coast. While in Victoria, B.C. he heard Oscar Peterson on the jukebox for the first time.

Meanwhile Oscar and Lil became parents in 1948 when Lynne was born. The next year Sharon was born.

The first tour did not earn Granz much money but he had recorded the live performances. He felt they offered an immediacy that a studio record could not. Ascher Records released it as Volume One *Jazz at the Philharmonic.* Jazz fans rushed out to buy the record and it became very popular. Granz would become one of the most successful record producers in the history of jazz.

Taking a taxi in Montreal to the airport Granz heard some jazz on the radio and asked the driver what station it was so he could find out who was playing the hot piano. The driver told him they were listening to a live broadcast from the Alberta Lounge and that was Oscar Peterson. Granz redirected the driver to the lounge and next thing you know Oscar is debuting in Carnegie Hall in New York City in one of his JAPT concerts. He did a duo with bassist Ray Brown. Oscar got rave reviews and Michael Levin of *Down Beat* magazine said, "Oscar Peterson stopped .... the Jazz at the Phil concert dead cold in its tracks." He dropped upon the American scene like a meteor hitting the planet.

Granz paid his musicians better than most and took care of his troupe. Oscar was soon one of the most recognized and respected jazz pianists anywhere. There were some testy situations with the Jim Crow laws that were entrenched in the southern States. Even though there was discrimination in Canada, Oscar was not prepared for what he faced in the South. It went way beyond disrespect. In some places if you stood up for your rights you risked your life.

On the other hand he was now in the big leagues. He met and played with Ella Fitzgerald, Roy Eldridge, Lester Young, Gene Krupa,

Buddy Rich, Ben Webster and too many others to mention. They drew sell-out crowds and brought down the house nightly with their performances. Granz pushed for change and insisted promoters sign a contract that allowed both black and white patrons to attend the concerts. On many occasions he chartered a plane to get his musicians out of towns that seemed especially dangerous. He was called the scum of the earth and "a nigger lover." He stood by his musicians and was respected for his determined stand in the face of hateful bigotry.

There has been a long tradition of 'cutting contests' where musicians jam for hours trying to outplay each other. Oscar was always competitive and in fine form, for his dad expected him to be 'the best.' Oscar did not disappoint.

Oscar hit it off personally and musically with Ray Brown. They were inseparable and challenged each other to greater heights.

While in Hamilton, a barber refused to give Oscar a haircut. The story made the *Spectator*, May 5, 1951 and caused quite a controversy. Even the mayor of Hamilton, Lloyd D. Jackson waded into the fray and soon the city had a discrimination policy. It raised the question of prejudice in other parts of Canada as well.

In 1954 the Oscar Peterson Trio debuted with Herb Ellis on guitar and Ray Brown playing bass. They had a special closeness and became lifelong friends. They could communicate through their instruments. Where ever they went Oscar loved a practical joke or prank. He would detune guitars during breaks or they threw steel balls on his ivory strings. Still there were too many long waits at airports, lonely hotels, meals on the run and they rarely got enough sleep.

The trio still played for JAPT and toured the world. In 1954 they played 50 concerts in 25 European cities, 24 concerts in Japan and 75 in the United States and Canada. He eventually met Art Tatum and was awed to make his acquaintance. In 1956 both Tatum and his dad died. Oscar lost two of his best friends.

On August 8, 1958 the trio recorded live at the Stratford Festival and the album became a classic. Oscar uprooted his family and moved to Scarborough, a suburb of Toronto.

In 1960 Oscar and some friends opened the Advanced School for Music (ASCM) in downtown Toronto. It was a school ahead of its time. The students received formal lessons and featured were jam sessions with their teachers. He still traveled and in 1962 cut *Night Train* one of his biggest-selling albums. Oscar wrote *Hymn to Freedom*, which was featured on this album. It became a well know song within the civil rights movement. ASCM closed in 1964 the same year Oscars' marriage fell apart.

He met Sandra King and they were soon married.

Herb and Ray needed a rest and the trio broke up. Oscar decided to go it alone and played his first solo concert at Carnegie Hall in 1972. That same year he was pleased and honoured with the Order of Canada. He was successful but loved to play in a group so he formed a new trio with guitarist Joe Pass and bassist Neils-Henning Ørsted Pederson.

When his marriage to Sandra ended in 1976 he met and married a young Swiss flight attendant named Charlotte Huber and they had a son Joel. It did not last long and they were soon divorced.

His family has a history of arthritis and his hands were suffering stiffness. He played in a lot of pain. The old trio with Ray and Herb reunited in 1990 picking up where they left off thirty years earlier.

In 1993 Oscar suffered a stroke that paralysed his left side. Still many would argue that Oscar plays better with one hand that many pianists do with two. In 2002 at Queen Elizabeth II's Golden Jubilee he was the featured artist at the performance. The way he tinkles the ivories is still much loved by his adorning fans.

Mary Pickford
'America's Sweetheart'

Gladys Louise Smith was born in Toronto, Ontario on April 9, 1892 to Charlotte Catherine Pickford Hennessey and a dreamy man with a moustache and golden-brown brown hair named John Charles Smith. They had a second daughter name Lottie in 1893 and a son John (known as Jack) in 1895. Her father suffered a blow to the head from a pulley on a paddle wheel boat that caused a blood clot on his brain. He died a year later in 1898 leaving his wife Charlotte and three children in a state of near-destitution.

Charlotte ran a penny candy counter on Queen Street, sewed at night and took in boarders. Gladys went to school for only six or seven months over two years at the McCaul Street School. She was often sick and saw a great deal of Dr. G.B. Smith (no kin) at the Children's Hospital. It was said he saved little Gladys' life at least four times.

Charlotte took in a married couple and rented the master bedroom to them. The husband was the manager of the Cummings Stock Company. He asked Mrs. Smith if Gladys could try out for the play being cast. She did and soon appeared at The Princess Theatre in the production of *The Silver King*, she was only five.

Gladys appeared in quite a number of Broadway plays and traveled extensively. David Belasco offered her a role in *The Warrens of Virginia* but said her name would not do. He picked Mary and Pickford, which was her great-grandmother Hennessey's maiden name. Belasco found it remarkable how young Mary could visualize a story; illustrate it with her ever-changing expression and subtle delicate movements of her body.

Thomas Edison was experimenting with moving images but lost interest and handed it over to William Dickson to develop the new medium. In 1893 the first registered movie was *Record of a Sneeze*. Soon the motion picture industry would grow then blossom.

Mary saw her first movie, *Hale's Tours* for a nickel at a 'nickelodeon' in Chicago. Though she could see the economic potential of 'flickers' as entertainment she had reservations about the medium for at the time it was a big step down from real acting in many people's opinion.

In the spring of 1909 Mary arrived at the four-story brownstone in New York where she met David Griffith who worked for the Biograph Company doing just about everything. The young girl's golden locks caught his attention. One of the permanent actors, a handsome,

Irishman named Owen Moore showed an interest in the new girl and asked, "Who is that dame?"

Mary over heard his comment and hit him with the full force of her indignation saying, "How dare you insult me!"

Mary was soon negotiating her contract, which was $25 for her first three days and $5 a day after that. She appeared in *Violin-Maker of Cremona* that was her first film released on June 7, 1909. She was given a contract for $40 a week. The first film she acted in, *Her First Biscuits*, was released on June 17. She starred in seventy-nine Biograph Studios films. The public first knew her as 'Little Mary' or 'The Girl with the Golden Hair.'

In *A Call to Arms* Mary fell off a horse and as a result she could not bear children.

Mary's twelfth film *They Would Elope* received her first movie review though the reviewer did not know her name for all the Biograph players were anonymous at first. She received another of her countless salary raises and was now making $100 a week.

Mary had a restrained style of acting from her decade of stage work. Most of the other players were melodramatic but not Mary she riveted the audience's attention by standing still. She said whatever the temptation she would never overact. One day Griffith grabbed her shoulders, shook her and bellowed, "What's the matter, can't you play it with feeling?"

Mary seethed, "How dare you lay your hands on me!" She bit his hand.

Lottie jumped on his back and began pulling his ears screaming, "How dare you hurt my sister!"

Griffith called them wildcats and told them to get out which they did. As they were crying and walking down the sidewalk Griffith came running and apologized. Mary returned and did her scene again with more tears than were really needed.

By this time Mary and Owen were starting to fall in love. She went to California to do three films. The last one was *Ramona* written my Helen Hunt Jackson. Biograph paid $100 for the rights and it was filmed on the actual site of the story, a first in movie history. It won acclaim and was the most successful of her early films.

Mary missed Owen but her mother was warned and concerned about his drinking habits. She told Mary not to see him and that he was not welcome in the Pickford home. They conspired to see each other and the more Charlotte forbade the romance the more they saw one another. Defying her mother made her miserable but Owen cut to the quick proposing to her. When she objected, he threatened to quit the company and never see her again. They were secretly married at a justice of the peace on January 7, 1911. Mary continued to live at home and they still only saw each other in stolen moments.

Carl Laemmle of the Independent Motion Picture Company (IMP) offered Mary $175 a week and Griffith refused to match it so Mary jumped ship. He first IMP picture was *Their First Misunderstanding*. By now Owen was insisting Mary tell her family about the marriage. She did and her mother cried for three days.

IMP decided to shoot a film in Cuba and the cast sailed on the *SS Havana*. Her brother Jack accompanied her, as did Owen. It was supposed to be a honeymoon but Mary felt like the greatest sinner alive and it was in her opinion more like a funeral.

Mary did at least thirty-five films with IMP but none have survived. She was unhappy, felt she was losing her acting ability and her films were not well received. Despite her salary she longed for the higher standards of Biograph. She cancelled her contract and signed with the Majestic Company for $225 a week. She made five pictures with Owen directing most of them at Mary's insistence. They were all lost. By now her marriage was beginning to crack. His drinking was a problem and they quarrelled often but not in public.

In 1912 Mary returned to Biograph though Owen went to Victor. Belasco asked her to play Juliet, a blind girl, in *A Good Little Devil* that opened at the Republic Theater in New York on January 8, 1913. They teamed with Adolph Zukor the founder of Famous Players that formed Paramount Pictures and made a five-reel motion picture of the play. She was paid $500 a week. The actors read their entire speeches to the silent camera. It was a disaster. Her next movie, *Heart Adrift*, was a success and Zukor doubled her salary to $1,000 per week. With the success of *Tess of the Storm Country* again her salary was doubled.

It was about this time the Thomas Edison labelled her 'the sweetheart of the Americans' which soon became 'America's Sweetheart.'

At a Sunday afternoon party in late 1915 Mary and Owen met Beth and Douglas Fairbanks. It would change all their lives in the years ahead.

Zukor offered Mary half the profits of her films, a $10,000 a week guarantee as well as a $300,000 signing bonus. Zukor exclaimed, "Sweetheart, I don't have to diet…I lose ten pounds every time I talk over a new contract with you!" She also got her name on films and marquees.

Mary was the first actress to fly in a picture called *A Girl of Yesterday*. It was assumed she would use a double. She didn't. One of the innovations she was responsible for was using artificial light from below to flatter her face. They became know as 'baby spots.'

With World War I raging she adopted the second battalion of the First Field Artillery and presented each of the men with a gold locket containing her picture. They became known as 'Mary Pickford's Fighting 600.' She helped raised millions of dollars in war bonds and traveled with Douglas Fairbanks and Charlie Chaplin to promote the war effort.

Her next triumphs were *Poor Little Rich Girl* and *Rebecca of Sunnybrook Farm* released in 1917. Charles Rosher assisted with photography and became her favourite cameraman. Unbeknownst to Zukor she played an ugly girl, Unity as well as the lead role in *Stella Maris*. Much to Zukor's surprise it was a success. Again her salary jumped to $675,000 per year or $350,000 per film in a time when taxes were non existent or minimal to say the least. It was an unheard of sum for those days.

Mary went to work on *Daddy Longlegs* helping write the script and as it turned out, made a smashing début as a producer.

Douglas Fairbanks divorced Beth in 1918.

On April 17, 1919 Mary Pickford, Douglas Fairbanks, Charlie Chaplin and David Griffith formed United Artists. They agreed to produce and finance their own pictures prepared to accept losses, which they never did, or garner the rewards that were more bountiful than they could have imagined. Their first three films were blockbusters with Mary appearing in *Polyanna*. I was a huge hit in Russia. By filming through black maline, a fine silk net, the actors appeared ten years younger. The results were extraordinary.

Mary and Owen divorced March 1, 1920 with her vowing she would not marry for a year. Mary gave him a $150,000 settlement and he threatened to shoot Fairbanks.

Despite her promise Mary married Douglas March 28, 1920 and he gave her Pickfair as a wedding present. When she finished *Suds* in June of 1920 they sailed to Europe for a six-week honeymoon. They encountered crowds so thick it became the most public honeymoon in history. Word was cabled ahead. England, France, Holland and Italy knew they were coming and they were royally welcomed everywhere they went. Only in Germany were they ignored to their consternation. When they returned to New York aboard the *Olympic* they were met by throngs of adoring fans.

Mary's first movie after the honeymoon was *The Love Light*. Douglas starred in *The Mark of Zorro* turning him into the favourite male star of the time. Mary of course had reigned as the female favourite for some time. Fairbanks produced and starred in *The Three Musketeers* and his popularity soared. Next he did *Robin Hood* with a budget of $1 million in the most expensive film ever produced. It broke records at the box-office.

Ernst Lubitsch from Germany directed Mary in *Rosita* in 1923. It was spectacular and one of the best films of the silent era though Mary called it the "worst picture, bar none, that I ever made.."

In the spring of 1925 a plot to kidnap Mary was uncovered and four men were arrested. Watchmen and dogs began to guard Pickfair round-the-clock. They went to Germany and Italy and when *Il Duce*, Benito Mussolini, received them she gave him an autograph book to sign. From that point on whenever they met royalty she had them sign her book. When they went to the Soviet Union 25,000 fans greeted them at the Moscow railway station. They were also swarmed at Warsaw.

During the filming of *Sparrows* in 1926 director William Beaudine shot a scene with live alligators. Douglas was furious and Mary never forgave Beaudine for endangering her life and the life of the baby she carried on her back.

In 1927 Douglas Fairbanks bought Mary a pink, white and gold porcelain tea service that Napoleon gave to Josephine in 1807.

During this period Mary bought as many of her old films as she could including 80 Biograph short films. She forbade the screening of her work and planned to destroy them on her death but Lillian Gish and others talked her out of it.

A première of any picture in Hollywood didn't start until Doug and Mary were seated. She started charity work and was a patron of the Los Angeles Orphans' Asylum. She started a club with Loretta Young, Ruby Keeler, Billie Dove and others to assist new actresses.

Buddy Rogers, only twenty-two, appeared in *My Best Girl* and his incredible good looks made him a star. Mary even kissed him, the first time she had ever touched the lips of any of her leading men. Douglas appeared on the set one day and Mary and Buddy were doing a love scene. He left abruptly in a jealous rage.

Mary asked him, "Mr. Rogers do you consider me a great actress?"

He replied, "My favourite is Norma Shearer." Mary would kid him about his response for many years to come.

Douglas founded the Motion Picture Academy with the help of Louis B. Mayer in 1927. In 1928 the first Oscars were awarded and the picture *Wings* won the Best Picture award. It was a silent film about the fliers of World War I. With the advent of 'talkies' directors, who had always shouted, now had to learn to be silent.

When Mary's mother died on March 21, 1928 she went out of her mind and even hated God.

On June 21, 1928 Mary went to a hairdresser and had the most famous locks since Medusa's cut off. Six of her curls survived and two are in a case at Pickfair. She would no longer hold up production on days of high humidity where she would have to put her hair in curlers and the cast would sit there while it dried.

Mary won an Oscar as Best Actress in 1929 for her part in *Coquette*. It was the first award for a sound film. The award was undoubtedly as much for her past performances as it was for her service to the industry.

The parties they threw at Pickfair were regal and her guest lists flush with the likes of the Crown Prince of Japan, Crown Prince of Prussia, Alfonso XIII, Lord and Lady Mountbatten as well as Einstein, Earhart, Marconi, great authors, painters and politicians. Only Marion Davis and her lover Randolph Heart could challenge their posh parties.

Even with such acclaim Mary had few friends and almost no girlfriends. She was the queen of the hill though a phantom and a legend in her time.

Douglas smoked a lot and his muscle-bound condition let to circulatory problems that led to his premature death.

Mary starred in the first Shakespearian talkie, *The Taming of the Shrew* in 1929. Critics loved it but after the film was finished Mary's confidence was shattered.

Less than a third of the way into filming *Secrets* she ordered production shut down. She wrote off the $300,000 loss and burned the negatives. She was hired in 1931 for *Kiki* and though it featured Betty Grable's legs it was a total box-office failure. Mary resumed the making of *Secrets* from the ground up. When released it went unnoticed by critics and fans alike. After only four sound pictures Pickford was through. She would never grace the silver screen again.

January 3, 1932 her brother Jack died. Officially it was progressive multiple neuritis. Some think he died from too many good things like women, drink and wild living. He was married three times to beautiful Ziegfeld girls, had countless affairs and was an alcoholic.

Mary and Douglas's marriage was falling apart. He would have fits of jealousy while at the same time he would be having affairs. Mary liked to say home and Douglas liked to travel. She wanted to withdraw from the world - he liked to live in it. Douglas tried to reconcile offering her a diamond bracelet but she received him coldly and turned it down. They got divorced on January 10, 1935 but it would not be finalized for one year. She was close to tears when she left the courtroom.

Eleven months later Douglas came crawling back to her. She held her ground. The day she received the final papers he again appeared with an impassioned plea. With her heart wrenched she again refuse. He flew to New York despondent. His son, Doug Jr., watched him pine for days and sent Mary lengthy wires that she didn't answer. Suddenly he left for Europe. The day he left his son discovered Mary had both called and wired him telling him to come back to California. She called her newly ex-husband on the ship but he had proposed to Sylvia Hawkes and said, "It's just too late." The divorce was issued on January 10, 1936 and signed by Doug and Mary on January 14. On March 7 Douglas married Sylvia. They moved into the Pickford-Fairbanks Santa Monica beach home. Doug began to phone Mary and ask if he could come and sit by the pool at Pickfair. Mary allowed him to come and they would sit for hours saying nothing. Once he said, "What a mistake."

She said, "I'm sorry."

Her sister Lottie, who had the only child in the family - Gwynne, died December 9, 1936. She had married four times.

Mary stayed active as a producer and to fill voids she began drinking cocktails. She saw Buddy Rogers when he wasn't travelling with his band and her niece thought she dangled him in front of Douglas for spite. Mary felt that Buddy more than any one else gave her back a desire to live. They were married on June 26, 1937.

Douglas died on December 12, 1939.

In 1943 Buddy and Mary adopted Ronnie from an orphanage and Roxanne in 1944. When they were young they were a source of joy and amusement. After they reached twenty-one Mary had no more contact though she provided monetarily for them.

During World War II the pool and gardens of Pickfair were always open to military personnel. Servicemen were still welcomed well after the war was over.

Mary did some radio work and published her autobiography *Sunshine and Shadow* in 1955. She hung on to her shares of United Artists until a year later selling them for $3 million. She became a recluse at the lavish estate she built with Fairbanks called Pickfair. In 1966 she had a cataract operation and after that rarely got out of bed and never left the house again except to go to the hospital.

In 1976 Mary received her last Academy Award for lifetime achievement. The recluse who had a life full of accomplishment, romance and glamour died May 28, 1979.

Piskiart
The Lone Warrior

The greatest feat of this brave 'Lone Warrior' was when he stole into enemy country, a war party of one. He was a tall fellow with the agility of a panther and the face of an eagle. However, he was more of a lone wolf for he preferred to hunt at night - alone.

The setting of this most unbelievable story was the 1640's in Algonquin and Iroquois territory. Piskiart, an Algonquin from Ottawa County, took actions into his own hands after his tribe returned to find their favourite spot by the lake inhabited by an Iroquois tribe called the Mohawk. They had built longhouses indicating their long-term intentions.

It was late at night when Piskiart approached the Mohawk village. He spotted a huge pile of branches from the construction at the edge of the nearby forest and made a den under it to hide in. He then stole into one of the longhouses where all the occupants were soundly sleeping. He killed every member, never using more than one blow to split the victim's skull. From his secret hiding place in the early morning he heard the wails of anguish as the catastrophe was discovered. Shouts of rage and lamentation of relatives rose and the young braves organized and dispatched war parties. They looked high and low, far and wide, for the culprits of this most dastardly crime. The braves returned at the end of the day empty handed but sure the villains were long gone. Sad and exhausted, the village fell into a troubled sleep.

Again Piskiart stole into the village and massacred another longhouse in the same manner as the night before. The following morning a similar scenario unfolded. Wails, cries and another war party of young braves set forth to avenge the slaughter of their village members. Alas, they looked in vain for the culprit of the crimes.

The third night when Piskiart tried to enter a longhouse he found ones occupied, guarded by sentries. In the dead of the night he gave a mighty war cry and tomahawked one of the guards. Hearing the commotion the other sentries and the braves gave pursuit as the villain fled into the night. As dawn was breaking some of the war party was still hot on his trail. The chase continued throughout the day. The pursuing braves took turns setting a blistering pace. However, Piskiart was very fleet of foot and at dusk the Mohawk party lost him. They finally gave up and settled down to an exhausted sleep. The bold Algonquin warrior doubled back to finish the war party off with his well-reddened tomahawk.

Little more is known about this copper-skinned warrior other than he later became the well-respected chief of the Algonquin tribe.

Jacques Plante
The Man with the Mask

Jacques Plante was born in a farmhouse near Mt. Carmel, Québec on January 17, 1929. He was the first child, ten more brothers and sisters would follow. He liked hockey but couldn't afford skates or the ten cents it cost to get in the arena. He would stand at the doorway and offer to play goal, which was not a favoured position. They took him up on his offer fairly often. He always wore a toque that he knitted, for is mother had taught that skill. He had asthma and quickly got winded when he skated hard.

In 1948 he played for the Québec Citadels and because his defensemen were not that good he took to coming far out of the crease leaving a gaping net behind him. It would become a signature of his play.

In 1949 he married Jacqueline Gagné and their first son Michel was born in 1951. In 1952 when the Habs goaltender Gerry McNeill broke his jaw, coach Dick Irvin brought Plante in. He still wore his toque and stood his ground against Irvin who threw his toques out before they played the Rangers beating them 4-1. The press began to call him Jake the Snake. The Montreal Canadiens signed him but sent him to their farm club, the Buffalo Bisons.

On April 3, 1953 with Chicago leading the Stanley Cup semi final series 3-2, Irvin pulled McNeill and sent Plante in. He registered his first shutout and in the next game led his team to a 4-1 victory. In the finals against Boston he won one and lost one but the Canadiens won and Plante's name appeared on the Stanley Cup for the first time.

McNeill retired in 1954 and Jacques joined the team as their starting goaltender. On March 13, 1955 a nasty brawl broke out and NHL Commissioner Clarence Campbell announced that Maurice 'The Rocket' Richard was suspended for the remainder of the season. The next game was in the Montreal Forum on March 17th and when Campbell entered the arena he was physically attacked. A tear gas bomb went off and the game was forfeited to Detroit. The building was cleared and the riot spread along Ste Catherine Street. Hundreds were arrested and Detroit won the Cup that year.

Toe Blake took the helm as the coach and the Canadiens would win an unprecedented five Stanley Cups in a row from 1956-60. Toe hated Plante because he wanted to be in control but he couldn't move Jacques around like he did the other players. Just the same, there was no other goaltender that had the great glove hand, confidence and panache that Jake did. He was outstanding and even Blake admits that begrudgingly. Still it irked Toe that Plante would not stay in the net and that he still wore that silly toque in practice. It was almost more than he could bear when in 1959 Plante was injured by a shot from Andy Bathgate of the Rangers and he put on a facemask that he had developed with Bill Burchmore. Blake bullied and threatened to fire him but Plante stood his ground and they won the Cup in eight consecutive games. The mask was there to stay.

In 1961 even though Maurice Richard retired and Doug Harvey was traded, Plante still won the Vezina and Hart Trophies. Blake had had enough and complained about the mask, then he traded him to the New York Rangers. After two unremarkable years there Plante retired.

In 1965 Scotty Bowman asked Plante to come out of retirement to join his Canadian team against a genuinely superior opponent, the Russians. Plante shocked the Russians letting in only one goal while the junior Canadians scored twice.

In 1968 when the league expanded Plante joined the St. Louis Blues and shared the goal with Glen Hall. They won the Vezina that year. He surprised everybody when he went and played for the Toronto Maple Leafs, his old arch enemy.

Before he hung up his skates he had played almost fifty thousand minutes in more than eight hundred games and had a remarkable goals against average of 2.34. He also had a record number of playoff shutouts with fifteen that he shared with Clint Benedict until Patrick Roy broke that record in 2001. He won the Vezina Trophy for the NHL's best goaltender a remarkable five consecutive years, seven times in all and he has his name on the Stanley Cup six times.

He started a new business Fibrosport, making goaltenders' masks. He wrote a book *Devant le Filet* (Before the Net). In the Series of the Century between Canada and the USSR in 1972 he was Radio-Canada's principal analyst.

In 1973 he negotiated a ten-year $1 million contract as coach and general manager of the newly formed Quebec Nordiques of the World Hockey Association. However his personal life was in disarray. His marriage was over and his son Richard committed suicide. When he took a slapshot in the side of the head in Edmonton he retired once and for all. He married again and went to live in Sierre, Switzerland. He came back briefly for his induction into the Hockey Hall of Fame in 1978. He died of cancer on February 26, 1986. Another legend for all time.

Poundmaker
Great Chief with a Lost Cause

Poundmaker was born near Battleford, now in Saskatchewan, in 1826. He was named after his father, Seka-Kinyan, a medicine man for the Stony tribe. His father was known as a maker of 'pounds' or traps into which the buffalo were chased. Poundmaker's mother was Métis and her brother was head chief of the Plains Cree. She returned to her family, fell ill and died. Her sons grew up as orphans. With no parents to care for him, Poundmaker learned to be independent at a young age. He learned to speak Cree but never learned to speak English or French.

He grew up with the customs of the Cree and believed in a Creator whose essence was earth, the home for all plants and animals. Since humans were dependent upon the plants, animals and the earth they felt that humans ranked last in the order of life. Belief in the natural spirits was a daily part of their lives.

As a boy and young man Poundmaker watched and participated in the sacred Sun Dance ceremony each spring. Everyone looked forward to meeting other people and renewing old friendships. During the ceremony vows were made for the new season and they fasted. They would dance and the orphans, elderly, widows, blind and lame received gifts of food.

Buffalo meat was a staple food of the Cree and that which was not used immediately was dried and made into pemmican. In the winter the meat was frozen.

Poundmaker became a good hunter and knew how to trap the buffalo in pounds like his father. They would slaughter the beasts and this would provide food for the band for days and the pemmican could last well into winter. As he grew older Poundmaker became one of the tribe's best hunters. He could imitate various animals like the coyote's howl, the gopher's whistle and the hawk's cry. Hunting taught him to be patient as well as courageous.

Though the men were expected to provide for their own families, the Cree led a communal life and shared whatever they had. With no family Poundmaker was generous with his share and spent time talking to the lonely and infirmed as he understood their plight.

From the plants that grew on the land Poundmaker learned how to make medicines. Ground or boiled root was used for headaches and toothaches and was also given to teething babies. The inner bark of pine trees helped soothe a sore throat. He learned of many other remedies for burns, fever and other ailments. For those who suffered from lumbago and rheumatism they used the sweat lodge. Poundmaker's ability to treat the sick made him well known among the Plains Cree.

When he acquired some status he married Little Beaver and took her sister, Grass Woman, as his second wife. He was appointed headman of the band. Always independent and daring he wandered into Blackfoot territory and met their chief, Crowfoot, who eventually became his stepfather. For the first time in many years there was peace between the two tribes.

The natives believed the land, like water and sky was not owned by anyone and in fact was shared by everyone. This idea conflicted with the white man's tradition of land ownership and private property. Many native people were driven off their ancestral lands. Migratory routes of the buffalo were disturbed and the great herds grew smaller. The railway brought more settlers and for their protection the North-West Mounted Police was established in 1873.

Poundmaker's people became discontented but when peace and rectitude were offered they agreed to meet. Poundmaker was one of the leaders at Fort Carlton who discussed a treaty. The Cree agreed to surrender their lands, obey the law and bring justice to offenders. The government agreed to many conditions including; farmland or reservations, schools, hunting and fishing rights, an allowance for ammunition and twine, clothes, hoes, spades, ploughs, harrows, axes as well as access to medical treatment. Treaty Number Six was signed on August 23, 1876. Though Big Bear, a highly esteemed chief, refused to sign, there was a great celebration and festivities. This was also the year Sitting Bull massacred General Custer and his 7th Cavalry. The renegades fled across the border and settled in Cypress Hills, now on the border between Alberta and Saskatchewan.

For two years Poundmaker and his band remained on the open plains but the hunting was poor. The buffalo herds could not migrate as the Americans set fires to prevent them from reaching Canada in an attempt to starve Sitting Bull and his band into surrender. Of course this had dire consequences for other tribes as well.

These were troubled times for the Cree and Blackfoot. They heard what had happened to the tribes in the States who tried armed resistance and Poundmaker did not want his people to suffer the same fate. Leading their people drained the leaders as starvation and tuberculosis stalked many tribes.

Reluctantly Poundmaker took his people to the reservation where the Battle River joins Cut Knife Creek. The land was hard and dry. The crops they grew were poor and not bountiful enough to sustain them.

They had to resort to slaughtering the oxen provided for farm work and settlers accused them of stealing their cattle.

Poundmaker led his people off the reserve and found some game before arriving at Fort Walsh where he arranged to get some food. The Governor General, the Marquis of Lorne, came west that year and Poundmaker traveled with him acting as a guide and assuring him a safe passage.

The winter of 1882 was very hard and cold. With little food the very young, sick and elderly perished. The next year was no better and their gaunt children went to school mainly for the little morsels of food they received. Still Poundmaker argued against violence.

In 1884 tensions between the Cree and white men ran high as they watched their children grow thinner from lack of food. Food and other provisions promised by the government in the treaty had been cut back and the starving tribe felt helpless in the face of government officials and regulations they did not understand.

It was time for the annual thirst dance called *Nipahakwesimowin*. Cree from all around had gathered on the reserve of Chief Poundmaker for the ceremony. The new Indian agent, fearing trouble, ordered Big Bear to return to their reserve near Frog Lake. Big Bear refused and the agent ordered all supplies and rations to be cut off immediately.

Anger rose especially when the agent shouted disrespectfully at Big Bear.

Despite the trouble, the religious ceremony went ahead. It had been hot and the elders who knew how to communicate with the spirits, prayed for rain that was much needed for the crops. They danced, chanted and drums were heard throughout the night.

On the nearby Little Pine reserve the Cree asked Agent Craig for emergency supplies for a sick native child. He refused and a scuffle broke out and one of them, Ka-wee-chet-way-mot, picked up an axe handle and hit Craig who managed to break loose and run for help.

Superintendent Crozier of the North-West Mounted Police rode right into the centre of the chanting Cree on Poundmaker's reserve. They were perturbed by the brash interruption of their ceremony and drove the Mounties out of the circle.

Crozier went to Poundmaker's lodge. The chief awaited him in full ceremonial costume with his face painted red, arm bands and his long braided hair waving in the wind. Crozier asked the chief to hand over Ka-wee-chet-way-mot but Poundmaker refused and would not speak to any outsiders until the ceremony was over.

The next morning Poundmaker offered to go in Ka-wee-chet-way-mot's place but Crozier wanted the actual offender. Another scuffle broke out and Poundmaker's steady voice told his young warriors to hold their fire. Finally Ka-wee-chet-way-mot's friends persuaded him to give himself up and blood shed was avoided. Emotions ran high and there was talk of war.

In nearby Batoché the Métis were becoming stronger and more vocal about their grievances against the government. Louis Riel returned from the States and with Gabrielle Dumont they prepared for open warfare.

Poundmaker knew that his people would be less likely to fight if the Department of Indian Affairs would issue them some food rations. He went to Battleford to meet with Agent Rae. The town was abandoned as the town folk thought it was a war party. Rae refused to talk to the chief and remained in the well-fortified barracks.

A fire broke out in town and the angry band broke windows and took supplies they needed. Poundmaker could do little to stop the looting. Inside the crowded barracks people awaited the attack but Poundmaker led his people back to the reservation, set up a war camp at Cut Knife Hill and waited for the militia.

Colonel William Otter set out to punish Poundmaker. As the leader Poundmaker was in a precarious situation. Many called for war while others that favoured peace saw it as a less viable alternative considering their dismal treatment.

News arrived that Big Bear's band had killed nine people at Frog Lake April 2, 1885.

On May 2 in a surprise attack at dawn Otter's troops opened fire and cannon balls and bullets fell on Poundmaker's camp. They used the Gatling gun for the first time in British history. Foolishly Otter had set up his troops in a ravine rather than on high ground. Poundmaker knew from the onset that the soldiers would lose the battle and would have to retreat. Though many of the braves wanted to annihilate the soldiers Poundmaker held his braves back and let Otter escape.

Though Poundmaker was opposed, some Métis persuaded other band members to head for Batoché. On May 14 they encountered a wagon train loaded with food supplies. They stopped the wagons and took the supplies but spared the driver's lives. A few days later they met Métis travellers who informed them that Riel had been captured and Dumont had fled. The government had ruthlessly put down the rebellion.

Poundmaker sent word with Father Cochin to Major-General Frederick Middleton that he was prepared to negotiate peace. Middleton, a fighting man, sent word that they must surrender unconditionally. Poundmaker said to his people, "I prefer to surrender myself at the risk of being hung rather than to shed streams of blood in a resistance which has no more reason to be."

When Poundmaker surrendered to Middleton he was disgraced in front of his people. He was taken to jail along with two Stoney murderers. In the newspapers of eastern Canada Poundmaker was seen as gallant and wise. He aroused much sympathy.

The trial of the leaders of the Rebellion was held in Regina. Poundmaker was tried for treason-felony, which was a charge that was difficult to translate and came out as "fighting the Queen and chasing her out of the country" or "kicking off Victoria's bonnet and calling her bad names." Poundmaker felt he had done nothing to Queen Victoria and had only tried to get better and fairer conditions for his people. Poundmaker did not speak in his own defence and it was not told at trial that he went to negotiate with the Indian agent but was spurned and rejected. The jury found him guilty and Judge Hugh Richardson sentenced him to three years in prison.

Poundmaker thought he would be hung and protested being imprisoned asking to be hung at once. The judge did not listen and the chief was hurried out of the courtroom.

Crowfoot threatened reprisals and Edgar Dewdney, Commissioner of the Department of Indian Affairs, worked quickly to prevent a major uprising. He also got a prison concession that allowed the chief to keep his long hair.

Prime Minister John A. Macdonald got a letter from a man who asked that Poundmaker be released from prison to join Buffalo Bill's Wild West Show. He would join Sitting Bull who brought in large crowds. Macdonald recognized it would degrade the dignity of the proud chief and he ignored the request.

After seven months Dewdney secured Poundmaker's release. He returned to his tribe but found little the same. Grass Woman had left him; settlers and townspeople who claimed victory had looted his reserve. Traditional dances and rituals were condemned. Children were not allowed to speak their native language in school and his people were now required to get permission from the Indian agent to leave the reserve. The will and the spirit of his people had been broken.

Dispirited, Poundmaker spoke out against the white man as never before. He spoke out against the government's efforts to destroy their religion and ancient traditions.

In 1886 Poundmaker's third wife Stony Woman trekked with him to Crowfoot's camp 650 kilometres away. He was sick with a fever when he met his friend. Death came swiftly the cause unknown. His remains were buried at Blackfoot Crossing. In 1967 they were carried back to Cree country and buried at Cut Knife Hill.

Louis Riel
Champion of his People - Martyr for their cause

Louis Riel was born at Red River Settlement on October 22, 1844. He studied for the priesthood at Collège de Montrèal but turned to law in 1865 studying under Rodolphe Laflamme.

The federal government of the fledgling country expected the Hudson's Bay Company (HBC) to transfer its vast lands into their jurisdiction. Anticipating this Prime Minister John A. Macdonald appointed William McDougall as the lieutenant-governor of the territory. Survey crews were sent to the area in 1869. The Métis were still suffering economically from the grasshopper plague the year before and were fearful of the Anglo-Protestant immigrants from the east. They had seen how they treated the natives.

The Métis organized a 'National Committee' making Riel the secretary. With his education and his father's background it marked him as the obvious leader. The Committee halted the survey and prevented McDougall from entering the Red River area. November 2 they seized Fort Garry. The Hudson's Bay officials offered no resistance. Riel invited people both French and English to send delegates to Fort Garry to discuss a 'List of Rights' the Committee had drawn up.

John Schultz, a doctor and owner of the Nor'Western fur trading company and John Dennis, in charge of the survey team, organized armed resistance. After some heated words and a number of shots Dennis and McDougall returned to Ontario. Schultz and his men surrendered to Riel who imprisoned them in Fort Garry.

Riel issued a 'Declaration of the People of Rupert's Land and the Northwest' declaring himself head of the provisional government December 23.

Macdonald sent special commissioners to the region to bring 'goodwill.' The ambassadors were Abbé Thibault, Colonel Charles de Salaberry and Donald Smith. Smith persuaded Riel to summon a general meeting held January 26, 1870. The 'delegates' debated a new 'List of Rights', endorsed Riel's provisional government and any prisoners who had not escaped were released. Plans were made to send 3 delegates to Ottawa to negotiate the entry of the Red River colony into confederation.

Meanwhile Schultz, who had escaped, surveyor Thomas Scott, a militia officer, Charles Boulton and some others gathered at Portage la Prairie trying to enlist the support of the Scottish parishes. Alarmed, the Métis promptly rounded them up and imprisoned them again in Fort Garry. They convened a court-martial and condemned Boulton to death.

Donald Smith, the HBC representative, intervened and the sentence was remitted. With Riel absent, second in command Ambroise Lépine held another court martial and sentenced the boisterous and unruly Scott to death. Smith's appeals were rejected and Scott was executed by firing squad on March 4, 1870.

Bishop Alexandre Taché, who was summoned from the Ecumenical Council in Rome, reached the Red River four days after Scott's death. He carried a copy of the federal proclamation of amnesty that he believed included any actions up to that date. Taché persuaded Riel to free all prisoners and send delegates to Ottawa. The Orange Lodges of Ontario, of which Scott was a member, opposed Riel and his delegates but never the less their agreement was embodied in the Manitoba Act passed May 12.

The government agreed to a land grant of 1,400,000 acres for the Métis and to provide bilingual services for the fledgling province. However there was no mention of amnesty though verbal assurances were given.

A new lieutenant-governor Adam Archibald was appointed and a military force under Colonel Garnet Wolseley marched into Red River on a 'mission of peace.' Riel fled to the United States but soon returned quietly home. Riel was denounced as Scott's murderer and a $5,000 reward was offered for his arrest. In Québec he was a hero and a defender of the Roman Catholic faith as well as the French culture. Macdonald tried to persuade Riel to remain in exile, even provided him with money but Riel chose to enter federal politics. He was elected in 1874, went to Ottawa, signed the register then was expelled from the House on a motion introduced by the Ontario Orange leader Mackenzie Bowell. Riel was re-elected in absentia but did not attempt to take his seat again.

Lépine was arrested, tried and condemned to death but the sentence was commuted to 2 years' imprisonment and loss of political rights. In February of 1875 the federal government approved a motion granting amnesty to Riel and Lépine on the condition that they were banned from 'Her Majesty's dominions' for 5 years.

Riel suffered a nervous breakdown and was admitted to the Longue Pointe Hospital. He was transferred to the mental asylum at Beauport, Québec. When released in January 1878 Riel went to the States, became an American citizen and married Marguerite Monet. They soon had two children. In 1883 he became a school teacher at St. Peter's mission on the Sun River.

In 1884 some Métis asked for his help to obtain their legal rights on the prairies. Riel went to Batoché and conducted peaceful agitation and prepared a petition. It was acknowledged in Ottawa and the government promised a commission to investigate the report on the western problems. The Métis viewed this as stalling as the railway edged ever closer.

March 19 Riel and his followers seized the parish church at Batoché and formed a provisional government. The Riel Rebellion was short lived. In two months the Métis as well as the native leaders that joined them like Poundmaker and Big Bear were routed. Riel was arrested May 15. It was claimed that he did not fire a shot.

July 6 he was formally charged with treason and on July 20 the trial began. Riel's counsel proposed they defend him on the grounds of insanity but Riel repudiated that defence. The all white jury found him guilty but recommended clemency. His case was appealed to the Court of Queen's Bench of Manitoba and to the Judicial Committee of the Privy Council. Both appeals were dismissed. The federal Cabinet decided in favour of hanging. November 16 the sentence was carried out. The Métis were heart broken and French Canadian nationalism was strengthened. The execution has remained a contentious issue even today and some demand a retroactive pardon. It is a sad chapter in Canadian history.

Marguerite de la Roque
Isle of Demons Castaway

On January 15, 1541 François I signed a commission for Jean-François de la Roque de Roberval to colonize New France with the help of Jacques Cartier. Roberval sailed in 1542 with his niece the lovely Marguerite de la Roque. She was only twenty-two. Cartier met up with Roberval in Newfoundland on June 8 but they quickly parted, Cartier for France and Roberval to colonize the New World.

On their journey up the St. Lawrence River Sieur de Roberval discovered Marguerite had a lover on board. He went into a rage and swore revenge. Roberval gave the command to lower a launch and load it with guns and ammunition. He ordered supplies and clothing be included. A hard taskmaster not one to be made a fool of, he ordered Miss de La Roque and her maid Damienne to descend into the launch. As the launch slipped away her lover broke free, dove into the water and swam furiously toward the launch and was able to climb on board. Roberval had the sails hoisted and departed.

He would abandon colonizing the new land for he arrived far too late to plant crops and successfully build a settlement that could survive the harsh winter. He sailed for home unmindful of the plight of his niece.

Initially the hunting, supply of food and shelter was adequate for the castaways. However the skiff of land they were deserted on was open to the tremendous gales of driving freezing rain. The sound of the wind whistling over the land gave it the name Isle of Demons for it sounded like the crying of a thousand possessed evil spirits.

Marguerite had a son but claims during the first winter all that was precious in her world was lost to her save her own life. Her son, lover and maid all died leaving her alone. She became proficient with the gun claiming to have killed three bears in one day; one of them she said was white. Still food was scarce during the hellish winters and the wind whipping the froth from the sea making life miserable.

She kept a constant vigil for rescue but no ships passed by. She was beginning to lose hope when in the fall of 1544 a fishing vessel noticed smoke. Though initially inclined to flee, for it was an island of superstition, they were puzzled by the figure that stood on the rocks and waved. The crew was mortified and thought they were seeing an apparition, but the captain took things in hand and landed the vessel to investigate. They were astounded when the darkened, scruffy woman in tattered animal skins spoke to them in fluent French.

When she reached France, Marguerite told her story to Andrew Thevet, the French Royal Geographer. When Samuel de Champlain read her story he used this as evidence that Europeans could indeed survive in the new land. She became the toast of Paris as there was endless fascination with the young woman, still only 24, who had survived in the wild new world for two years on her own.

Jamie Salé and David Pelletier
Figure Skating Pairs Event Fiasco

At the Salt Lake City Olympic games in 2002 the pairs event garnered a lot of controversy. The Russian pair, Yelena Berezhnaya and Anton Sikharulidze, skated a good program but Anton had a slip during their performance opening the door for Salé and Pelletier. They skated a flawless performance but when their scores were announced there was a storm of boos and Salé collapsed in tears.

Scott Hamilton, the NBC commentator and ex-skating champion, whipped up the furor describing the results as disgraceful. Sophie Moniotte, a recently retired French ice dancer tells *Newsweek* magazine, "Our sport has gangrene. In most sports doping is the problem. With figure skating, it's deals and manipulation."

So the controversy dragged on for days affecting the International Skating Union (ISU), the International Olympic Committee (IOC) and even dragged President Putin of Russia into the controversy.

Salé and Pelletier, linked romantically as well as professionally, allege they had received half a dozen messages saying they had not deserved to win the previous year's World Championships and would not win at the Olympics.

The next day Marie-Reine Le Gougne, the French judge, broke down and claimed to have been put under pressure to vote for the Russian pair as part of a reciprocal deal whereby the Russian judge would support the French ice dance pair.

After receiving evidence of the judges' post mortem, the ISU knew they must investigate but the IOC sensed the need for a quick resolution. Hyper-sensitive to scandal they did not wish an 'unfair' decision involving possible judging malpractice to further stain the Olympics' good will.

Richard Pound, a Canadian on the IOC said of the ISU, "You've fouled up our festival, sort it out now, this is a contrived situation, not a random error." The Canadian National Olympic Committee lodged a complaint to put further pressure on the ISU.

In the end a second set of gold medals were awarded to Salé and Pelletier but the damage had been done and the truth of an injustice had emerged. This brought past injustices to the forefront. This controversy will undoubtedly continue because the evaluation of this sport, like gymnastics and diving, is subjective and as a result will continue to be fertile grounds for political pressure rather than truly objective assessments of the athlete's performance by unbiased judges.

Jamie Salé and David Pelletier were married December 30, 2005 at the Fairmont Banff Springs Hotel in Alberta.

Sir Charles Saunders
Canada's Wheat King

Charles was born in London, Canada West on February 2, 1867. His father was a druggist and self-taught horticultural scientist. Prime Minister John A. Macdonald appointed him as the first director of the Dominion Experimental Farms and Stations in 1886.

Charles first love was music but he yielded to his father's pressure and earned his doctorate in chemistry at Johns Hopkins University in 1891. His wife was a mezzo-soprano and together they ran a music school in Toronto. In 1902 his father informed him that he had appointed him to become dominion cerealist. He accepted his fate and moved to the Manitoba farm.

Charles immediately applied scientific methods to his new task and meticulously selected individual heads of wheat from the breeding material. He crossed Hard Red Calcutta, an early maturing variety and Red Fife to make a new variety called Markham.

Markham did not produce uniform offspring so he selected those that produced stiff straw. Each plant was grown separately with no mixing of strains until he had refined the seed into the one he called Marquis. By 1907 he had enough seed to distribute to 407 farmers. By 1920 the wheat grown in western Canada was 90% Marquis. It matured early avoiding frost damage. It also milled nicely and was in high demand by millers and bakers around the world. Millions and now billions of dollars worth of Canadian wheat are shipped around the world annually. That is how we got the title, 'Bread basket of the world.'

Charles continued to work on the farm applying his research skills to barley, oats, peas, flax and beans. His delicate health collapsed in 1922 and he retired. He was given a pension of $900 a year. In 1925 the government increased his pension to $5,000 annually.

When questioned about his achievements and asked who made Marquis wheat he replied with a smile, "God Almighty." He was knighted in 1934 by George V. He died in Toronto on July 25, 1937.

He added more wealth to this country than any other individual and is undoubtedly one of the most influential Canadians of all time.

Norma Shearer
Silent Silver Screen Star Who was a Gold Mine for MGM's 'Talkies'

Edith Norma Shearer was born on August 10, 1900 in Westmount, a suburb of Montreal. She was named after her mother Edith Fisher. She had a sister Athole who was two years younger and a brother Douglas who was two years older. Early in her life she dropped the Edith to avoid confusion with her mother's name and besides she felt Norma was more glamorous.

Norma took a lot of kidding when she called a young neighbour boy her husband. He had blonde hair and she liked him a lot. A truck killed him when riding his bicycle. Norma was grief stricken and cried for nights.

She always liked the boys, had a gentle influence on them and on occasion would stand her ground if it was necessary. In her own words she was 'boy crazy.' She took piano lessons from Blossom Connelly and was within days of taking the Royal Academy of Music final examination when her frail teacher died suddenly and another dream crashed in ruins. It was about this time that her father's business failed and they had to move from her childhood home. She felt the pinch of poverty and experienced a profound disappointment in her father. Norma went with her mother and sister to Manhattan in February 1920 but they were poor and it was a difficult experience. Everything bewildered the Shearer's, the fast pace, lights and the frenzy of the people. Norma loved the garish billboards; brilliantly lit theatre marquees and movie houses were popping up everywhere.

They noticed the gleam in the eyes of the men that their father's had lost. They paid $7.50 a week to board in a flophouse. The winter was biting and the room was inadequately heated so they slept together in a double bed to keep warm.

Norma went to Jimmy Quirk with a letter of introduction from a Montreal film producer. He introduced her to Ziegfeld though he had reservations about her teeth and the cast in her eye. She was short and petite at 5' 2" with legs that were unappealing. Ziegfeld was non-committal and chastised Jimmy for sending him a 'dog.' Jimmy advised Norma to do something about her eye and to cap her teeth.

She landed a part in *The Flapper*, her first silent film. She haughtily informed the assistant director that she needed better clothes so she asked for $100 that she used for a simple operation that disguised the cast and careful makeup concealed the imperfection.

She got some bit parts and began to get modeling jobs with Rolf Armstrong, a famous illustrator and artist. She soon got her teeth capped and wore braces for a time. Soon she was posing for Kelly-Springfield and her face peered out from behind tires that were plastered on billboards all over. She was dubbed 'Miss Lotta Miles.'

She got jobs for toothpaste, housecoat and rouge ads. She claims she mastered facial expression from the men who photographed her. Norma resorted to playing the piano in movie houses when modeling jobs ran dry but she did not have a union card. She had some distinctive portrait photographs made by Arnold Genthe at this time on spec complete with a pay later plan. They never helped but opportunities soon came.

A talent agent named Eddie Small signed Norma. She appeared in *The Sign on the Door* but the film did not appear until 1921. She had a substantial part in *The Stealers* that attracted the notice of a young Irving Thalberg of Universal Studios in California. He contacted her agent who felt his proposal did not warrant the expense of travelling to Los Angeles but Norma thanked him anyway.

Norma appeared in her first leading role in *The Man Who Paid* opposite Wilfred Lytell in 1922. Again Thalberg made note and began keeping a file on her for he felt she didn't look or act like anyone else. Various trade papers heralded her as a girl with beauty and screen personality. Her next film was *The Bootleggers*. Her leading man was Channing who made advances and she dated him for a time much to her mother's dismay. When he suggested candlelight dinner at his place her mother put down her foot.

Jimmy Quirk, who published *Photoplay*, was married but was enamoured by Miss Shearer. He helped her career immensely. He eventually divorced his wife and married the beautiful silent-film star May Allison.

In 1923 the Shearer's moved to Hollywood under contract to Louis B. Mayer. Norma met the 'Boy Genius', Irving Thalberg, who was frail, often bedridden and had a rheumatic heart condition however he was immensely creative, literate and intelligent. Norma thought he was an office boy but he soon set her straight. She was loaned out to a firm called Iroquois to do *The Devil's Partner*. She appeared in her first Mayer film *Pleasure Mad*. She was loaned out again to do *The Wanters, Lucretia Lombard, The Trail of Law* and *The Wolf Man*. She was heralded as having done her best work to date in *Broadway After Dark* in 1924 and was in *Broken Barriers*, the first film to carry the official Goldwyn logo. Critics went all out in their praise of Shearer for her role in *He Who Gets Slapped*.

Norma developed a crush on Victor Fleming, the director of *Empty Hands*. He was part Cherokee and the ladies found him irresistible.

Norma showed her versatility in the delightful comedy *Excuse Me* in 1925. She was now twenty-four years old and seemed to fall in love with one handsome actor after another. Her mother kept her on a short leash and she began to rebel. She gave another moving performance in *Lady of the Night*. She was farmed out to do a Jack Pickford film called *Waking Up the Town* and she appeared with Mary Pickford's brother in a film that reviewers declared put the town to sleep. Jack Pickford was smitten with Norma and pursued her relentlessly for a time but he was a heavy drinker, was rumoured to take drugs and Norma was afraid of him.

On the set of *Pretty Ladies* in 1925 she met Lucille LeSueur who would become better known as Joan Crawford. They would both go on to prestigious films and their running feud, whether actual or publicity inspired, sold a wealth of news copies in the subsequent years.

Norma introduced her brother, Douglas, to Louis B. Mayer who was impressed with the young man's grasp of technical matters and his fascination with talking pictures. With the success of *The Jazz Singer* in 1927, Douglas was hired and would garner twelve Academy Awards for his work.

Norma was linked to a number of handsome leading men and many more chased her but it seemed the she couldn't snare the ones she seemed to want most. She was a first class tease and had her sights set very high but she tried not to lead a man on. She was honest from the beginning and found that if there was that spark it could be wonderful. As one gentleman said all who worked with her or knew her fell in love with her. Louella Parsons remarked, "Whatever man eventually gets her, and she has had the pick of the best in Hollywood, will be a lucky guy. She'll stick with him to the end..."

It was Irving Thalberg who fell in love with Norma and they married on September 29, 1927. Louis B. Mayer was the best man and his daughters Irene and Edith were bridesmaids. Norma felt she had no particular religious direction and converted to become an Orthodox Jew. They were both in agreement that Norma would continue her career because so much had been invested by both of them.

Norma's last silent film *A Lady of Chance* was released in December of 1928. The studio then began a quest to find a strong film to make her debut into the 'talkies.' They chose *The Trial of Mary Dugan*. Norma had her voice analysed and found it was pleasant, lilting and high-pitched but never the less distinctive and intriguing. Many silent film stars would become casualties of sound productions.

Norma urged her husband to pick up *Ex-Wife*. It was renamed *The Divorcee*. The book was not a classic but the movie was. For her role Norma received her first and only Oscar, which elevated her status making her one of the first ladies of the silver screen.

August 25, 1930 Norma had her first child they named Irving Thalberg, Jr. He would become an important part of her life though acting still was centre stage. She decided they needed their own home as they had been living with Irving's mother. They built a home in the French provincial style at the foot of the palisades in Santa Monica. Thalberg's mother Henrietta was very upset, indeed livid but Norma had her way in this regard.

Though it appeared she had everything Norma became the classic sex-starved wife. On screen she would kiss and hug and love and as soon as the producer called, "Cut!" she instantly turned it off like an iron butterfly. It was speculated that she conducted discreet affairs to ease her tension and afterwards felt guilty.

She fought tooth and nail to procure the rights to *A Free Soul* (1931) where she appeared with Clarke Gable. In her role Norma simmered, seethed and scintillated the audience. Lionel Barrymore won an Academy Award for his performance. The next year *Smilin' Through* won millions of hearts all over the country and abroad. Irving was at his height of power and influence when he suffered a heart attack in late December 1932. After recovering somewhat the family set out to vacation in Europe.

They were soon both back into the grind churning out films with Norma appearing in *Riptide* and *The Barretts of Wimpole Street*. Irving failed to underscore dramatic highlights with appropriate music that robs some of his best films of the emotional impact of the moment.

Norma had daughter Katharine in 1935. She then appeared amid a splendid cast that saw John Barrymore win an Oscar for his performance *Romeo and Juliet*. September 14, 1936 Irving suddenly died and Norma went into seclusion. She considered retiring but rose from the ashes like a phoenix taking the lead role in *Marie Antoinette* directed by Woody (One Take) Dyke. Norma was at her best for she rallied the cast and brought out the best performances she could and the film was shot in record time.

In the 1939 making of *The Women*, Norma recommended Joan Crawford as her love rival. It was an unusual film as there was not a single man in the production. It was a cat fight royal with Shearer's character telling Crawford's that what she is wearing was too vulgar for her husband's tastes to which Joan spits, "When Stephen doesn't like what I'm wearing I'll take it off."

Crawford asks, "But what about your pride?"

Norma replies, "Pride is a luxury a woman in love can't afford."

After the film Norma took some time to relax. When she went to New York she met George Raft. He allegedly had mob connections and seemed to be an unusual match for Miss Shearer. Their red-hot affair lasted through '39 and 40. Raft could not secure a divorce from his wife Grayce who sued him for half a million dollars. Norma put an end to the affair for her main concern was still her children.

She was like a lioness on the prowl, restless and anxious. She turned down roles in *Gone with the Wind, Pride and Prejudice* and later *Mrs. Miniver*.

Norma appeared in *Escape* (1940), a gripping spine-tingling story. She embraced the aging Russian star, Alla Nazimova, with a soul of kindness for she sensed tragedy in her life. With the war in full swing she did not want to have anything to do with tragedies and appeared in two comedies in 1942, *We Were Dancing* and *Her Cardboard Lover*. Always a perfectionist she insisted on camera angles and lighting to get her face as "snow white as possible." Both films were really trifles and unworthy of her enormous talent. They were comedowns from the great work she had done. There was no one to blame but herself and she did have the grace to admit it to others in later years.

That spring she took a trip with her children to Sun Valley, Idaho. There she met Martin Arrougae, a ski instructor. Though he was a shy unassertive man, he had a great physique and virility and was 14 years her junior. He didn't chase her letting her come to him. There was a mutual attraction and sexual excitement that led to a romantic fulfillment she had never known. She converted from the Jewish faith to Catholicism for him and Father John O'Donnell, the Padre of the Stars, married them August 24, 1942. In addition to the wedding band they both wore heart shaped rings with the inscription 'Everything leads me to thee.' Martin attended navigation school and became a naval aviator and was posted to Oakland, California.

Norma still had a financial interest in MGM and discovered Janet Leigh at the Sugar Bowl Ski Lodge and promoted her to the movie moguls. In the 50's she placed her mother in a sanatorium where she died in 1958 at eighty-five. Norma had to quit skiing in 1957 after suffering a severe leg fracture. Movie offers continued to come in but she said she was happily married, deeply contented and had more money than she would ever need. She continued to state that, "It was better to go, when I did, while still on top of things."

In 1971 she mourned the death of her brother Douglas. By 1976 Norma's health was failing. She had arterioscleroses and her eyes began to fail. In September of 1980 she entered the Motion Picture Country House and Lodge, the famous retirement hospital for film people in Woodland Hills, California. The brilliant charismatic star died June 12, 1983.

Joshua Slocum
1ˢᵗ to Sail Around the World Alone

Joshua Slocum was born in Annapolis Valley, Nova Scotia on February 20, 1844. He was the fifth child of a Loyalist family from New England. According to Joshua, his father, John, was an autocratic master in his boot factory. Joshua worked there but dreamed of sailing.

Joshua quickly tired of his father's tyranny and ran away from home. He became a cook on a schooner and then joined a deal drougher as an ordinary seaman. A *deal* was an old word for a slow awkward coastal vessel that sailed tons of rough-hewn pine and spruce. Much of the wood was destined for Britain and indeed Joshua sailed for Liverpool.

He studied and acquired the skills needed to navigate by sun, stars and compass and became confident handling rope and canvas. He learned how to repair broken spars. Through the 1860's and 70's he sailed the Atlantic, Caribbean, Pacific and South China Sea.

In 1871 he was in command of a ship that sailed to Australia where he met and married Virginia Albertina Walker. The captain of a vessel had their own private quarters and the right to bring their wife along on voyages if they wanted to. Virginia was a courageous woman who saved her husband's hide during a mutiny. She also bore a number of children and all were born on the high seas. He sailed around the world five times, commanded some of the finest ships afloat and at forty became the captain and part owner of *Northern Light*.

Things started to go sour on Joshua when he lost his share in the ship as well as his beloved wife in 1884. He married a distant cousin and took the *Aquidneck* to Brazil with a cargo of pianos. The ship wrecked off the coast of Brazil leaving Joshua penniless with an unhappy wife, two sons and no way to get home.

An experienced boat builder, Joshua salvaged what he could of the vessel from the rocks and with his sons help, built a seagoing canoe he named *Liberdada*. He sailed it 5,800 miles to Washington, D.C. then up the waters of the intercoastal waterway. He wrote a book about his experience in The *Voyage of the Liberdada*. His wife had all she could take and never sailed again. She decided to live inland with relatives, safely away from the water. Slocum's life was in shambles. He had no wife, no money and his profession of sailing was endangered by the advent to steam powered ships.

He heard that Herman Melville was coming to Massachusetts to give a reading from his novel *Typee*. Slocum loved to read and had already printed a book. After the reading Slocum was intrigued with the idea of sailing a ship around the world and then writing about the adventure. He considered applying for command and again eating his bread and butter on the sea. However there were not enough ships to go round besides nearly all the tall vessels had been cut down for coal-barges and were being ignoramiously towed by the nose from port to port. He could work at a shipyard but would have to pay fifty dollars to a society.

He met a whaling captain named Eben Pierce who had made a fortune in the industry. Pierce offered Slocum a rotting 100-year old oyster boat that was sitting in a field with trees growing through it. The derelict was called the *Spray*. The 39-foot sloop had a broad beam and good cabin space below.

Slocum decided to rebuild the decaying vessel. He soon had a steam box and began to rip the old planks off the frame. The old oak frame was as decayed as the exterior but Slocum got permission from some of the amused farmers about to cut down a few oak trees. It was a big project and to finance it he took odd jobs to feed himself and pay for the few articles he couldn't scrounge. It took thirteen months but when it was finished it had a prime white oak frame and was planked with 1 ½ inch thick Georgia pine. He confidently launched the *Spray* in the spring of 1894.

He spent a year fishing off the New England coast and put a little cash away. More importantly he got a feel for his new ship. He was delighted to discover that once he set a course he could lash down the wheel and the *Spray* would hold the course until the wind changed. This reduced the burdens for a single-handed fisherman but more importantly it would allow him to rest below and conserve his strength on the round the world journey he had decided he would embark upon.

Officially he launched his circumnavigation of the world from Fairhaven on April 24, 1895. He called on a few ports including Boston where he met the heiress of the Funk and Wagnell publishing empire, Mabel Wagnall. She promised to help with the book detailing his journey. She was enthusiastic about his travels and Slocum sent her letters from around the world.

He headed north to Brier Island, Nova Scotia where he had an eye for the ladies and took a few around the island. His sister at Westport gave him a big fruitcake before he departed. His tale is full of wonder and as a sailor he liked to tell stories that he no doubt embellished. His claims raised some scepticism in the sailing and navigation circles.

On July 2 he left Cape Sable in Nova Scotia and sailed into a fog so thick one could almost 'stand on it.' The *La Vaguisia of Vigo* passed him a bottle of good wine and a card along a line on the fifteenth. He passed *Java of Glasgow* in his little sloop and passing the great ship had an effect upon the captain somewhat akin to waving a red flag in front of a bull. He reached Fayal on the 20th and a young naval officer fearing for his safety offered his services as a pilot. He no doubt could have handled a man-of-war but the *Spray* was too small for the amount of uniform he wore. She was soon moored and the pilot expected 'gratification' which was not forth coming because Slocum's budget was nil.

He stopped at the Azores and painted his name, date and ship's name on the seawall and it is still carefully preserved there. He sailed to the Straits of Gibraltar and was welcomed by the British Navy who entertained him royally. He birthed among battle-ships like the *Collingwood, Balfleur* and *Cormorant*. Joshua claimed not even her Majesty's ships were as well looked after as the *Spray*.

He was invited on board the *H.M.S. Collingwood* but he hinted about his limited wardrobe. "You are expected, sir, in a stovepipe hat and clawhammer coat."

Joshua replied, "Then I can't come."

"Dash it! Come in what you have on; that is what we mean." He did and had a grand time and felt right at home.

Commander Reynolds warned him about pirates. On August 25 one of her Majesty's tugs helped him depart. He soon encountered a felucca that followed in his wake. Slocum changed course and the felucca did the same. They were sailing fast and the distance between them was growing less. Slocum piled on the sail carrying too much for safety. The distance shortened and he saw the tufts of hair on the head of the crew. The pirates were preparing to strike a blow. The exultation on their faces changed in an instant when they broached to on the crest of a great wave carrying too much sail. The same wave overtook the *Spray* and shook her in every timber. The main boom broke short on the rigging. Slocum sprang to the jib-halyards and instantly downed the jib. With the head-sail being off and the helm put hard down the sloop came in the wind with a bound. He secured the broken boom, not a stitch of the sail was broken. With the mainsail secured he hoisted the jib and stepped quickly to the cabin and snatched his loaded rifle and cartridges. Fortunately the wave and squall dismasted the felucca and the thieving crew were struggling to recover their rigging from the sea. By the time he had things in order for the dark he was too tired to cook and found he was too fatigued to sleep.

Another gale came on and the sea was discoloured with the reddish-brown dust from the African shore. He passed a number of ships and lamented there once was a time when they backed their topsails and had a 'gam' and on parting fired guns but the good old days were gone. He entered the doldrums and progress was painfully slow logging only three hundred miles in ten days.

On November 5 he arrived in Rio de Janeiro. December 11 he grounded on the coast of Uruguay and nearly drowned. At high tide he dislodged his sloop and sailed to Montevideo. It was over hauled in dry dock. Fortunately a British steamship agent picked up the expense in exchange for news of his adventure. They installed a makeshift stove contrived from a large iron drum. It would stand him good off the coast of Tierra del Fuego.

He entered the legendary waters through the Strait of Magellan on the southern tip of South America on February 11, 1896. This was the most harrowing experience of the entire voyage. Slocum was one of the earliest adventurers to have ventured into the Strait, being preceded by Ferdinand Magellan and Sir Francis Drake.

Going through a part of the strait required tacking into a howling wind. At night he navigated by sound. He cast anchor at Sandy Point after three days. He was advised about Indians who had recently massacred a schooner's crew. Samblich gave him some carpet-tacks to thwart anyone trying to come on board at night. He experienced terrific squalls called williwaws. He encountered natives in canoes who charged his sloop but Joshua fired shots narrowly missing them and they retreated. He had to weigh anchor in coves until gales blew themselves out. A Chilean gunboat *Huemel* came and towed him to Notch Cove. There was little life except for dogs owned by savages, a few shy seals and the odd steamboat duck. There was an abundance of mussels that were sumptuous. Never the less he was relieved to leave the towering piles of bleak granite mountains astern.

A savage storm pummelled the *Spray* but she was noble and brave in the mountainous seas. The mainsail was torn to rags and the squaressail on the boom was bent. Despite the pounding he did not have to pump once. Hail and sleet cut his flesh and blood trickled down his face. He passed the Milky Way and Thieves' Bay and that night when he weighed anchor he spread tacks on the deck making sure the 'business end' of a good number were up. That night around twelve o'clock he heard howls and he came on deck and fired several shot to let the rascals know he was home.

Joshua got out all his spare canvas and sewed the mainsail as best he could. He encountered the *Columbia* at Fortescue Bay and was provisioned with some cans of milk and cheese. At night he watched the steamer off and on just for the pleasure of seeing electric lights. It took seven attempts to clear the strait as he was driven back each time by bad weather and unfavourable winds. The last big wave broke over the *Spray* fore and aft on April 14 as he left Cape Horn in his wake. Finally there was an ocean unblemished by land.

Once clear he had favourable winds to Juan Fernandez Island, the site of the legendary Robinson Crusoe story. The trade winds pushed him on a course so steady he read, mended clothes, cooked meals and contemplated the universe.

July 16 he cast anchor at Apia in Samoa. Three young women welcomed him and sang. He visited the widow of Robert Louis Stevenson who gave him some of her husband's charts. Friends and admirers made sure he was well provisioned with fresh supplies.

He cast off for Australia on August 20. He reached Sydney October 10 and was soon sporting a new suit of sails compliments of Commodore Foy. He cast off for Melbourne and was charged tonnage dues, the only place on his voyage to do so. He squared the matter by charging people for coming on board. When his business waned he caught a twelve-foot shark to add to the entertainment. He made enough money to bank some. He gave lectures and was provisioned with jams and other preserves as well as bottles of raspberry wine. They hauled the *Spray* out in Devonport, Tasmania to make repairs but none was required though a coat of copper paint was applied.

It was April 16, 1897 when he weighed anchor and with winter blowing in he decided to reverse his direction and resume his course along the east coast of the continent. He experienced the 'rain of blood', which is the phenomena of fine dust from the deserts that mixes with rain and falls as mud.

From Sydney he sailed with a full set of admiralty sheet-charts of the Great Barrier Reef. He made Cookstown on May 31 and reported the warrior aborigines he saw in Queensland were lithe and fairly well built but with repulsive features and their women still more ill favoured.

After celebrating Queen Victoria's golden jubilee and being well fitted, on June 24 Slocum departed from Thursday Island with the trade winds holding steady. He wound by Booby Island where sailors stored provisions for shipwrecked and distressed wayfarers. There was also an improvised post-office where sailors dropped letters to catch the first homebound ship. The Arafura Sea had milky white water that glistened with a green and purple shimmer. At night on the last quarter of the moon the dark nights produced a phosphorescent light effect on the water that was breathtaking. Sea snakes slithered on the surface.

July 2 he sighted the island of Timor with Christmas Island sighted on the 11th. He saw terns the islanders call the 'pilot of Keeling Cocos' where he cast anchor July 17. He had run 2,700 miles in twenty-three days and spent only three hours at the helm. He stayed eight days at Rodriquez and arrived at Mauritius on the 19th. Had to muster all the crew for inspection and Slocum smiled while allowing them to board. With storms still raging off Cape Good Hope he was resolved to wait for better weather. Much to his delight he talked a small group of young girls into going sailing. They were gone two days and Slocum discovered they could hoist the sails like old tars and trim the sails too. They would clap a bonnet on the jib and could put the sloop in stays. No ship had a fairer or prettier crew.

The *Spray* set out to sea on October 26. On the 30 it was calm with a motionless sea and hushed world. By November 6 thunder and lightning precede a gale that lashed her as much as anywhere except Cape Horn. He arrived in Port Natal in Durban. Many were amazed that he sailed his sloop alone and some said it couldn't be done.

He met President Krüger of Transvall (now South Africa) and argued with him about whether the earth was flat or not. As they said in Australia he was "off on her alone" December 14. Christmas day the *Spray* was trying to stand on her head and while at the end of the bowsprit reefing the jib she ducked him three times and he did not like it a bit. He had never been put under so many times in such a short duration, three minutes. Gales kept blowing him back. When another threatened to blow he tucked into Simons Bay. After the hard weather he ran into calm under Table Mountain in South Africa.

He was towed into the Alfred Dry-docks in Cape Town and Slocum spent three months travelling the country being accorded a free railroad pass by the colonial government.

On March 26, 1898 he headed out into the south Atlantic. The *Spray* was happy to be leaping among the white horses, gambolling with the porpoises and sailing among her old friends the flying-fish. A booby with its harsh quack announced St. Helena where Napoleon spent his last dreary days in exile. He was given a goat that once it got his sea legs ate his charts of the Caribbean but he was so familiar with the area he didn't replace them. He cast the goat off at Ascension Island happy to be rid of it.

May 14 the *Spray* was overtaken by the *Oregon* that asked if there were any men-of-war about? War with Spain had been declared. Tobogo came into view and at night a sudden flash of breakers, not far off, startled Slocum. The current pushed toward them while he tacked without much altering the bearing of the danger. That's how matters stood for hour after hour as the flashes of light beat ever closer. He lamented the day he had allowed that damn goat on board. Alas he rejoiced when the flashes turned out to be Aladdin's lamp on the island of Trinidad that featured a great revolving beam of light. It was thirty miles away.

At Grenada and Antigua he was tendered free and audiences filled the hall to listen to him talk about the seas the *Spray* had crossed.

Then it was up that familiar coast when her sails flapped limp in a calm known as the horse latitudes. She bobbed like a cork for eight days and he saw three full rigged ships on the horizon also becalmed. As if to make up for lost time a gale began to blow on June 18. The *Spray* was jumping like a porpoise and seemed only to hit the high places. His rigging began to give out. The jib broke at the masthead and fell into the sea.

June 25 off Fire Island a storm with lightening and a tornado welcomed him home after it swept over New York City wrecking buildings and parted ships at docks from their moorings and smashed them against other one another.

The *Spray* with the now fabled lone Captain Slocum aboard eased into Harbour, Massachusetts on June 27, 1898. Many had assumed he was dead but he had just achieved what no other person had ever achieved, becoming the first to circumnavigate the world alone. His voyage had taken him 3 years, 2 months and 3 days. The culmination of his journey was the book he wrote *Sailing Alone Around the World*.

In 1901 he took the *Spray* to the Pan American Exposition in Buffalo, New York. He sold a small souvenir pamphlet and autographed pieces of cloth he cut from the tattered mainsail he'd used on the voyage. President William McKinley signed his logbook and was shot dead an hour later by an anarchist.

Slocum sailed Jamaica, the Bahamas and Caymans but the *Spray* was starting to look weathered and beaten. In 1908 he told President Theodore Roosevelt he planned to sail up the Orinoco to the headwaters of the Amazon. The old sea dog took off into a November gale and was never seen again.

Louis Slotin
Tickling the Dragon's Tail

Louis Slotin was born in Winnipeg, Manitoba on December 1, 1910. He received his Bachelor's and Master's degrees at the University of Manitoba in 1932 and received his doctorate from the University of London in 1936.

In 1942 Slotin became involved in the Manhattan (Nuclear Bomb) Project first assisting at Oak Ridge, Tennessee and then moving to New Mexico in December of 1944 where a secret laboratory was set up. He worked with such notable scientists as Robert Oppenheimer and Albert Einstein.

Slotin was a member of the critical assembly group who conducted experiments to establish the best method for assembling the central core of an atomic bomb. It was essential to determine the precise detonation point without actually reaching that critical threshold.

He conducted dozens of experiments successfully for he had the patience and courage to complete the assembly. The first experimental bomb was detonated July 16, 1945.

He couldn't be present because he was not an American.

On May 21, 1946 Slotin was demonstrating the perilous technique to his successor, Alvin Graves, at the secret Omega Site Laboratory in Pajarito Canyon, Los Alamos, New Mexico. The screwdriver slipped from between the two beryllium-coated plutonium spheres. They began to go supercritical and there was an instant blue glow and a wave of unbearable heat. Those present experienced a dry prickly sensation on their tongues, a sign of excessive radiation. Slotin grabbed the two spheres with his bare hands and wrenched them apart ending the chain reaction and soon the blue glow was gone as was the unbearable heat. Louis had received almost 1,000 rads of radiation and began to die.

His parents, Israel and Sonia, were flown in from Winnipeg to be with him. His hands were swollen, he suffered severe diarrhoea with diminished output of urine. He developed massive blisters on his hands and forearms, gangrene and a total disintegration of body functions. Nine days after the traumatic event Louis quietly died. He became an unsung hero. His parents, though opposed to autopsies due to their Jewish faith, allowed it for the sake of science of which their son was such a great part. His body was shipped home in a lead lined casket to Winnipeg where he was buried.

'Snoopy' was a Canadian
Roy Brown and Wop May

On November 23, 1916 Baron Manfred Albrecht von Richthofen downed Lanoe Hawker the #1 British ace. When he learned of his accomplishment he painted his plane red out of joy.

On January 4, 1917 the 'Red Baron' became the leading living German ace with 16 kills. He was awarded the *Orden Pour le Merite*, the 'Blue Max', Germany's highest military honour. Richthofen's red Albatros was making a name for itself among the Allies. He ordered his squadron, Jasta 11, to paint their planes red to camouflage his. The German propaganda machine worked it for all it was worth. Fan mail, mostly from adoring German women, arrived at the airfield. He became Germany's #1 war hero.

On July 6, 1917 the Baron had his closets call when a chance shot cut a 2-inch long groove in his skull. He was temporarily paralysed and blinded. Falling out of control he regained the use of his limbs a few thousand feet above the ground. He made an emergency landing and was transported to St. Nicholas' Hospital in Courtrai, Belgium. Against doctor's orders he put himself back on duty three weeks later. He was plagued by headaches and nausea while flying.

At the end of August the new Fokker F1 triplanes arrived. Richthofen was among the first to take them into combat. His kills mounted and despite pleas from his men and superiors he refused to 'retire.' With at least 80 kills to his name he was unquestionably the leading ace and his Flying Circus was the pride of the Imperial German Air Force.

'Bloody April' was a slaughter, as Jasta 11 alone accounted for 83 kills and 316 airmen lost. The Germans controlled the skies over the Somme battlefield.

On April 21, 1918 Roy Brown, captain of the 209th Squadron of the Royal Flying Corps, counselled 'Wop' May to stay out of the action during his first few sorties and just watch. He had less than twenty flying hours and no combat experience in a Sopwith Camel. Brown knew they would be up against some of the most experienced German pilots including the legendary Red Baron.

May however was a risk-taker and Brown's prudent warnings fell on deaf ears. When the battle ensued May joined in until his guns jammed, then he tried to dash for home. To the Baron, May looked like an easy kill so he took chase. Brown noticed the bright red trifolker take after the rookie so Roy broke away from the battle to try and help the rookie.

In the mean time Wop noticed he was being chased and was frightened. He flew close to the ground, skimming over the trees toward Morlancourt Ridge. The Red Baron anticipated the move and swung to cut May off. By now Brown had caught up and began firing as they passed over the ridge where numerous Australian ground troops opened fire. Everyone watched as the Baron's plane crashed.

When the soldiers realized who it was they ravaged the plane taking pieces as souvenirs. It was determined that a single bullet entered through the right side of the Baron's back and exited about two inches higher through his left chest. The ace of aces was dead and Roy Brown and Wop May's names went down in history. It has become a controversy as to whether Brown killed him or the Australian troops. The question, though explored on the television show *NOVA*, may never be fully answered.

For his efforts Roy Brown was awarded the Distinguished Service Cross Bar on June 21, 1918. It was his last victory for he was too valuable to be allowed to return to active combat duty. After the war he retired from the Royal Air Force (RAF) and went back to civilian life as an accountant. He started a small airline in Québec and Ontario that was reasonably successful but sold it when the Canadian government decided to get into the business. When World War II began he tried to enlist with the Royal Canadian Air Force (RCAF) but was rejected. He took a job as an advisory editor of the *Canadian Aviation* magazine. He gave it up on the advice of his doctor. He purchased a farm near Stouffeville, Ontario and turned it into a prosperous business. He died of a heart attack on March 9, 1944.

Wop May received the Distinguished Flying Cross and returned home a decorated hero. In 1920, Wop May and a friend named George Gorman flew two Junkers JL6 aircraft from New York to Edmonton a distance of 6,000 kilometres in the dead of winter, six years before Lindbergh flew across the Atlantic. Wop was a pioneering bush pilot and flew prospectors and supplies into northern locations.

In 1928 he married Vi Bode with whom he had a son. They would later also adopt another son. In 1929 there was a diphtheria outbreak at Little Red River, six hundred miles north Edmonton. Wop was asked if he could fly some anti-toxin in, he agreed without hesitation. It was 30 below zero and the whole area was deep in snow. Wop's Avro Avian was an open cockpit cloth-covered biplane on wheels, not skis. They wrapped the anti-toxin in woollen rugs around a little coal burner and placed it on the floor of the Avian to keep it from freezing. When word reached Edmonton that 'Wop' had made it and was on his way home it seemed all of Edmonton turned out to welcome him back from his historic flight. Vi, his wife was the first to welcome him and when she unwound the silk scarf covering his face the skin on his lips was frozen to it. You can see raw patches in the photograph, taken that day, where the skin came away from his lips. The story made its way around the world. In 1931 Wop was back in the news again as he flew supplies to RCMP officers who were on the trail of the Mad Trapper of Rat River. He spotted for them and when they finally killed the murderer he landed and took the body back to Aklavik along with an officer who had been wounded.

During World War II he was instrumental in the training of numerous pilots from around the world: Australia, New Zealand, South Africa and many from the United States. Just think what the young boys thought training under one of the men credited with downing the Red Baron.

After the war he was eventually hired by Canadian Pacific to help expand their overseas markets. Now his ports of call were Hong Kong, Tokyo and Bangkok instead of Aklavik, Snowdrift and Rat River. On June 22, 1952 while on a vacation with his son Denny, they were exploring the Timpanogos Caves near Provo, Utah when he died suddenly of a heart attack.

Springhill, Nova Scotia
Greatest Endurance Feat in Canadian History

Background:

One of the worst enemies of miners is the gas that they call firedamp, blackdamp and afterdamp. It can kill in and of itself but can also cause explosions. Ventilation is of vital importance in mines to reduce these risks. February 21, 1891 at 12:34 P.M. a cataclysmic gas explosion occurred and the force of the wind was like a tornado hurling timbers and clouds of dust through the dark passages. One hundred and twenty-five men died in the Springhill mine, as did seventeen husky little pit ponies.

Another mishap occurred November 1, 1956 when a section of a coal train broke loose on the Back Slope and rolled backward into the depths. It became airborne and scraped its cables along the roof of the mine igniting a standing haze of coal dust. A roaring fireball burst from the mouth of the mine shooting men high into the sky. A fiery cloud billowed into the air like a mushroom cloud. All the buildings that covered the No. 4 portal burned and some men were trapped in the burning buildings. The fires were quenched and volunteer rescue workers called draegermen, specially trained in the use of gas masks, groped their way down the main slope and many lives were saved. However 39 miners died that day.

Thursday October 23, 1958 8:06 P.M.

A beautiful Indian summer day bright and full of promise had passed. Springhill was infamous for 'bumps' (explosions) and on this day a bump rocked the #4 mineshaft at the Cumberland Rail & Coal Co. at 8:06 P.M. Before folks could catch their breath they heard another bang! as the rock floor rose and slammed into the one above it. The mine under them was in convulsions.

The miners worked the No. 2 mine around the clock and there were 174 men on duty that evening. According to the miners' code they had to believe someone was alive down there so it was their duty to go to their rescue. Soon the Wrecking Crew, a group of volunteers, assembled and prepared to rescue survivors.

Bowman Maddison in a panic grasped the water cans and dumped two buckets over his head to dispel the gas. He would come to regret this action in the days to come. Wails of men could be heard. Joe Holloway stumbled across the head of Hughie Guthro and he nearly had a heart attack. In terror Joe investigated and found Hughie was buried alive and with the help of Harold Brine they took on the task of freeing him. All the miners who survived and were not seriously injured were soon moving about in search of other survivors.

Within twenty minutes a dozen miners emerged limping, holding their arms, some bleeding from their noses and all wearing black masks of coal dust. Floyd Gilroy, Dr. Arnold Burden and others put on their breathing apparatus and descended into the depths.

Over the next few hours that stretched into days there was little sleep to be had as they returned time and again to the pit. Journalists arrived from Halifax and Toronto with cameras and lights.

Friday October 24 5:00 A.M.

By the early morning hours seventy-five survivors had been led or carried out to safety. They had reclaimed their brass tags from the board where children returned time and again to see if their father's were alive. Ninety-nine tags still dangled from the board.

The Red Cross, Salvation Army, Royal Canadian Legion, a fleet of ambulances and local restaurants provided services and food for the miners and their families at the pithead. Queen Elizabeth II sent her condolences and expressed her concern.

Journalists and photographers rushed to Springhill from around the world. They came from New York, Chicago, London and Paris to cover the story. There were one hundred and thirty-seven reporters on the site in short order.

Another five men were rescued and now 94 tags remained unclaimed. Pockets of gas and mountains of debris hampered the draegermen in their rescue efforts. As the days wore on, letters, cards and gifts arrived from around the world. Prayers were said for the coal miners trapped a mile underground in the deepest mine in the world at the time.

Saturday, a volunteer manager from New Glasgow arrived and announced that because the gas was up to 10%, rescue operations would be suspended. The draegermen took exception to his mandate and felt their time was well spent despite the danger for it was in the Miners' Code. The general manager of Dominion Steel and Coal Corporation, Harold Gordon, called a press conference and said, "I regret very much to have to tell you this. There is no hope, whatsoever, for any of the men who are on the 13,400 wall or the 13,800 wall."

Gordon's announcement was like a slap in the face to the crowd gathered at the pithead and it spread like wildfire throughout the community.

Life for the families of the 94 missing men became surreal. Sleep became a thing of the past. Night and day mingled and the only constant was an overwhelming sorrow. The community pitched in and steaming dishes of soup or stew magically materialized for the distressed families.

Sunday night on the *Ed Sullivan Show* comedian Shecky Green appeared and quipped, "You say you're hurt? Nah, you weren't hurt. That was soft coal!"

When Green came off the stage Sullivan was livid and said, "You are sick, sick, sick. You are the sickest son of a bitch I've ever known."

Little did the rescuers know that there was a group of twelve survivors. Joe McDonald was injured when the men pushed a fan off his broken leg. Ted Michniak and Fred Hunter were also injured. However Levi Milley, Eldred Lowther, Bowman Madison, Gorley Kempt, Caleb Rushton, Joe Holloway, Hughie Guthro, Harold Brine and Larry Leadbetter were shaken and had some minor injuries but were otherwise in good health. Elder and some of the others looked for a means of escape. Using the few tools at their disposal, the men found every route to be a dead end and their chances of clawing their way to freedom impossible. Still they tried and used up precious food and even more precious water as they frantically searched. Soon their lamps diminished and they became physically and emotionally spent.

There was another group of seven survivors in a shaft above Group 12. They included: Maurice Ruddick, Herb 'Pep' Pepperdine, Currie Smith, Garnet Clarke and Frank Hunter. However one survivor, Percy Rector, was caught by one arm in a standing slouch. He cried in agony, "Help me! Help me! Oh Jesus Christ!" He pleaded with the men who inspected the timber that held his arm in a vice grip. They took a saw and began to cut into the timber but it was holding the pocket from collapsing. Percy begged for them to cut off his arm but the men feared he would bleed to death before help arrived. As a result they did nothing while Percy was transformed into some kind of primeval animal screaming, "Aaaarrrrgggghhhh!" It was a pitiful sound that gurgled from his larynx. Some men covered their ears while others covered their eyes. As time moved along they shared their water and poor Percy's tongue would thrust about for water like a small wild frantic mouse bursting out of its hole and his sorrowful cries continued unabated. As the days passed his cries diminished and became a miserable moan.

Though some men had watches that glowed in the dark they lost track of days and they would speculate. It was 8:00 o'clock but was that A.M. or P.M., was it Sunday or Monday or Wednesday. As time ticked by they calculated their odds of getting out and turned to the state of their soul and the chances of getting a heavenly reward. It was hard to believe that in each other's company the misery seemed to be multiplied rather than diminished. All the water was gone and they began to chew on splinters of wood but their thirst drove them to the edge of insanity. The surface of their tongue, the papillae, seemed petrified and scraped against the roof of their mouth like bristles on a hairbrush.

They started to collect their urine and some began to wet their lips with it but found it repulsive. They found other's urine less offensive and they collected it in a communal pail and added some Tums. Each in turn was driven by their unquenchable thirst to wet their lips.

Tuesday October 28

Percy Rector stopped moaning and died. His corpse hung by his arm and thankfully in the darkness no one could see. The silence that his death brought was a relief to the men's long suffering ears.

Wednesday October 29 3:00 P.M.

Gorley Kempt and Harold Brine hear rescuers who were crawling on their bellies in search of survivors. They struck a pipe and yelled and screamed and they got a reply. The men became jubilant, hope burst like fireworks in July. Word was soon out that 12 men were alive at the 13,000-foot level. Like wildfire the word spread and school was dismissed and in no time throngs of people amass at the pithead sensing a miracle.

The men parched and fearing death by dehydration pleaded for water. The rescuers laid a copper pipe in and discovered they have 82 feet between them and the survivors. The men at the end of the pipe continued to cry for water. Soon their thirst was quenched and their animal instincts were quelled and the first slops of sugar-sweetened coffee relax the men and their souls seem to return.

Thursday October 30 4:20 A.M

When they finally break through the last of the debris the men are overwhelmed. They said it looked like a line of lights along the highway of life shining the way to the surface of the world. All twelve men are evacuated on stretchers and Floyd Gilroy and Dr. Burden were preparing to leave when they think they hear a noise but are not positive.

Friday October 31

His Royal Highness Prince Philip visits Nova Scotia after a trip to Ottawa and he goes straight to All Saints Hospital and visits the twelve miracle men for over an hour and a half.

Saturday November 1

A rescuer stumbles over a hole and finds a man who moans. He calls, "He's alive!" They excavate and find Barney Martin at death's doorstep in a semi-coma and severely dehydrated.

A well respected couple, Norma and Maurice Ruddick have 12 children, named: Colleen, Sylvia, Valerie, Alder, Ellen, Dean, Chuckie,

Revere, Leah, Jesse, Iris and newborn Katrina. Maurice is unwilling to just lay down and die. He rallies the men to pound on pans and make some noise. This time, much to their surprise, they get an immediate reply. Someone says, "How many there?"

"Seven," answers Currie gasping.

Soon lights are sweeping them and Jewkes cries, "It's like angels, angels."

John Calder calls, "Ruddick? You in there, Maurice?"

"I'm here."

"Man, the workmen's compensation board sent me down here specifically to get you out!"

"Why is that?"

In high spirits Calder said, "Why? They said they'd have to pay so much for your wife and twelve children, if we don't find you, there won't be enough for the others."

The last man is out by 8:45 P.M. There will be no more miracles but the town is joyous for the 19 who prevailed.

Reporters that had left the town flocked back to report the miracle but they find the men a quiet lot. One asks, "What was it like down there?"

"Well sir, I can tell you this - it was dark."

The final tally: 174 trapped, 75 died, 99 rescued.

November 5

Dr. Burden, Gorley Kempt and Caleb Rushton were were invited by Ed Sullivan to his show for he wanted to honour the heroes especially since he felt his comedian had done irreparable damage the previous Sunday.

November 6

The last body that of Fidel; was brought out and buried.

Somehow the story got out that Maurice said, "Give me a drink and I'll sing you a song." He didn't remember and could not confirm or deny the story. He was singled out for honours earning the Man of the Year in Canada for 1958.

November 18

All the miners and their children were invited for a week holiday sponsored by the state of Georgia. They were to be treated to a recently completed tourist development on Jekyll Island. Unfortunately in the segregated south at the time Mr. Ruddick and his family posed a problem as they were Negroes. Maurice said they would comply with rules and show that Canadians were above such discrimination. Maurice, his wife and children were segregated at the end of the island in a trailer hastily parked there. Never the less they all had a wonderful time.

Maurice and his family were entertained by the generous and loving coloured folk of Georgia. He felt it was like a homecoming. He was treated to Fats Domino, Little Richard, The Platters, Nat King Cole and Jackie Wilson's *'Lonely Teardrops'* on a record player of course. He was given record albums, hand-me-down clothing for the children and home-canned onion relish and peach jam. It was a time to remember and unprecedented in the annals of Canadian history.

Miners' Code

An unwritten miners' code is the cornerstone of their friendship and devotion to each other. They stick together and refused to give up on a man lost in the pit until he was brought up dead or alive. One basic principle is to believe in the possibility that men are still alive. Don't give up hope. The Springhill miners formed the first miners' union in 1879. They inspired the formation of the United Mine Workers of America.

Sam Steele
Lion of the Yukon

Sam Benfield Steele was born in Purbrook, Ontario on January 5, 1851. He enlisted in the Canadian militia in 1866 as an ensign in the 35th Battalion of Infantry. He participated in quelling the Fenian raids that year. He joined the 1st Ontario Battalion of Rifles on May 1, 1870. He served in the Red River Expedition that recaptured Fort Garry from the rebellious Métis under Louis Riel. In 1871 he left the army to enlist in the newly formed 'A' Battery of the Royal Canadian Artillery.

When the North-West Mounted Police (NWMP) formed in September 1873, he joined as a staff constable. With barely 300 men they were to uphold Canadian law over the Western wilderness populated by Indians, whisky traders and desperadoes on the run from the States.

Steele trained the young recruits teaching them how to ride. June 8, 1874 the NWMP began its westward trek with 275 men, 20 Métis scouts and two 9-pound cannons. There were torrential rains and hordes of mosquitoes. With a shortage of water and feed their mounts grew weak.

Sam wrote:
July 19, 1874 locust attacks eat the paint the wood on the wagons and carbines. Tents had to be packed away to save them from destruction

On July 25 they reached La Roche Percée and some inscribed the rock with their initials. Commissioner George French set up Fort McLeod while Inspector William Jarvis and Steele staggered on with their group of men to Fort Edmonton. They built their own post at Fort Saskatchewan.

Sam was promoted to chief constable in 1875 and given the rank of inspector in 1883. He oversaw and enforced an alcohol free zone as the tracks of the Canadian Pacific Railway (CPR) were laid across the prairies. In 1884 he established a new NWMP post at Beaver, also called Beaver Crossing or Beavermouth.

He was stricken with mountain fever and became bedridden. He still had to control the enraged men who had laid the CP rail track and had not been paid for an extended period of time. The disgruntled men were so startled to see the legendary Mountie that they stopped when he commanded, "Halt." The leader of the rowdy group, Hugh Behan, was dragged off to jail. Magistrate Johnston came out and read the Riot Act. Steele stepped forward and said if more than 12 men stood together or any large crowds assembled he would open fire. He demanded that they disperse. Steele's fever broke and in no time he was on his way to Calgary for the North-West Rebellion was raging.

Fortunately the influential Blackfoot Chief Crowfoot came out on the side of peace. However Poundmaker laid siege to the settlement of Battleford and looted the residences. Cree Chief Big Bear incited by the shaman, Wandering Spirit, attacked the hamlet of Frog Lake killing the Indian agent and eight others and took three survivors captive.

With the unfolding rebellion William van Horne, manager of the CPR mobilized the North-West Field Force, composed of the army, militia and Mounted Police. This move instilled confidence in the financial supporters of the railway and aided with its completion.

Steele joined Major General Thomas Strange and they marched from Calgary to Edmonton hoping to trap Big Bear's Cree. They engaged his clan of braves at Frenchman's Butte on May 28 and had to retreat. Sam and his Mounties followed Big Bear to Loon Lake and a brisk firefight ensued injuring three Mounties and killing four Cree. The Cree released the white prisoners and pleaded for the Red Coats not to shoot them. Soon the Cree were turning themselves in at Fort Pitt. Big Bear surrendered, July 2 at Fort Carlton 100 miles to the east.

The revolution was over. Louis Riel was hung November 16 as were eight Indians including Wandering Spirit on November 27.

Steele was promoted to superintendent. In 1887 he led 75 Mounties to British Columbia to settle a dispute with the Kootenai tribe. He built Fort Steele and stayed a year.

He married Marie Elizabeth Maye de Lotbinière Harwood of Vaudreuil in 1890. They had two daughters and one son. He was posted to the Klondike gold rush from 1896-98 and was in charge of the NWMP post on the White and Chilkoot Passes. Here it was said he 'patrolled the biggest beat in the world.'

He served during the Boer War and attained the rank of major general in 1914. With the outbreak of World War I Steele raised and trained the 2nd Canadian Division and accompanied them to England. He was not allowed to go to the front, instead he was placed in command of the Shorncliffe area in eastern England. Shortly after the war he was discharged. His retirement was short lived as he died January 13, 1919.

Sir William Stephenson
The Spy called 'Intrepid'

William Stephenson was an important clandestine agent during the war and was in a position where relatives, business associates and friends could become possible targets for reprisals, kidnapping and blackmail. For this reason and due to the nature of a spy agency that it is as involved with misinformation as well as real information, it is hard to know what is true and what isn't. There are a number of books on Stephenson including: *The Quiet Canadian* (1962) by Harford Hyde and *A Man Called Intrepid* (1983) by William Stevenson, who is not related. Bill Macdonald hoped to dispel some of the mistaken information in other books when he wrote *THE TRUE 'INTREPID' Sir William Stephenson and the Unknown Agents*. This the story of the master spy of World War II Intrepid.

William Samuel Stephenson was born William Samuel Clouston Stanger on January 23, 1887 in Winnipeg, Manitoba to Sarah and William. When his father died of progressive muscular atrophy in 1901 his mother fell into financial distress. William was cared for by his adoptive father named Vigfus Stephenson and his wife Kirsten. They were Icelandic Canadians. William soon took their surname.

William attended Argyle Elementary School and evidently had a photographic memory. He left school after grade six. He worked for the Sprague Lumber Yard and later worked as a telegram delivery boy for the Great North West Telegraph Company.

On December 3, 1913 a robber named John Krafchenko shot and killed H.M. Arnold, a local bank manager. Young Bill was instrumental in his capture. His job as a delivery boy took him all over the city and he identified the fugitive who was soon arrested.

January 12, 1916 Stephenson enlisted in the 101st Battalion, Winnipeg Light Infantry. He sailed to Britain on board the *SS Olympic* and arrived in Britain on July 6, 1916. He was soon transferred to the 17th battalion and sent to France in July 1916. He was wounded and gassed less than a week later. He returned to England and took courses in the theory of flight, internal combustion engines, communication and navigation during the year it took him to recuperate.

In April of 1917 he joined the Cadet Wing of the Royal Flying Corps and was soon a member of the 73rd Squadron. Only 5' 5" tall he won the featherweight boxing championship of the Inter Allied games and became friends with Gene Tunney. He was awarded the Military Cross and Distinguished Flying Cross in 1918. There is some controversy as to how many aircraft he shot down. Some say 12, others 18 and still another reports 26. What is known is he was shot down with a bullet through his leg. When he tried to escape he was shot again in the same leg and captured. He was interned at Holzminden. In prison he was impressed with an unusual can opener that he stole then escaped.

After the war he started a company called Franco-British Supply and marketed the can opener as Kleen Cut. With a partner he incorporated Stephenson-Russell Limited on February 2, 1921. They marketed various goods including the can opener. When they went bankrupt on August 13, 1922 Stephenson slipped out of town in the dark of night.

He surfaced in Britain and invested in the General Radio Company and Cox Cavendish Electrical Company Limited. He conducted research into wireless photography. He was the managing director of both companies by August 1923.

He returned to Canada and displayed his company's x-ray apparatus and radio sets at Toronto's Canadian National Exhibition. On his way home he met petite Mary French Simmons whose family were wealthy tobacco manufacturers from Springfield, Tennessee. He married her on July 22, 1924.

Mary ran a tobacco shop on Upper Street in London while William patented a wireless photography process and was a millionaire before he was thirty. He headed a mission of technical experts to India in 1934 and traveled to Afghanistan and Tibet covering some Himalayan trails on horseback.

In 1934 when his entry in the King's Cup air race won, he met German military and aviation officials. He learned about Nazis doctrine and the strategy of blitzkrieg. He reported his finding to British officials thus beginning his 'spy' career.

The Nazis began building aircraft in 1934 though forbidden by the Versailles Treaty. November 28 of that year Winston Churchill warned parliament of the threat. Some Brit's thought they were building 100 aircraft a year while Churchill claimed they were building 125 a month.

Stephenson joined the board of the Pressed Steel Company in the spring of 1936. With his numerous undertakings he came in touch with many of the great names of the twenties and thirties including: H.G. Wells, George Bernard Shaw and Greta Garbo and such politicians as Lord Beaverbrook and Winston Churchill. He was also associated with Reginald Mitchell and encouraged him to complete the Spitfire. He also assisted Fran Whittle's efforts to produce a jet engine.

Adolf Hitler came to power in 1933, occupied the Rhineland in 1936, marched into Austria and the Sudetenland in 1938 and was given Czechoslovakia by British Prime Minister Neville Chamberlain in 1939 proclaiming, "Peace in our time."

Albert Einstein fled Germany in August 1939 and warned about the possibility of an atomic bomb.

Stephenson's father Vigfus died in 1937 and his mother Kirsten in 1940. William did not attend either funeral.

When the Nazis invaded Poland September 1, 1939 it triggered the Second World War, so much for peace Neville. Joseph Kennedy thought the war was lost but President Theodore Roosevelt followed developments closely and corresponded with Winston Churchill who was First Lord of the Admiralty. Neither the United States nor Britain had a comprehensive intelligence service at the time. Military Intelligence 6 (MI6) was the British equivalent but it was far from effective. Churchill appointed Stephenson to the Office of Strategic Services.

The intelligence personnel in Britain did not know where Stephenson came from or where his authority began or ended. Admiral Sir Barry Domville, head of British Naval Intelligence, liked Hitler and was jailed during the war. The Earl of Cottnham left Military Intelligence 5 (MI5) because he could not accept war with Germany. Frederick Winterbotham the head of MI6's air section wanted Britain and Germany to unite against Russia.

In any event MI6 was circumvented when Roosevelt requested intelligence assistance. Churchill began casting lifelines to North America and he gave the rope to William Stephenson.

Stephenson contacted Gene Tunney who knew J. Edgar Hoover, the chief of the Federal Bureau of Investigation (FBI), and a clandestine meeting was arranged. Even the Ambassador from England was not informed. In April of 1940 he met with Hoover who insisted they get the president's approval. A lawyer named Ernest Cueno was the intermediary who set up a meeting with the President Franklin Roosevelt. It took place shortly there after and he was offered the position of Passport Control Officer of New York City.

Churchill became the prime minister of Britain on May 10, 1940. Stephenson's assignment was to do all that was not being done and could not be done by overt means to assure sufficient aid for Britain and eventually bring America into the war. As it turned out his first assignment was to obtain destroyers, aircraft, military supplies and equipment as the British were forced to leave most of their weaponry behind on the beaches of Dunkirk. General William Donovan went to

England to assess the situation. Stephenson characterized the trip as one of the most important missions in the history of western civilization.

Joseph Kennedy, the U.S. Ambassador to Britain, objected calling it the height of nonsense but he was ignored. Donovan reported the British would fight to the last ditch but could not hope to survive unless they got supplies from America. A deal was struck for the delivery of fifty mothballed American destroyers by August. Through covert operations Stephenson also obtained 100 Flying Fortresses, a million rifles, wireless equipment and a variety of other greatly needed equipment. Stephenson set up shop in the Rockefeller Center, which Nelson Rockefeller leased inexpensively as his contribution.

Stephenson recruited staff through newspaper ads. They were mainly Canadians and mostly women in the 1,000 recruits he hired. Who and what this large contingent of Canadians did in New York during the war still remains largely unknown. Stephenson took aim at the isolationists in America. There were nearly a million with such prominent people as Charles Lindberg in the fold. British Security Coordination (BSC) agents were dispatched all over the country to attend meetings, keep track of members, design and implement effective counter propaganda measures and harass members. Stephenson sought out sympathetic journalists and media moguls such as Walter Winchell and A.H. Sutzberg, president of the *New York Times*.

Donald Downes became an agent and discovered America First was receiving funds from the Nazis for activities in many cities including New York, Washington, Boston, Chicago and San Francisco.

President Roosevelt set up the Coordinator of Information (COI) and the Office of Strategic Services (OSS) as the U.S. intelligence network. Stephenson trained many of the agents in a parcel of farmland outside Whitby, Ontario in America's first spy school known as Camp X. They were taught self-defence, lock picking, map reading, codes, ciphers, listening devices, second story entry, explosives and a host of other pertinent skills. The camp became a communication centre linking, Washington, London, Ottawa and New York.

During the war Stephenson made as many as 43 trips to Britain but few are documented. In Bermuda British censorship intercepted letters and found invisible ink as well as the first micro-dot. The unit was very efficient and after the war analysing Nazi documents it was discovered that very little was missed.

Donovan made a trip to Yugoslavia with phoney papers that were prepared in New York. They were stolen and a revolution outraged Hitler who diverted many forces from the eastern front to subdue

Yugoslavia. As a result, the invasion of Russia was delayed by six weeks. Eventually the Soviet forces defeated the Nazis and a great deal of the credit goes to the Russian winter they encountered due to the delay instigated by the covert operation.

Stephenson was also the representative of the Special Operations Executive (SOE), that trained foreign nationals and organized numerous drops into occupied Europe. They slipped the Danish physicist Niels Bohr, a nuclear expert, out of Europe in a fishing boat away from the Nazis and he eventually worked on the Manhattan (Atomic Bomb) Project.

The BSC intercepted mail, which they covertly opened and closed. To decipher them they hired interpreters and linguists and provided them with all manner of books on Dutch, Portuguese, engineering and chemical terms, Who's Who, Banker's Almanac, directories from a host of countries and any other books relevant to uncover spies, saboteurs and other pertinent information.

Stephenson conferred with a variety of atomic scientists including: Albert Einstein and Chaim Weizmann. In 1941 Stephenson's job status was officially renamed Director of Security Coordination in the U.S.

Stephenson extended intelligence services to South America at the request of the FBI. One of his agents named Stagg discovered a large meeting at the German Legation in Bogotá, Columbia. Stagg, one of his men and his wife walked down the street. Stagg memorized the license plate numbers of every vehicle and was thus able to trace every car owner.

A letter was intercepted from the Bolivian Military Attaché in Berlin to the German minister in La Paz. It was altered to warn of a military coup aimed at overthrowing the president. The Bolivian government threw the German minister out of the country and broke off diplomatic relations. Bolivia was a major source of wolfram used in steel and arms production. Evidently after the letter was intercepted, it was forged and altered with fallacious information. It was then clandestinely planted to produce the desired results.

During the course of the war Stephenson had a hand in every intelligence operation there was including: MI6, MI5, BSC, COI, SOE, OSS, the Political Intelligence Department, Office of Naval Intelligence, the Security Executive and a Special Branch of Scotland Yard.

After the D-Day landings Stephenson was given some recognition for his contribution as he was knighted and awarded the

American Distinguished Service Medal though it was not made public until 1946.

Ian Fleming worked for Stephenson who had a pension for gadgets of every description and was undoubtedly the model for the 007 spy of movie fame.

After the war the files of the BSC were packed into semi-trailers and transported to Camp X. Grace Garner, Eleanor Fleming and Meryl Cameron cross-referenced the material. Tom Hill, Golber Hyatt, Roald Dahl and Montgomery Hyde wrote a history of the organization. Twenty copies were printed in Oshawa. It is often referred to as 'The Bible' and is still classified. It is one of the most astonishing documents in history. One went to Churchill and the heads of security intelligence organizations. Tom Hill held the remaining ten copies and eventually burned them. Stephenson regretted not keeping a copy for himself. None of the remaining ten copies have surfaced for more than a few hours.

In early September 1945 Stephenson heard about Igor Gouzenko (see Gouzenko) from Norman Robertson the Undersecretary of State in Canada's Department of External Affairs. The Soviet Embassy cipher clerk had defected but it seems the Canadian government of William Lyon Mackenzie King didn't want anything to do with Gouzenko as Russia was considered an ally. Stephenson intervened and Gouzenko and his wife were shuttled to Camp X where they were guarded in seclusion. He was the most important defector of the era and his revelations are often regarded as the beginning of the Cold War.

The Stephensons moved to Montego Bay, Jamaica. Here they entertained many guests and friends such as Noel Coward, Beaverbrook and Ian Fleming who bought residences on the island. In 1951 the Stephensons moved to New York and lived in an apartment above the recluse, Greta Garbo. He was one of the originators of the British American Canadian Corporation that was renamed World Commerce Corporation. It worked at getting around currency restrictions that slowed trade and helped develop poorer countries.

In the sixties Stephenson suffered a serious stroke that affected his speech. He fought back and soon there after retired with his wife to Bermuda. Pauline McGibbon, the Lieutenant-Governor of Ontario, visited Bermuda and heard Stephenson wanted to see her. They clicked and she visited him for many years after that.

Stephenson's beloved wife Mary died in 1977 from terminal cancer. In 1980 Governor-General Edward Schreyer traveled to Bermuda to present the Companion of the Order of Canada, a much-delayed award for the vital service he rendered. In 1983 he was awarded the

William J. Donovan medal and the ceremony took place on the aircraft carrier *USS Intrepid*.

Stephenson died January 31, 1989 in Bermuda. His adopted daughter Elizabeth, with her son Rhys, were present along with four other people.

Dorothy Stratton
Playboy Tragedy

Dorothy Hoogstratten was born in Vancouver, British Columbia, February 1960. At seventeen Paul Snider spotted her at a Dairy Queen serving ice cream. Nine years her senior, he courted her intensely and they got married in Las Vegas in June of 1979. He convinced her to send her pictures to *Playboy* in Los Angeles. Hugh Hefner sent for her only two days after seeing her pinups. He took an immediate liking to her and she became the October '79 Playmate. Hef took an immediate disliking to the greasy Snider so he decided to introduce her to some of the upper echelons of Hollywood society.

At one mansion party Hugh introduced her to filmmaker Peter Bogdanovich who directed/produced hits like *Paper Moon*. He had recently ended a relationship with Cybill Sheperd. The two hit it off immediately and he was going to make her a star.

Snider, out of his mind with jealousy, forbade her from drinking coffee and poisoned her dog for he thought it took too much of her attention. He even hired a private detective to follow her around. Their relationship was seriously deteriorating and Dorothy moved in with Bogdanovich in Bel Air.

Dorothy was honoured as Playmate of the Year in the June 1980 *Playboy* issue.

On August 14th, 1980 she agreed to meet with Snider at an apartment he was sharing with Dr. Stephen Cushner and some other roommates. She flew all the way from New York where she was filming *They All Laughed*, directed by Bogdanovich. She had withdrawn $1,000 cash to give to Snider hoping to settle their split once and for all. At 12:30 the private investigator called Paul and was informed that, "Everything was going fine."

At five in the afternoon two female occupants who also shared the apartment came home and noticed their vehicles but assumed they wanted privacy. At 7:00 P.M. Dr. Cushner arrived home and also gave them their privacy. At around 11:00 the investigator called the doctor and suggested they take a peek into the room. Did they get a cruel surprise.

The police arrived at 12:30 A.M. Dorothy was laying across a low waterbed with ants crawling all over her. A blast from a 12-gauge Mossberg shotgun blew her face off and she was missing the tip of her left index finger. He then turned the gun on himself and blew out his brains.

Dorothy was cremated and buried August 19th, at Westwood Memorial Park.

There are two films about her tragic life: *Death of a Centrefold* and *Star 80*.

Maurice Strong
Custodian of the Planet

Maurice Frederick Strong was born in Oak Island, Manitoba on April 29, 1929, the first child of Frederick and Mary. Times were hard during the depression especially when his dad lost his job with the Canadian Pacific Railway. Maurice was an excellent student and skipped four grades. He also liked to skip school and go to a large hole he dug in the side of a hill he called the 'dungeon.' Here he would watch the animals pass by, it was his initiation to ecology.

He ran away from home and tried to enlist in the Army in 1943 with World War II raging. He was too young and was sent home agreeing he would complete high school. Upon graduation he was off again getting a job with the Hudson's Bay Company at Chersterfield Inlet in the Northwest Territories. He was fascinated with the Inuit. Unhappy with the way his boss treated the natives he left the trading post and moved in with an Inuit family. He learned their language and met Bill Richardson who was looking for valuable rocks. They became friends and Richardson offered Maurice a job in Toronto. Bill's wife introduced him to Noah Monod, a Frenchman who was an official at the newly formed United Nations (U.N.), a world organization dedicated to ending poverty and promoting world peace. Strong's imagination was fired and with Noah's help he got a job at the U.N.'s headquarters in Queens, New York.

Though his job was simply to supply delegates with pencils, paper and such items he was convinced that his future lay with the U.N. Lacking qualifications he quit and returned to Toronto. Having grown up poor he was deeply prejudiced against business.

Maurice married Pauline in 1950 and they spent two years travelling the world. He was sympathetic with the Mau Mau cause in Kenya in 1953. He learned Swahili and would talk to people and listen to their hopes and fears. Working with Bill Richardson he found he had a real knack for business. Climbing quickly he was president of the Power Corporation by thirty-five.

In 1966 he left the business world and became the head of Canada's External Aid Office. He reorganized the office, doubled the aid to foreign countries to $80 million and renamed it the Canadian International Development Agency (CIDA).

In the 60's the world was changing. In the last sixty years the population of the earth had almost doubled from 1.61 to 3.02 billion. This put an enormous strain on the earth's wildlife and natural resources.

Problems arose like smog, dying lakes and rivers, over population and endangered species. From this sprang organizations to protect the ecology like Greenpeace and the World Wildlife Fund.

In Sweden in 1967 as they switched from driving on the left side of the road to the right meant stopping traffic for a while in various parts of the country. Swedes were astonished when the air became clearer. Swedish diplomats persuaded the U.N. to hold its first meeting on the environment.

In the spring of 1972 the U.N. Conference on the Human Environment was convened in Stockholm, Sweden. The man who was the secretary-general of the conference was Maurice Strong.

For seventeen months prior to the conference Maurice traveled the world talking to presidents, prime ministers and other powerful people. He asked scientists to prepare reports on the state of the environment in their country. Many countries were reluctant to even attend the conference. Brazil for example feared it would stop them from developing the Amazon River Basin. Other countries had similar concerns. Strong weighted in and by the time the conference opened he was considered an important environmentalist.

June 5, 1972 the conference opened with 1,200 delegates from 130 nations. More than 1,500 journalists were present and the conference made headlines around the world. Maurice personally spoke of polluted oceans, the destruction of forests, loss of animal life, global warming and the 'greenhouse effect.' It awoke many nations to environmental and ecological concerns.

The conference spawned the creation of a new organization called the U.N. Environment Program (UNEP). Strong was chosen to head the program and opened the UNEP October 2, 1973. Forest rangers and game wardens marched by and when the trumpets died Jomo Kenyatta, president of Kenya shouted, "Harambee", which is a Swahili word meaning 'lets pull together.' Maurice over saw many projects like Earthwatch and helped enforce the Ocean Dumping Convention that calls for an end to dumping hazardous wastes and toxic chemicals into the ocean.

After four years he resigned and returned to Canada and joined the government of Pierre Elliot Trudeau. He set up Petro-Canada then moved on to other jobs.

In 1985 the U.N. called again. Central Africa was in crisis with war and famine. Strong helped raise $4 billion and managed the difficult task of getting the food and supplies to those who desperately needed them. He confronted hostile leaders and found the suffering in Africa was much worse than the Great Depression he endured. People were so underfed they looked like living skeletons and a million perished. U.N. relief saved millions more. The land there was too stressed. They had cut down large expanses of forest for firewood. The soil turned to a hard crust that couldn't grow crops. Strong encouraged African governments to stop cutting trees.

Strong returned to his second wife Hanne Marstrand and their large piece of land in southern Colorado. They have five children including a foster child from Hungary.

He was a tireless worker for the environment and planned the Earth Summit that opened on June 3, 1992 in Rio de Janeiro, Brazil. It was the largest gathering of world leaders in history. It looked like the conference would collapse when the arguments grew so heated. The Roman Catholic Church objected to an agreement on population control because it involved birth control. As a master negotiator Strong helped settle disputes. In the end most delegates signed a treaty concerned with global warming with the aim to control the production of greenhouse gases like methane and carbon dioxide. The second was to protect the planet's biodiversity and protect wildlife habitats around the planet. The third major accomplishment was the creation of a new U.N. commission on sustainable development.

His impact has been so enormous that the *New York Times* hailed him as the 'the custodian of the planet.' He has been a tireless worker for our precious planet.

Superlative Canadian Geography

Physically Canada is the world's second largest country with an area of 9,976,139 square kilometres. The Soviet Union once was 22,402,000 square kilometres but is now said to be 17,075,400 square kilometres. Some areas of their still vast country, would like to leave their control like the Chetchens and vast areas are little populated like Siberia and Mongolia.

Canada's population was 31,700,020 in 2005 with a population density of 3.1 people per square kilometre. Russia, with a population of 144,500,000 in 2003 has a density of 8.4 people per square kilometre thus making Canada one of the largest least densely populated countries in the world. Australia at 7,690,000 square kilometres has a density of 2.5 people per square kilometre and challenges our supremacy in this regard.

Canadians are privileged to live in a country with plenty of free wide-open spaces filled with an abundance of wildlife. Canada is relatively young being born July 1, 1867. Strategically placed between the super powers, Russia and the United States of America, Canada has been a leading nation to champion the cause of 'world peace.'

Few Canadians know very much about this great country that shares the longest undefended border in the world with the United States of America. Given its size, Canada has numerous geographical superlatives. In fact Prime Minister William Lyon Mackenzie King remarked,

"Some countries have too much history, Canada has too much geography!"

Alert, Northwest Territories - world's northernmost habitation, is only 800 kilometres from the North Pole

Athabasca Tar Sands, Alberta - one of the world's largest oil deposits, major oil reserve development, billions invested, 350,000 barrels per day produced 2006

Baffin Island, Northwest Territories - fifth largest island in world at 507,000 square kilometres

Bathurst Island, Northwest Territories - present location of the North Magnetic Pole which moves 24 kilometres per year

Bay of Fundy, Nova Scotia - world's highest tides at 15 metres

Calgary Stampede, Alberta - world's largest rodeo inaugurated in 1912

CN Tower, Toronto, Ontario - was the world's tallest freestanding structure at 553.3 metres, completed 1997

Campbell River, British Columbia - 'Salmon Capital of the World'

Canada - 'The Bread Basket of the World'

Capilano Suspension Bridge, Vancouver, British Columbia - world's longest at 135 metres, built 1899

Columbia Icefields, Alberta - hydrographic centre of North America, Columbia River flows to Pacific, North Saskatchewan River flows to Hudson Bay and Athabasca River flows to the Arctic Ocean

Davis Strait - widest strait in the world at 965 kilometres, between Baffin Island andGreenland, named in honour of John Davis who sailed it in 1587

Della Falls, British Columbia - Canada's highest waterfall at 440 metres, southern edge of Strathcona Provincial Park on Vancouver Island, discovered in 1899 by Joe Drinkwater and named after his wife

Dinosaur Provincial Park, Alberta - 1979 UNESCO named it a world heritage site

Elliot Lake, Ontario - world's largest uranium deposit discovered in 1952

Esterhazy, Saskatchewan - 'Potash Capital of the World'

Great Lakes system - largest reserve of freshwater in the world

Hartland, New Brunswick - world's longest covered bridge at 391 metres

Hudson Bay - bay with the world's longest coastline at 12,190 kilometres and is the second largest bay in the world at 822,352 square kilometres, Bay of Bengal is the largest

Isle de Bonaventure, Québec - one of the world's largest operating windmill at 36.5 metres

Lake Superior, Ontario - largest freshwater lake in area in the world at 18,024 square kilometres, not the largest by volume, Lake Bakyal, Russia has that honor

Mackenzie River - Canada's longest at 4,241 kilometres

Manitoulin Island, Ontario - largest freshwater island in the world at 2,766 square kilometres

Manitoulin Lake, Ontario - world's largest lake on an island in a lake

Mica Dam, British Columbia - 6th highest in the world at 242 metres, Canada's highest

Montreal, Québec - is the second largest French-speaking city in the world

Mount Logan, Yukon - Canada's highest mountain at 5,595 metres

Mount MacDonald Tunnel, British Columbia - spiral tunnel 14.7 km, longest in North America

Nanaimo, British Columbia - 'Bathtub Capital of the World'

Niagara Falls, Ontario - 3rd largest waterfall in the world in volume of flow, 6,000 cubic m/sec, Sete Quedas, Brazil/Paraguay 50,000 cu m/sec and seven falls of Guiara Brazil/Paraguay larger, Canada's Horseshoe Falls, 670 metres wide and 54 metres high

Shediac, New Brunswick - 'Lobster Capital of the World'

Signal Hill, Newfoundland - Marconi received the first trans-Atlantic message in 1901

Slingsby Channel, British Columbia - has the world's strongest current at 16 knots

Sudbury, Ontario - 'Nickel Capital of the World'

Trans-Canada Highway - is the longest paved road in the world at 7,280 kilometres

Wapusk National Park, Manitoba - one of the largest denning areas for polar bears in the world, est 1996

Wasaga Beach, Ontario - claims to be the longest and safest in the world at 14 kilometres

Wood Buffalo National Park, Alberta/Northwest Territories - is the largest park in the world at 44,807 square kilometres

All this in Canada you say…really…

David Suzuki
Environmental Guru

David Suzuki was born in Vancouver, British Columbia on March 24, 1936 and lived in the back of his parent's dry cleaning shop. Because his parents were Japanese they were relocated to an internment camp in Slocan, B.C. during World War II. During their incarceration David was alienated from his peers because he could not speak Japanese. After the war they relocated to Lemington, Ontario.

He studied at the University of Amherst and Chicago where he received his PhD in 1961. He did his doctoral thesis examining the chromosomal crossover of the fruit fly. He had a passion for genetics and became a professor at the University of Alberta in 1963. A year later he became Professor of Zoology at the University of British Columbia. David bred a mutant fruit fly strain that died when the temperature reached 29° C. It was a breakthrough in biological pest control as they would breed and produce offspring that would die during the first hot spell.

In 1971 he hosted the television series *Suzuki on Science*. He appeared on shows like *Quirks and Quarks*, *Earthwatch* and *Discovery*. It was the television series *Planet for the Taking* in 1985 that confirmed his belief that the biggest threat to the human species is its own desecration of the environment. He wrote *Metamorphosis* 1987 and is the host of *The Nature of Things* that is broadcast in more than fifty countries.

David was married to Setsucko Joane Sunahara from 1958-65 and had three children Tamiko, Laura and Troy. He married Elizabeth Cullis in 1972 and they have two daughters Sarika and Severn.

He has become a leading environmentalist and one of the most recognized Canadians on the planet. In a 2004 Canadian poll he was voted the 5th greatest Canadian.

Frederick 'Cyclone' Taylor

Frederick Wellington Taylor was born on June 24, 1884 in Tara, Ontario. He was the second son and fourth child of Mary and Archie Taylor. He was named after the town veterinarian. His father was a travelling salesman for the Cockshutt Company of Brantford.

When he was five years old he borrowed his sister Harriet's clamp skates and went skating under the eye of Jack Riggs, the town barber, famed throughout the region as an outstanding speed skater. Riggs gave young Fred the first skates he ever owned for his sixth birthday. In 1891 the family moved to Listowel and Fred continued to learn to skate on Maitland Lake. At age 17 he lead the Listowel Mintos to a second league championship when he quit school and went to work in the local piano factory for $5 per week. In October 1903 Fred was contacted by Billy Taylor of the Ontario Hockey Association who asked him to play for the Marlboros but he refused the invitation. Billy was offended and vowed that Fred would not play anywhere. Taylor sat out the season and never forgave him.

In 1905 Fred accepted an invitation to play for Portage la Prairie of the Manitoba Hockey League. He played for room and board plus $25 per month pocket money. Near the end of the Canadian season an American team in Houghton gave him a call and he joined them January 30, 1906. He was an immediate success and stole the headlines. In one of the last games of the season he scored 3 goals to help Portage Lake defeat Pittsburgh 3-2. Honus Wagner, a baseball superstar, saw Taylor and said was as fine an athlete as he had ever seen.

The next season Taylor negotiated a contract with the Ottawa Senators for $500 and a job in the Immigration Department at $35 per month. It was here he met Thirza Cook who later became his wife. The Senators lost that year to the Montreal Wanderers who went on to defeat Toronto St. Pats for the Stanley Cup. It was in Ottawa that Governor General Earl Grey gave him his nickname 'Cyclone.' He was named to the All-Star team. The Senators and Wanderers were invited to New York to play in the Big Apple. The *New York Times* headline was: TAYLOR MAGNIFICENT. Every time he touched the puck he received a thunderous ovation. He was called 'Little Jeff' for his resemblance to Jim Jeffries the heavyweight-boxing champion of the world.

At this time Cyclone became a Scoutmaster and his troop was the eighth in Canada. In 1908-9 Cyclone sustained a nasty 3" gash in his right foot from a skate while leading the Ottawa Senators to a successful year. Interestingly enough they won the Stanley Cup by default.

In 1909-10 two leagues, the Canadian Hockey Association and the National Hockey Association of Canada vied for Cyclone's services. He signed with the Renfrews, known as the Millionaires, for $5,250 and a steady job, for twelve games. By comparison Ty Cobb, the brightest star in baseball, had a salary of $6,500 for a seven-month season and 154 games.

When the Renfrews went to Ottawa to play the Senators, Cyclone was reported to have said he could score a goal skating backwards against them. The fans bombarded him with boos, hisses, bottles, pennies, fruit, etc. He was cool as a cucumber, brilliant at times but did not score in their 8-5 loss. Cyclone was the first to congratulate the winners. Three weeks later at home in Renfrew, Newsy Lalonde bagged six goals in a 17-2 blowout but Cyclone stole the headlines again. He scored but one goal when he stole the puck, sped down the boards past the defence, wheeled and skating backwards for the last few strides and flipped a backhand past the startled goalie Leseur. With a season of 8 wins and 3 losses they placed 3rd and the Wanderers went on to win the Stanley Cup. After receiving a tremendous welcome in New York, the Renfrews beat the Wanderers 9-4 in an exhibition game and again Cyclone stole the ink.

In the 1910-11 season the Ottawa Senators won the Stanley Cup and the Renfrews folded. Cyclone was invited to the Big Apple to play for the Senators because the invitation was conditional that Cyclone be on one of the squads. The Senators swept the Wanderers in both New York and Boston where Cyclone once again captured headlines:

TAYLOR'S CYCLONIC RUSHES ELECTRIFIED AUDIENCE

With the Renfrews disbanded there was a draft and the Montreal Wanderers picked up Cyclone. Ottawa immediately asked to purchase his rights but Sam Lichtenhein wouldn't sell. Cyclone had purchased a house in Ottawa and the rebel that he was said he would not go to Montreal. He sat out another season but made a full season's salary of $1,200 and set a new high in salaries for no work at all.

In 1913 Cyclone joined the Vancouver Millionaires. On March 24, 1914 Immigration Officer Frederick Taylor boarded the *Komagra Maru* in Vancouver harbour. A new federal law curbing Chinese, Japanese and East Indian immigration into Canada had recently been passed. Taylor took his turn aboard the ship while tempers flared. Finally on July 23 the *Rainbow* chased the *Komagra Maru* out of the harbour.

In the 1915-16 season the Vancouver Millionaires won the Stanley Cup. Cyclone played until 1921 and won five scoring championships. He played brilliantly but failed to win the Stanley Cup again. Despite an injury that hampered his play, Cyclone scored three goals in his last game to go out like a true champion.

Cyclone and Thirza had five children, Frederick, John, Edward, Mary and Joan. He retired gracefully and resided in Vancouver. He toured the world as a hockey ambassador. Cyclone is a hockey legend and the first 'star' to fiercely fight for his right to negotiate a fair contract.

Cyclone died June 10, 1969.

The Water Rats
The Taking of the Scheldt Estuary

In 1944 the German resistance stiffened with their backs to the wall. Supplies became a big problem for there weren't enough ports to handle the supplies required by the vast armies on the continent. The port of Antwerp was captured in tact but it was useless as long as the Germans controlled the Scheldt Estuary. This is an ugly piece of land that is more river, bog and mire than anything. It was given to the Canadians to secure. The men who did the job became known as the Water Rats. The esteemed soldier named Ben Dunkelman (see Dunkelman), known as 'Mr. Mortar', took part in the mission. In a mere five weeks the Canadian First Army suffered 6,500 casualties. The first ship to bring its cargo to Antwerp was the Canadian-built *Fort Cataraqui*.

Field-Marshal Bernard Montgomery said, "The Canadians have proved themselves magnificent fighters. Clearing the Scheldt was a job that could have been done only by first-rate troops. Second-rate would have failed."

Sir John Thompson
Prime Minister who died in Queen Victoria's Castle

John Sparrow David Thompson was born in Halifax, Nova Scotia on November 10, 1844. He was the youngest of seven children given birth by Charlotte and her Irish husband John. He articled for the bar under Henry Pryor and was called in 1865. John, a Protestant, married Annie Affleck, a Roman Catholic, on July 5, 1870. They lived with John's mother and sister. He became a Roman Catholic some time later. They would have two sons and three daughters while four other children died in infancy. Though reluctant to enter politics he went from alderman in 1871, to provincial attorney-general in 1878, to premier of Nova Scotia in 1882; but his government was defeated in that years election.

By this time the 5' 7" man weighed 180 pounds and his eating habits were less than ideal as he loved coconut caramels. He was handsome but his waistline had begun to bulge. Still he was a man on the move, had charm and was known for dealing with things in a fair manner with an Irish wit that bordered on sarcasm. Politics seemed to take him away from home far too often and as a result there is a treasure trove of correspondence between him and his wife.

He was appointed to the Supreme Court of Nova Scotia and three years later Prime Minister John A. Macdonald persuaded Thompson to take the Justice Portfolio. He ran in the federal by-election in Antigonish and won. He represented Canada, negotiating fishing rights and copyright laws with Britain and the United States.

On August 28, 1888 Lord Salisbury cabled, "The Queen has been pleased to confer on you a Knight Commandership…in recognition of your services at the Conference at Washington." Thompson was both surprised and delighted though he consulted Sir John A. Macdonald who encouraged his acceptance, which he did.

Sir John Thompson shouldered more and more responsibility. He undertook the huge task of revising the Criminal Code of Canada and getting it passed by the House.

Over the years Macdonald had come to rely upon Thompson for the way he wrote laws as they were more coherent, more compact and tougher than Macdonald's. Their relationship was warm and slowly over time the accumulation of trust brought the men closer together. They admired each other and it could even be said they were affectionate friends.

When Macdonald died on June 6, 1891 many thought Thompson would accept the party leadership but he declined. John Abbott served but due to health problems soon fell ill and was forced to resign on November 24. Thompson reluctantly took the reigns of power December 5, 1892 and became Canada's first Roman Catholic prime minister.

The Thompsons were very busy entertaining with various state dinners at Rideau Hall and formal balls at Russell House. Annie even personally cooked dinner for 250 guests who dined at their house. She felt that things were in a "whirlwind." John was too generous and began to feel the economic crunch.

One of the first disputes was the education question and the role the church played. Legislation could affect every aspect of education including licensing of teachers, text books, history and even the kind of poetry taught as well as the prayers and religion. The Roman Catholic bishops demanded autonomy and strict guidelines. Thompson saw it more in legal terms and how the British North America Act applied. He felt the wrath of the Roman Catholics and Protestants alike. The sessions on the North-West school dispute drained Thompson's energy and the issue was put to rest with the defeat of D'Alton McCarthy's motion.

March 22, 1893, Sir John Thompson and his wife arrived in Paris. He negotiated the French Treaty that he said was "much ado about nothing." He sat for the French-Canadian sculptor Louis Phillippe Hèbert who was commissioned to make a white marble bust of Thompson, which now sits in the Nova Scotia Archives in Halifax.

Thompson negotiated with the United States over the seal hunt along the Alaska Panhandle. The arbitrated sixty-mile limit, seemed appalling but the $473,151.26 fine for recklessly seizing 17 Canadian vessels and their crews was fair compensation.

In 1894 when the Governor General's wife Lady Aberdeen started the National Council of Women he supported her wholeheartedly. Many men did not support the cause for it supported prohibition and women's suffrage.

Prison reform and tariffs were the hot topics of the day and on more than one occasion Thompson's patience was tried. Thompson felt prison should be a place not so much for punishment as reform. He also supported the idea of parole. Others felt the penal system was too lenient allowing the prisoners tobacco, as well plum pudding and cake at Christmas.

July 30 he took his family on a greatly needed holiday to Lake Rousseau. Thanks to George Eastman's new Kodak camera that used roll film, there are 'snapshots' of the Thompsons at this retreat. Thompson cruised the Muskoka Lakes with a gold braided cap denoting his high rank but he preferred to ride in the bow like he did as a child. So passed the halcyon summer days of August.

In the fall Thompson did not feel well and his legs were swollen. Dr. J.F.W. Ross of Toronto examined him. Ross found evidence of Bright's disease and that Thompson was suffering from valvular disease of the heart. Ross recommended a thorough examination and Sir John told the doctor he would get examined in London when he went to be inducted into Queen Victoria's Imperial Privy Council. Ross recommended he consult with Sir Russell Reynolds of London.

In Ottawa Thompson saw Sir James Grant the chief physician for the governor general who felt his heart was sound and a moderate reduction in weight and whisky should work. In Montreal he saw Dr. T.G. Roddick, who sided with Grant's optimistic diagnosis.

In the latter part of September Thompson found himself in a major physical examination by three doctors Wright, Roddick and Grant who were not so optimistic this time. They recommended he give up work for a year. Annie urged him to resign but he would not, he said, until he took his party safely through the next election in 1895.

On October 13 Thompson unveiled a bronze statue of Macdonald in Queen's Park, Toronto. It was a beautiful blue autumn day, the crowd was large and Thompson looked to be in good health and spirit.

Thompson boarded the *RMS Majestic* on October 31 in New York. Annie did not accompany her husband as she feared the financial burden she would impose. In fact she did not even see him off as she was attending to a recently broken wrist and she remained at the hotel before heading back to Ottawa.

When Thompson arrived in London he saw the specialist Sir Russell Reynolds who was more hopeful. He recommended rest and this lifted his spirits and he resolved to go to the continent for a holiday with Senator Sanford and his daughter Muriel. Thompson met his daughter Helena whom he was proud of. She reported he climbed to the top of St. Peter's dome, suffered from breathlessness and it took two days in bed for him to recover.

On December 1 Thompson returned to London and took up quarters at the Royal Palace Hotel. Sir Charles Tupper was upset that Thompson continued to work and he recommended he see Dr. Tavers who told him he had strained his heart and had to be careful. He rested in his hotel for three days then felt well enough to move on as he had baskets of invitations and was driven to fulfill his social obligations.

On December 12, 1894 he was inducted into the Imperial Privy Council at Windsor Castle. It was a short twenty-minute affair but it still taxed Thompson. They adjourned to the Octagon Room for lunch and before he touched any food he fainted. He was given some water and brandy that revived him somewhat. The Queen's personal physician, Dr. Reid, arrived and he told the doctor he had a pain in his chest and suddenly without a sound collapsed against the doctor. Reid felt for Thompson's pulse and there was none. Sir John Thompson was dead. It was 1:45 in the afternoon.

A telegram arrived in Montreal at 11:36 A.M. reporting from Windsor Castle that Sir John Thompson passed away after a meeting of the Privy Council. At first few could believe it but within a half hour the news confirmed the fact that their beloved Prime Minister was dead. Tupper made the final confirmation and Mackenzie Bowell cried. It was he, along with Douglas Stewart and Foster who went to tell Annie. One can only imagine her reaction. Flags dropped to half-mast and Lady Aberdeen rushed from Montreal to be by her side. Annie wrote, "never to hear his voice again, never to hear him come in the door, never to hear him come up the stairs again – never, never – oh! I am afraid of the nights and I am afraid of the days and I am afraid of the years and if it were not for the children…"

His body was laid out in Clarence Tower at Windsor Castle where a requiem mass was held just before midnight. His body was taken to London and embalmed by a French specialist, Dr. Charles Bayle. Helena was received by the Queen and attended the memorial requiem mass held on December 14 with many British statesmen in attendance as well as Cecil Rhodes, Charles Tupper and Lord Tennyson.

George Robinson, 1st Marques of Ripon, felt a precedent had been set when American philanthropist George Peabody was sent home in a British man-of-war. No less could be done for Sir John. His widow agreed and the *HMS Blenheim*, one of the fastest cruisers in the navy, sailed home from Gibraltar.

On Saturday December 22, like a British state funeral, a special train and a special car delivered Thompson's body to Portsmouth with the engine draped in black. A gun carriage met the train and was escorted by naval and military officers in full uniform. The *Blenheim*'s sides were painted black, the gang way draped in black. It was a blustery rainy day when Thompson's body was installed in the captain's stateroom. After a short service the *Blenheim* slipped out of port.

Helena arrived in time to accompany the family to Halifax aboard three private cars on the train.

On New Year's Day 1895 in mist and drenching rain the *Blenheim* arrived punctually at midday. As she came up the harbour guns from various ships and cannons at the Citadel reported her arrival. Everyone knew Thompson's body had arrived home.

The city streets were lined with soldiers of the 65th Halifax Rifles to control the crowds. In an official ceremony the coffin was escorted to a gun carriage with four powerful black Clydesdale horses that pulled the carriage through the rainy streets to Province House where Thompson's body lay in state.

January 3, 1895 was a beautiful day with the sun shining and the air mild and still. The city was overflowing. There were seven thousand applications for the seven hundred seats in St. Mary's Cathedral. Five lieutenant governors came as well as a row of archbishops and bishops. Bishop John Cameron performed the mass and Archbishop O'Brien performed the sermon.

The procession formed up in late morning outside the church with the sun still holding. It wound slowly to the cemetery only half a mile away but it took an hour and a half to get there. The crowds were huge. Everything looked so imposing and proper. There were soldiers from the Citadel in red, sailors in blue from the *Blenheim*, the military band played Beethoven's funeral march and Handel's death march. The crowd was quiet as they witnessed their most esteemed son's passing. He was buried that day in Holy Cross Cemetery only half a mile from where he was born.

Thompson was the second prime minister to die while in office. Macdonald had been the first. He was the first prime minister to die outside the country. Charles Tupper and Richard Bennett would also die beyond our borders. He was also the youngest prime minister to die, he was only 49 years old.

Ross Tilley
Guinea Pig Doctor

Ross Tilley was born in Bowman, Ontario in 1904. He graduated from the University of Toronto Medical School in 1929 and received further training in Vienna, Edinburgh and New York. He set up a practice in Toronto and joined the 400th Squadron as a medical officer in 1935. He studied plastic surgery with Canada's first plastic surgeon Dr. Fulton Risdon.

With the outbreak of the Second World War in 1939, Tilley became a captain in the Royal Canadian Army Medical Corps. He was soon transferred to the Royal Canadian Air Force (RCAF) Medical Branch. He went to Queen Victoria Hospital in East Grinstead and met Archie McIndoe a distinguished plastic surgeon from New Zealand. They took an immediate liking to each other.

They were swamped with an ever-increasing caseload of airmen who were badly burned. Their surgery required innovation as they did skin grafts modified to each patient's particular situation. They did Tiersch grafts, flap grafts, stamp grafts, pedicle grafts, dermatome grafts and other new techniques that they would pioneer with the men who would become known as the Guinea Pigs. Tilley's specialty was hands. This type of reconstructive surgery involved a series of operations that slowly, graft by graft, restores a hand, a nose or a face. Success was measured in incremental steps as the patient was slowly returned to better health. Their aim was to restore them to society so they could make further contributions and if at all possible return them to their passion, flying. This was not always possible.

All airmen faced the danger of being 'fried' as they called it. However the Spitfire and Hurricane pilots were at particular risk because their fuel tank was located in front of the instrument panel and if it was hit the gasoline would stream back into the cockpit. To protect their eyes and hands they were issued goggles and gloves. In their opinion it was more important to see the enemy to save ones hide. Goggles restricted visibility so many men did not wear them. On hot summer day's gloves were just uncomfortable.

As the war wore on Ward III filled to capacity sometimes with two or three members from the same crew. Dr. Tilley used his influence to persuade the Canadian government to build a Canadian wing to the hospital. Canadian Army engineers built a fifty-bed ward. Tilley and his anaesthetist, Dr. Norman Park, as well as Canadian surgeons, doctors, nurses, dieticians and orderlies staffed the wing. They would handle all the Canadian boys and would take any overflow from the parent ward. It opened in July 1944.

Most of the airmen were young boys in their late teens or early twenties. It was a terrible fate for a kid to be so terribly disfigured for life. Though there was anguish and pain, Tilley and McIndoe ran a most unconventional ship. They knew the attitude of their patients was the key to their success. They fought for and got permission to serve beer and it was always on tap. Furthermore they felt the men had earned the right to wear their uniforms even though they were not fighting. They also abolished rank so all the men felt equal. They also employed some of the prettiest girls they could muster to serve food and clean and this raised the spirits in the ward more than anything else. These things made the men feel special. And that was not all.

As soon as the men were mobile enough it was mandatory that they go out and scout around town and go to a pub. One of the most popular spots was Whitehall with host Bill Gardiner. No matter how disfigured the men might be, the waitresses didn't cast a second look and served them just like any other customer. Many locals would be sitting around them and they genuinely took an interest in the young lads for they were the ones who had been on the front line. They got invited to people homes for supper, out to the pictures and to dances. The people of East Grinstead were truly gracious and appreciative to have these wonderful men in their midst. It became know as 'the town that didn't stare.'

Many of the men were initially treated elsewhere. The standard treatment was gentian violet that was applied to counteract infection and tannic acid was sprayed on the surface. This treatment resulted in a hard crust forming that caused the limbs to become virtually useless. When they went to Grinstead the wounds were treated in a saline bath and then they were given an anaesthetic and the tannic acid was scrubbed off. The men endured the next painful step of skin grafts that were then bandaged. All their patients were welcome in the operating ward and could watch the doctors rebuild faces, noses, ears and fingers. However the men felt the greatest gift McIndoe and Tilley bestowed was the confidence they instilled in their shattered patients.

Great camaraderie was born of the nights at the pub and they decided to form a club they called the 'Guinea Pigs.' To gain entry into the club at the most basic level you had to be 'fried' and gone through surgery under the hands of Dr. Tilley or McIndoe. The next level was for the doctors, surgeons and medical staff for they made the magic. The last level, but just as important, was the Royal Society for Prevention of

Cruelty to Guinea Pigs. This included all friends, benefactors and people who genuinely cared for these men.

Many Guinea Pigs don't know how they got through the first few days after the crash but one phrase that echoed through out the ward was that: "There was always some one worse off than you." Yet it was amazing that the most severely injured and disfigured boys were the most cheerful. Archibald McIndoe's credo for the Club was:

> "We are the trustees of each other. We do well to remember that the privilege of dying for one's country is not equal to the privilege of living for it."

Special mention should be made of Marjorie 'Marge' Jackson for she was an extraordinary nurse and many of the men make special mention of this Florence Nightingale.

The real heroes of this story are the Guinea Pigs and here are the names of some of them; James Adams, Herb Aldridge, George Allen, Kenneth Allison, Harry Anderson, 'Bill' Anglin, George Beauchamp, Paul Branch, Kenneth Branston, Les Caddel, Lorne Cameron, Edward Carlson, Edgar Cecile, Cecil Cooper, John Cummins, 'Ken' Davidson, Ken Davies, Paul Davoud, 'Art' Doyle, Gerald Dufort, 'Stu' Duncan, Henry Ernest, John Everett, Geroge Fawcett, Everett Ferguson, Robert Fraser, Gordon Frederick, Donald Freeborn, Stanley Given, Frank Hanton, 'Jack' Harding, 'Reg' Harrison, 'Hank' Hastings, Cyril Hicks, Douglas Hicks, James Hicks, Frederick Hiley, Frank Hubbard, Lyall Hurry, Owen Jones, John Kerr, Zdzislaw 'Kras' Krasnodebski, 'Bud' Lacasse, Arthur Leitch, Ray Leupp, Robert Lloyd, David Lunney, Robert McCallum, 'Ben' Marceau, 'Hank' Marcotte, 'Jim' Martin, 'Bill' Martin, John Maxwell, Norman McHolm, Duncan McTavish, Garnett Moore, William Newsom, Ronald Noon-Ward, Sydney Noyes, Karl O'Conner, Howard Phillips, 'Al' Platsko, Tadeusz 'Teddy' Podbereski, 'Ken' Porter, 'Barney' Redding, Jacob Redekopp, John Reynolds, Stanley Reynolds, Donaldson Simpson, Ed 'Smithy' Smith, John Smith, Kenneth Smyth, 'Larry' Somers, John Southwell, Harold Stannus, Douglas Stephen, Bob Tait, William Tanner, 'Ray' Tarling, Douglas Thompson, Leonard Tremblay, Richard Turnbull, Les Wainwright, John Weber, George Wilkinson, George Wilson, David Wright.

The men were deeply touched by the personal concern and care shown by all the staff. They were also touched by the acceptance in town to their disfigurement and these factors are often cited as the big steps toward their eventual rehabilitation.

Dr. Ross Tilley was a great surgeon, and legendary healer with special abilities. He waged a personal battle against cancer until his death on April 19, 1988.

Pierre Trudeau
A Red Rose in His Lapel

Pierre Elliott Trudeau was born in Montreal on October 18, 1919. His father was French-Canadian and his mother was English of Scottish decent. He was educated at the Jésuit Collège, Jean-de-Brébeuf, Université de Montreal, Harvard and the London School of Economics, earning a law degree. He seemed to have little interest in a career; instead he roamed the world throwing snowballs at Lenin's statue in Russia, for which he was arrested.

In 1965 when Prime Minister Lester Pearson needed to improve his relationship with Québec he engaged Pierre along with his friends Gérard Pelltier and Jean Marchand. They were anti-nationalists and were amongst the separatist grumbling about the government of the day. Within two years Trudeau was justice minister and a year later, April 20, 1968 he was prime minister, carried into power on a wave of charm as Trudeaumania swept the country.

He was baptized in the arena of politics with the October Crisis in 1970 when he implemented the War Measures Act. It was his darkest hour culminating in the death of Pierre Laporte.

Still he charmed his way across the country and into the heart of Miss Margaret Sinclair whom he married May 4, 1971. He was the first and only prime minister to marry while in office. The country was enthralled.

Trudeau worked at bringing Québec into the fold of Confederation. He started by making the federal government a truly bilingual one. Millions were poured into teaching the Ottawa bureaucrats French. Québecers ascended to senior posts in his Cabinet. Around the country money was poured into second-language education and soon French immersion classes were the rage. Still these measures did not quell the dissatisfaction in his home province and it took his intervention in 1980 when a referendum in Québec pushed for separation. The margin was slim but NO won the referendum. He repatriated the constitution on the steps of the Parliament buildings signing the Constitution Act with Queen Elizabeth II on April 17, 1982.

Still pressure groups tried to amend it before the ink had dried. The new constitution's Charter of Rights and Freedoms created a mini revolution in the courts. He extended the social safety web and made an effort to check the growing American influence in Canadian society and culture.

What really endeared him to the people of Canada was his joyful pranks like the pirouette he did behind Queen Elizabeth's back and his widely reported, "fuddle duddle" statement. He had time to have three sons with Margaret, Justin, Sasha (Alexandre) and Michel before their separation in 1977. After their divorce in 1984 he retained custody of the children.

Trudeau retired from office June 30, 1984. His charismatic style would be missed as he became Canada's third longest serving prime minister. Perhaps he had not done as much for Canada as other prime ministers but he did it with a style that left a major imprint on his country.

On November 13, 1998 his son Michel was killed in an avalanche in Kokanee Glacier Park, British Columbia. His heart was filled with sadness but his son, an adventurer died in the great outdoors that he loved so much.

Pierre died September 28, 2000 but his story was not over. At his funeral at Montreal's Notre-Dam Basillica over 3,000 attended the ceremony including his former wife Margaret and his children Justin and Sasha. Also in attendance was his daughter Sarah whom he had conceived with Deborah Coyne. We will fondly remember Justin's eloquent speech that brought the nation to tears:

"I was only six....we went to Alert, Canada's northern most point...we drove past buildings...and came upon a red one...(he) boosted (me) up to the window, rubbed my sleeve against the frosty glass...I saw a figure, hunched over one of many worktables that seemed very cluttered. He was wearing a red suit...that's when I understood how powerful and wonderful my father was."

"Statesman, intellectual, professor, adversary, outdoorsman, lawyer, journalist, author, prime minister. But more than anything to me, he was dad."

"I was becoming politically aware. And I recognized one whom I knew to be one of my father's chief rivals...I told a joke about him – a generic, silly little grade school thing."

"My father looked at me sternly with that look I would learn to know so well and said: 'Justin, never attack the individual. We can be in total disagreement with someone without denigrating them as a consequence.'"

"He took me by the hand...introduce(d) me to this man...at that point I understood that having opinions that are different from those of another does not preclude one being deserving of respect as an individual."

"Simple tolerance…of each human being, regardless of beliefs, origins, or values - that's what he expected of his children and that's what he expected of his country."

"…Over the past few days, with every card, every rose, every tear, every wave and every pirouette, you returned his love. It means the world to Sasha and me…We have gathered from coast to coast to coast, from one ocean to another, united in our grief, to say good bye."

"But this is not the end. He left politics in '84. But he came back for Meech. He came back for Charlottetown. He came back to remind us of who we are and what we're capable of. But he won't be coming back anymore. It's all up to us, all of us now."

"The woods are lovely, dark and deep. He has kept his promises and earned his sleep. Je t'aime Papa."

Pierre Elliott Trudeau was buried next to his mother in the St-Remi-de-Napierville cemetery, Saint-Remi, Québec, a shrine for all-time.

Shania Twain
She is the One

Eileen Regina Edwards was born on August 28, 1965 in Windsor, Ontario. At age two she became Eileen Twain after her adopted father Jerry Twain. She grew up in the mining town of Timmins and planted trees with her native American stepfather wao was part of a forest crew. They were poor even by rural standards but her mother Sharon and stepfather found joy in Eileen's joy of music and that drove them to make great sacrifices to support her budding career.

Eileen started to perform country music in clubs, senior centres and telethons when she was only eight. She took a job at a northern Ontario resort, Deerhurst. In November of 1987 when a logging truck crushed her parents' to death, she moved to Huntsville, bought a house, a family truck and took care of her brothers and sisters. When they finally came into their own only then was Eileen able to resume her singing career.

With her friend Mary Bailey's help she cut a demo tape in Nashville in 1991. She adopted the name 'Shania' that means 'I'm on my way' in Ojibway; though she did not know what it meant initially, it certainly was prophetic. When Norro Wilson and Buddy Cannon of Mercury Records heard the demo they signed her and she released her first album *Shania Twain* July 6, 1993, but it contained only one of her own songs, 'God Ain't Gonna Getcha For That.' She garnered only moderate praise.

About this time she met Robert John 'Mutt' Lang, a famous rock producer with the likes of AC/DC, The Cars and Bryan Adams in his fold. They didn't actually meet until months after they had talked on the phone. The romance was a whirlwind and they married in December of 1993.

Her next album *The Woman in Me* was released in 1995. Shania and Mutt wrote or co-wrote every song. It seemed that every single off the album was a major hit somewhere. Each video was unique and set new creative standards and of course became wildly popular.

Any Man of Mine became her signature song and it became a smash #1 hit on all the charts in the U.S. and Canada at the same time. This miffed Nashville when this up start rocked the charts. They felt she had not paid her dues and she didn't go on tour to promote her album for it seems the video was sufficient.

It allowed her time and the energy to put together her next album *Come On Over* released in 1997. There were so many hits on this one that she completely rewrote the record books for weeks #1, longevity and to Nashville's despair it topped both the country and pop charts. *Your Still the One, From This Moment On, That Don't Impress Me Much, Man! I Feel Like a Woman* and *You've Got A Way* bust the charts. The album became a smash worldwide selling 19 million in the U.S. and 25 million worldwide. It became the best-selling female solo album in history, best-selling country album of all time and the 5th best selling album of all time.

Now Nashville was really irate but you can't argue with success. Though initially spurned, even Nashville had to bow and bestow upon her the honours she so richly deserved. Though late coming she garnered 5 Grammy Awards, Country's Album of the Year, Best Country Female Performance and so many other accolades that I would run out of space if I named all of them. Likewise she has graced the covers of numerous magazines: *TIME, Newsweek, Esquire* to mention only a few.

It is interesting that it took some time for Canada to embrace their own star as her sales lagged here compared to other countries that were quick to embrace her talent and beauty of her songs and her being.

August 12, 2001 Mutt and Shania welcomed their first child, a boy named Eja (pronounced 'Asia'), into the world. She released *Up* in 2002.

Though initially Shania did not perform live she has since made the rounds playing to packed venues wherever she stages her show.

Shania is on her way and I'd say she has arrived so eat your heart out Nashville.

Joseph Burr Tyrrell
Dinosaur Slayer

Joseph Burr Tyrrell was born in Weston, Canada West on November 1, 1858. At the time Weston was about as far out in the wilderness as you could get. He did not see or hear well and sought solitude as a child. His parents were of the gentry class and had difficulty appreciating what their son saw in pieces of earth, which he would collect along with spiders, grasshoppers, bark and whatever he could scavenge and meticulously catalogue.

At school he loved to look at maps and imagine what was there. He would fill in the gaps with what he thought he would find: rivers, lakes, geological formations, forests and the promise of mountains on the other side of the uncharted continent.

His parents introduced him to John A. Macdonald in the hope that he would intervene and motivate their son to do something, like perhaps become a lawyer. But Joseph wanted to work in the great outdoors. He went to Upper Canada College, pushed on to the University of Toronto and then came down with tuberculosis. He survived but the doctors said he should find work outdoors if he wanted to reclaim and retain his health.

Again his parents appealed to Macdonald, now the prime minister of Canada. Their request was answered when Joseph landed a job with the Geological Survey of Canada and was posted to Ottawa in a cellar packed with crates of fossils and stuff sent back by explorers. His self-taught taxonomy skills stood him well but he hated the bureaucratic politics. The head of the team, director Joseph Selwyn, thought the lad needed a smartening up and sent him out in the field with George Dawson. Old George did not like him, perhaps it was because he was the PM's protégé, or because he had to drag him along and teach him the trade. Never the less Joseph loved being outdoors and exploring.

Their first trip in 1883 took them into totally uncharted territory in the Cypress Hills area now part of Saskatchewan. Dawson tried to make his days miserable assigning him to pull the tail end assignment where he would get all the dust and grime raised by the horses in front. Still the other members of the team were impressed with the young man's tenacity in collecting and writing up everything in sight including the fleas on the horses they rode. The men thought this was hilarious but Dawson didn't see the humour in it. The boys were soon treating him with affection and calling him 'JB.'

In 1884, JB was given his own expedition and area to explore northeast of Calgary, still uncharted land then, where he would find an eerie landscape the local Cree thought was inhabited by the Serpent People. There were coulees and curious pillars capped with huge flat boulders in colossal formations.

On the 7th and 8th of June, JB discovered one of the largest coal deposits ever found in Canada. On the 9th he saw a fossil he had never seen before with gigantic teeth in an immense jawbone. He would later say, "There was this great ugly face looking out of the cliff at me!" He looked further and saw the sharp serrated teeth of a carnivore.

What he did not know and we would not know for some time, was that it was the first complete carnivore dinosaur skeleton found in Canada: *Albertosaurus sarcophagus* and it was 64 million years old. This is one of the richest sources of dinosaur remains in the world but he did not know it at the time.

His 1885 expedition was hampered by the Métis civil war. Batoché and the near vicinity was a hotbed of animosity. In Calgary he received word that he could continue to explore but was told to avoid the battle zone. He went straight to the native village on the edge of town, the Stoney Camp and hired a guide whose name was William. It was an unusual name for a native at the time but he had adopted it to avoid the hostilities aimed at his people.

The young Stoney put JB in touch with his spiritual side and how everything, the trees, breeze, canyons, skeletons and the fleas all possessed spirits. He gained respect for the native people and he was heartbroken when William died of tuberculosis.

In 1886 JB met Edith Carey, known as 'Dolly.' He was taken with her but was not in a position to further his romantic inclination and he bid her farewell. He was sent to explore north of Winnipeg. He traced the shoreline of Lake Manitoba in a boat called the *Pterodactyl*. He hired a group of Mohawk paddlers as William had convinced him that wilderness exploration needed the instinct and experience of the native guides. They paddled Lake Athabasca, where at the end of civilization, he pressed a blue flower into a note and sent it to Dolly. He headed into fly infested muskeg, pushing through it to the bleak habitation of the tundra. On July 25 they scared a group of Inuit away but Joseph Tyrrell left some steel needles and tobacco as a token of friendship.

They followed a river that kept running north; he hoped to get to Hudson Bay. The vegetation grew sparser. Their stomachs gnawed for food and supplies diminished. They felt the earth vibrating and when they came around a bend, there before their eyes was a huge herd of caribou. Within two days they had a month's supply of dried meat.

He had been out of contact with civilization for months. He pushed on and finally arrived in Fort Churchill. Everyone thought he was dead. He had traveled 1,400 miles and lost fifty pounds. He snowshoed to Winnipeg and caught a warm train to Ottawa. He married Dolly on February 14, 1887. Present were Governor General Lord Aberdeen and his wife. He impressed them with his stories of wilderness, bones and native folklore. Later that year their first son was born.

The trip he had completed was hotly debated in parliament for it had cost $7,000 and produced nothing. As one cheeky member of parliament said, "Hell, they even starved on that money. Imagine what it would have cost if they'd eaten well!"

Lord Aberdeen intervened and procured the funds for his next expedition, which was to navigate the Kazan River to its source. During their travels they came upon a silent group of Inuit in their kayaks. These natives gave them food and wood. When they asked nothing in return this further elevated the status of natives in Tyrrell's eyes. He loved the deep sense of peace he felt while in the north. However he was paid only $800 a year, a pittance, even in those days. He was sent to the Dawson area in the spring of 1898 to his great joy.

When he landed at Skagway he got a fever. He arrived at the ponderous hill of picture fame just before an avalanche killed some of the gold rushers but the line on the hill barely wavered. Soon he was at the city that carried the name Dawson, a name he had grown to despise. The area was teaming with crazed moilers for gold, as many as 100,000 and most were in tents for there were few buildings. He struck a claim below Hunter Creek one valley over from Bonanza and quit the Geological Survey team. Over the next six years he extracted all the gold he could find from his claim. Dolly visited him twice. It seems most of their discourse was by letter.

When he returned he and Dolly moved into a fashionable Toronto home. He became an agent for a London-based investing syndicate. They asked him to look at the abandoned mines at Kirkland Lake. He took Dolly and quickly assessed that there was a fortune in gold in veins that were far from exhausted. It took ten years but when the Kirkland Lake Mine opened he became chairman of the board and a millionaire. The rest of his days were full of serenity. He and Dolly had two more children, boys. He survived his sons and Dolly who died in 1945. JB died one year short of a century in 1957. The Royal Tyrrell

Museum of Palaeontology was still on the horizon, little did he know what a stir he had caused, perhaps even more so after his death.

Underground Railway
Last Stop Canada

The Underground Railway brought thousands of runaway slaves to freedom in Canada. The stories and personal accounts surrounding the Underground Railway are difficult to obtain. The emancipated slaves and their sympathetic rescuers were sworn to secrecy to protect the routes and the people who assisted them. In addition, many of the slaves were illiterate and therefore their tales often died with them.

The first slave ships landed at Jamestown, Virginia in 1619 with a cargo of twenty black men and women. Many thought slavery was wrong and the Quakers preached against the enslaving of other people. They became known as abolitionists. Southerners who supported slavery had the mistaken belief that African Americans could not take care of themselves so in their misaligned eyes slavery was beneficial.

Of course this was never the case. Many black people then and now are upstanding citizens with talents, skills and the determination to succeed. In order to have a chance they first had to be liberated.

There was little chance of freedom until Britain ended slavery with the Emancipation Act on August 28, 1833. With that, British soil became synonymous with freedom for fugitive slaves and many fled to Canada. There were annual Emancipation Day celebrations that first began in 1834 and continue to this day.

Many arrived in Toronto but some ended up in Chatham, St. Catherines, Windsor, Hamilton, Amherstburg, Niagara Falls, Owen Sound, etc.

Many of the routes were old Indian or military trails and there were at least half-a-dozen major routes and numerous secondary routes.

The term Underground Railway was coined in 1831 when a slave from Kentucky, Tice Davids, escaped across the Ohio River and his master remarked, "The f*cking Abolitionists must have a rail road under the ground by which they run off with the niggers." With the steam locomotive emerging the term caught on and even the terminology evolved around it. They had 'stations' or 'stops' and 'stationmasters' who took them in to their safe houses. Their 'cargo' or 'freight' was all human and all black.

Courageous people risked their lives to help provide shelter, food, clothing and secrecy to assist them. 'Conductors' sometimes drove wagons, carts or carriages with slaves hidden in compartments. Sometimes fugitives were disguised as slaves driving their 'owners' about but who were actually Underground Railroad workers.

The Abolitionist Society was organized in 1844 to fight against discrimination.

In 1850 the Fugitive Slave Act re-ignited fear and black people south of the border who were fugitives or 'freemen', risked being enslaved again as slave catchers hunted them down. The next year the North American Convention of Coloured People was called in Toronto and chaired by Henry Bibb. He would also establish Canada's first black newspaper, *Voice of the Fugitive*.

One of the most famous 'conductors' was Harriet Tubman. She worked out of St. Catherines and made nineteen trips into hostile territory to liberate her kinfolk. She eventually had a $40,000 bounty on her head, a considerable sum in those days. She was unstoppable and as a credit to her tenacity she was called 'The Black Moses of Her People.'

Some fugitives hid in crates that were being shipped north. One such man was Henry 'Box' Brown who acquired his middle name as a result of his method of escape.

One of the heart-breaking aspects of escape was that children often had to be left behind. That was not always the case as Ann Maria Jackson, a fugitive slave, left Delaware in 1858 with her remaining seven children. Two of her children had been sold and that spurred her into action.

When fugitives arrived they often boarded with established families. If they arrived in Toronto, children could attend public schools free without regard to their colour. Elsewhere this was not the case.

Many of the newly arrived fugitives were skilled at carpentry, cooking, blacksmithing, masonry and barbering. Others found jobs working the ships that sailed the Great Lakes or as waiters, dockworkers, porters, labourers, housekeepers and washerwomen.

James Mink did well in Toronto for he operated the city's largest livery stable as well as a fancy hotel, the Mansion House. He was part of the well to do black community. His beloved daughter married a white cab driver from Yorkshire. He immediately took her on a honeymoon to the United States and sold his bride into slavery. It took her father many years and a good part of his fortune to finally secure his daughter's freedom.

Some liberated slaves rose to become leaders of their community and even went on to higher education like the brilliant medical doctor Alexander T. Augusta. Wilson Abbott's son Anderson, became the first Canadian-born black doctor to graduate from Toronto's King College Medical School. He was one of eight black surgeons in the Union Army.

It is believed that at least 30-40,000 fugitive slaves made passage to Canada.

The raid on Harpers Ferry in 1859 by John Brown, set in motion events that led directly to the outbreak of the American Civil War in 1861.

November 15, 1861 a fugitive slave, John Anderson, was ordered to return to the States by Chief Justice John Robinson. While fleeing Anderson stabbed his master Seneca Diggs who died. There was an outcry over the ruling for everybody knew about Missouri's 'lynching laws.' His case was appealed to the Privy Council of England who ruled in his favour stating that Anderson was justified in defending himself against a man who wanted to enslave him.

On January 1, 1863 Abraham Lincoln, President of the United States, signed the Emancipation Proclamation freeing all the slaves in the states.

By 1865 the American Civil War was over but that did not end the suffering of the black people in America. Veterans of the Confederate Army founded the Ku Klux Klan in 1866. In southern states 'Jim Crow' laws were enacted to segregate the blacks from the whites. Lynching became commonplace and was used to terrorize the black community into compliance for many years to come. Slaves no longer fled to Canada for freedom for they were free though they still continue to struggle against racism to this day.

Marie Madeleine Jarret de Vércheres
Heroine of Castle Dangerous

It was a cool fall day when Marie woke to the smell of fire burning in the stove. In the poorly insulated palisade fort it was a rugged existence. The crisp air enfolded her as she tumbled out of bed. It was a foggy day and the temperature was decidedly cool. Some were already cooking breakfast as others prepared for a day in the fields harvesting the crop planted in the spring.

Marie quickly dressed and went to help make breakfast. After breakfast was done and the kitchen tidied up, Marie prepared to help in the field. She crossed the small parade square and went out the fort's main gate to the field. She had only walked a short distance when she heard blood-curdling screams. Suddenly from nowhere there were war whoops and screams of her brethren as they were slain. Indians lurking in the fog attacked the people in the fields. Marie turned and ran for the fort with Indians in hot pursuit. Fourteen-year-old Marie ran as fast as her little feet could carry her. She trembled as she swung the huge gate to the fort closed. Just as she secured the door she felt a thud as several Indians attempted to knock the door down. It held.

Amid all the screams Marie kept a cool head. When she was only twelve she saw her mother defend the fort against marauding Indians for two days. She screamed at the old men to help her defend the fort. She loaded the guns as the five men fired between the cracks of the palisade walls. The Indians soon retreated into the forest. Cries of the prisoners could be heard in the surrounding forest as they were tortured to death. Marie prepared the guns for another attack. They did not return during the day but Marie kept a close vigil. Late at night they came and tried to burn the fort. Marie and the men quickly extinguished each blaze while firing gunshots into the night.

Day and night young Marie kept a careful vigil and the Indians came two or three times a night to try to capture the fort. Finally a group of soldiers were paddling down the stream that went right past Castle Dangerous, now Vércheres, Québec . As they went past they noticed a flag being waved in the fort. The men pulled their canoes to shore. Overjoyed Marie marched proudly from the fort. It was October 30, 1692. She had kept vigil over the fort for eight days and nights without sleep. She surrendered the fort to the soldiers and collapsed into a much-needed sleep. Soon she was famous for her feat.

James Morrow Walsh
Sitting Bull's Mentor North of the 'Medicine Line'

The Sioux, under the chief Sitting Bull camped at a place they called Greasy Grass. General George Armstrong Custer ignored the advice of his head scout Arikara, named Bloody Knife, when he expressed concern that there were too many Sioux to attack. The 7th Calvary attacked and 264 soldiers of all ranks, as well as Custer, were annihilated at the Battle of Little Big Horn on June 25, 1876. The west was thrown into turmoil as whites were shocked by the slaughter and were frightened by the Sioux success.

James Morrow Walsh was born in Prescott, Upper Canada on May 22, 1840. He was the first of nine children born to Margaret and Lewis Walsh. He was a fair student who excelled at athletics especially cricket, soccer and canoeing. He became one of the new nation's leading lacrosse players; a game originated by the Algonquin tribes. The Prescott team was ranked as the continent's best.

James tried a number of occupations before enrolling in the Kingston Military School. He excelled at gunnery and cavalry and graduated with honours in 1862. In 1866 he fought the Fenians or Irish revolutionary movement who were founded in the States and were committed to overthrowing Britain freeing Ireland from British rule. In 1869 he graduated from the Militia School of Gunnery and joined Colonel Garnet Wolseley's military expedition that was sent to the West to suppress the Red River rebellion.

First he married Mary Mowat on April 19, 1870, settled her in Prescott and headed out on the Red River Expedition five weeks later. Soon their first and only daughter, Cora, was born.

In May 1873 Parliament passed a bill calling for a 'Police Force in the North-West Territories.' This force would travel to the great prairie and establish law and order among warring Indian tribes and protect them from whiskey traders.

'Old Tomorrow' as Sir John A. Macdonald was called, procrastinated until the Premier of British Columbia, Amor de Cosmos, traveled to Ottawa and reminded the Prime Minister of his promise of a rail link to the Pacific. Settlers and railway builders needed protection. A gang of wolf hunters killed 36 Assiniboine, this became known as the Cyprss Hills massacre. When informed of the incident Macdonald knew the time had come for action.

Walsh was appointed to the North-West Mounted Police on September 25, 1873 at a salary of $1,000 per year. James commanded 'A'

Troop that left Ottawa on October 1. Thirty-two men headed to Toronto where one was dismissed for drunkenness and eight more new recruits joined the ranks at Prescott, including James's younger brother William, as well as Sam Steele. (see Steele)

They reached Prince Arthur's Landing, now Thunder Bay, and headed along the 545-mile Dawson route to Lower Fort Garry. Steele soon became Walsh's right hand man as he had also served during the Red River Rebellion of 1869. The troop encountered swamps, snowstorms, rapids and ferry delays. After three weeks of difficult slogging they arrived at Lower Fort Garry, the Stone Fort. On November 3, 1873 Lieutenant-Colonel Osborne Smith swore in each recruit and the North-West Mounted Police formally came into existence. Soon there were 150 recruits stationed at the fort. The training was rigorous.

Though Walsh can be called the original Mountie, Lieutenant-Colonel George French became his commanding officer. French worried about the shortage of manpower and pressed Ottawa for more men. Another 201 men, 16 officers and 278 horses joined their ranks and went into training. Walsh was promoted to inspector and commanded one of the six troops.

Fred Bagley, the youngest member at 15, was the trumpeter and his diary gives one of the more entertaining accounts of the Mounties' earliest days. On July 8, 1874 a red-coated column of 275 men, 120 ox carts and 30 Métis drivers left Dufferin. Their mandate was to put an end to the whiskey trading.

Savage storms and vast stretches of arid country without proper food or water left the column straggling for miles behind Colonel French. On September 2 the hills began to move like a burnt umber mirage and the men cried out, "Buffalo" and the hunt was on. Major James Macleod, James Walsh and Sam Steele were in their element but George French was out of his.

Tempers and patience flared and waned. Colonel French ordered two sentries into irons accusing them of stealing biscuits. Macleod stepped forward and spoke firmly, "Sir you can't do that. Our regulations give you no authority for such a course of action…I can't allow this to happen." Both men stood silent with mutiny hanging in the air. He allowed French an opportunity to respond, but he didn't. Macleod saluted and returned to duty.

They were unable to find Fort Whoop-Up, and after carving their initials in La Roche Percée, they split up. Some men headed for Fort Edmonton while French continued to search for the whiskey fort. Their chief scout Pierre Leveille advised them to head south where they would find water and food. September 22 French left with the men's best wishes that he never return. He never did.

Major Macleod accompanied French to Fort Benton. A local trader Isaac Baker recommended a local Métis scout named Jerry Potts to guide them to the elusive fort. Macleod resupplied and headed back to meet up with the troops with Potts leading the way. Potts was a valuable acquisition as he spoke native languages, knew the country intimately and would prove himself time and again.

They camped for the night and found themselves surrounded by buffalo in the morning. Jerry insisted all weapons be holstered to avoid a stampede and led the column for half a day through a sea of brown fur.

Potts soon guided them to John Healy's notorious outpost Fort Whoop-Up. He immediately told Macleod the fort was abandoned, though a tattered American flag flew overhead. Macleod was not so sure. He cautiously scouted the surrounding area and focused his cannons on the fort. His troops were ready for a battle but suddenly Macleod and Potts urged their horses down the slope toward the fort. Potts grunted and inclined his head toward a small wisp of smoke. Macleod boldly pounded on the heavy door. An unkempt old man opened it and was startled to see a tall man in a gold-braided scarlet tunic and white helmet before him. Indeed the fort was all but abandoned but Macleod inspected every inch never the less.

With this done their next mission was to establish a fort before the winter blizzards swept in on them. Flights of wildfowl were streaming southward. Occasional burst of snow flurries swirled around them. The 'Great Lone Land' was living up to its name. Only 28 miles from Fort Whoop-Up Potts led them to a stretch of plain with a valley and a river named Ol' Man's that was beautifully fringed by tall cottonwoods. Here the men set to building a fort the men called Macleod in honour of their leader.

Macleod wisely sent Potts out to the surrounding native camps to spread the word of the great White Mother, the name used for Queen Victoria, and their mission to stop the liquor trade. Potts did his job well and soon various tribes began to trickle toward the redcoat's camp.

They were impressed by the respectful and courteous manner of Macleod. The crimson they wore reminded them of the honourable men their elders had met at Fort Garry in contrast to the blue coats of the hated 'long-knives' on the other side of the border.

On December 1, 1874 Crowfoot, the chief of the Blackfoot, made an appearance. Carrying an eagle feather and wearing a blanket over his buckskin shirt, the chief dismounted and walked through the gateway. Macleod extended his hand and Crowfoot reached out and touched his palm. Their trust grew rapidly and Crowfoot named the redcoat commander *Stamix Otokan* for he had a bull's head mounted over the entrance to his office. Crowfoot ended the meeting with, "You are a brave man, *Stamix Otokan*. The laws of the Great White Mother must be good when she has a son like you. We will obey your laws."

Jerry Potts was held in high esteem and his most annoying habit was that he said so little. He could reduce a long speech into a sentence or even a word. Macleod recalls when the Peigan and Blood rode into the fort and spoke to Potts for a long time. Finally Potts turned to Macleod and said, "Dey damn glad you here." In a winter blizzard he had saved ten men and three prisoners leading them through the blizzard to Fort Macleod.

In the spring, Major Walsh set out with Jerry Potts and his troops on the 160-mile ride to Cypress Hills where whisky traders had set up shop again. Macleod told Walsh to establish a fort.

At the headwaters of Battle Creek the men built Fort Walsh. The area was a beehive of activity as the fort took shape. One day there was a sudden and deepening silence. Walsh looked up and down the valley and soon saw the reason for the silence. A couple of hundred-armed warriors rode toward them. Potts grunted, "Sioux."

The bare-chested warriors, dark eyes darting everywhere, braids down to their shoulders, looked intimidating. One among them wore a white-man's hat and a checked shirt and was a Métis. They reined in close to the fort and the Métis rode to Walsh's table. Walsh asked Potts what they wanted but the Métis spoke English and replied, "Long-knives chase us 'cross border. Who you?"

"Redcoats of the great White British Mother," said Walsh pointing to the Union Jack behind him.

The Sioux spotted two men in U.S. Army blues and their eyes danced with hate and they shouted and pointed accusingly. In the next instant Macleod and his men found themselves looking down the Sioux rifle barrels.

"We're not long-knives! We're the British Mother's redcoats."

Realizing they were in mortal danger Macleod warned without a tremor in his voice, "If any of you fire a shot more redcoats will come, more redcoats than there are buffalo on the prairie and none of you will be left alive."

As the Métis translated one of the warrior's eyes widened and he pointed to the hills above. Suddenly the Sioux wheeled their ponies around and left hoof-flung grass and dirt behind as they thundered away.

Hundreds of Cree streamed through the trees into the valley pursuing the Sioux. They soon abandoned the chase and returned to the fledgling fort. They were friendly. The men shook hands, invited them to tea and a smoke of tobacco. It had been a close call.

Walsh declared they would keep their arms close at hand. It took six weeks to complete the fort. Walsh had the constant irritation of a painful skin disease, erysipelas also known as Saint Anthony's Fire and so he traveled to the U.S. to seek treatment. June 26, 1876 Walsh was informed about the Custer Massacre and was asked to return to duty as Sitting Bull was expected to flee across the border.

Walsh always made a point of looking good be it in his gold-trimmed scarlet tunic, striped pants, pill-box cap and polished black boots or in his buckskin trail garb. Walsh looked official and this would play to his advantage in the impending encounters with the most savage Indians of the time.

That winter Major Walsh and his guide Louis Leveille boldly confronted White Eagle and Black Moon of the Lakota Sioux, Long Dog, chief of the Hunkapapas, and Spotted Eagle, chief of the Sans Arcs. At the meeting when Walsh removed his hat they could see why he had been given the name White Forehead for his weathered face contrasted with the milk white complexion of his forehead. He told them of the White Mother's laws and they agreed to comply. After the ceremony he was asked if his men would eat with them and stay the night in their camp. Walsh knew he had made a good impression and promptly accepted.

The next morning as Walsh and his men prepared to leave, White Eagle asked him if they could have a few bullets to hunt buffalo for they had expended all their ammunition fighting the bluecoats. Walsh looked at their drawn faces. He knew if he delayed, the buffalo might migrate beyond the border and starvation was a distinct possibility. He made a decision on the spot and granted their wish warning them they must not use the ammunition for any other purpose. Tension evaporated into smiles.

The winter of 1877 Walsh confronted Four Horns, chief of the Teton Lakota and Hunkapapa people. He gave them his speech, which was by now becoming polished. They accepted the White Mother's laws and Walsh slept in their village again as a sign of trust.

Walsh had been waiting for the appearance of Sitting Bull for many moons. In May, word came that a large group of Indians were seen heading to the border. He took a small patrol and three guides and headed off to welcome the advancing tribe. Spotted Eagle and Black

Moon greeted Walsh when his patrol approached their tepee village. The great chief's attention was drawn to a muscular, pockmarked faced Sergeant McCutcheon who was standing a little apart from the others. Sitting Bull veered towards him and shook the hand of the surprised sergeant before Spotted Eagle pointed out Walsh and Sitting Bull was soon shaking his hand with a firm grip.

A meeting was called and they all gathered in the council lodge. In typical Walsh fashion he stated with Louis Leveille translating, "All people who live in the White Mother's country-white man and red man alike-must obey her laws. It is against the law to kill any man, woman or child. You must not injure any person, steal or give false testimony. You must not take another person's horses, guns, robes, wagons or anything else. You must not damage, burn or destroy other people's possessions. No woman or child may be violated and it is your duty to protect them. You must not cross the international boundary line what you call the medicine line or 'the big road.' You must not run off horses from other tribes or raid them. You must not make war on the American soldiers or American people. The Great White Mother lives at peace with the Americans."

Sitting Bull accepted the terms and pulled out a gold medal marked with King George III's image. He said his grandfather fought for the British. Walsh guaranteed them a safe sanctuary from the long-knives if they obeyed the laws. Walsh also granted him and his tribe a supply of ammunition to hunt game stipulating it must not be used otherwise. Once again he was asked to eat and sleep with the tribe.

The next day when three Assiniboine rode into camp herding five horses Walsh's scout Leveille over heard that they had stolen the horses from a black-robe. Walsh promptly arrested them and put them in leg irons. White Dog expected the Sioux to come to his defence but they did not. He protested that he did not know it was against the White Mother's law to steal property. Walsh relented and freed his prisoners but took the horses and returned them to the rightful owner. It was an effective demonstration of the redcoat's justice.

Chief Little Child of the Saulteau was struck in the head with the barrel of Crow's Dance's rifle and his warriors pulled down his camp. When Little Child reported the incident to Walsh he assembled a patrol of 14 men along with their surgeon Kittson. Little Child accompanied the men and they were soon on the trail of the Assiniboine renegades. The rode through the night for they were able to easily see where the travois' had been dragged in the moonlight.

Early in the morning they found the village with about 250 tents peacefully sleeping, not a sole stirred. Walsh made plans to surprise them and arrest the culprits. He sent Leveille and Kittson to a rocky butte to wait for them and to prepare a defensive position.

He took the rest of the men into the camp and directly to the war lodge entrance. He had his men surround the tent, loosen the tepee pegs and crawl under the barrier. Walsh walked in the main entrance and found two-dozen braves sound asleep. Not a single brave stirred and the men quickly collected their guns. Little Child indicated who had struck him as well as others that rampaged their village. Within minutes 21 astonished braves were in handcuffs. As they exited the lodge pandemonium swept the camp. Walsh and his men mounted their horses and herded their prisoners out toward the butte.

When they arrived a rock wall had been started that they further fortified. Drums were beating and the men prepared for an attack. Vastly outnumbered things looked grim.

A chief of the Assiniboine stepped forward and Walsh explained why he had arrested the men. The chief said he had tried to stop them but they would not listen. Negotiating through his interpreter Leveille, Walsh promised fair justice. The chief said the young braves had only followed the lead of their elders. Walsh released the nine youngest he had apprehended but said the remaining 12 would have to face trial for they were the accused, they were older and therefore responsible.

A very tired patrol returned to Fort Walsh with their prisoners in tow and justice was promptly dealt. Crow's Dance received 6 months confinement while others received smaller amounts of time. Walsh had defied all odds and once again came out a winner. Walsh's reputation was growing and in the face of insurmountable odds he seemed to be able to bluff his way through the most dire situations and emerge without a shot being fired. It was miraculous.

When three U.S. 'officials' turned up at Sitting Bull's camp they contacted Walsh who immediately departed with his superior Major James Irvine. The men turned out to be the Right Reverend Father Martin Marty, Colonel Miles and a scout John Halsey, an agency interpreter.

After much discussion Walsh and Irvine took the three men back to the border.

Another tribe, the Nez Percé, were in a running battle with the long-knives. White Bird, 98 warriors, 100 women and children had broken through the soldier's line and were headed to the medicine line. When they arrived Walsh was sickened by their condition which included grievous wounds, children with broken legs and arms and a woman shot through her breast and side of her head. The Great Father's promises meant death and heartbreak for the natives. Of course Walsh promised them a safe asylum in the Great Mother's land.

On October 16, 1877, Major Walsh and Macleod brought Sitting Bull before American General Alfred Terry and his delegation. They were offered a full pardon if they gave up their weapons and horses and returned to their reservation peacefully. Sitting Bull did not believe the forked tongue of the bluecoat and steadfastly refused to return. Walsh supported Sitting Bull's position as witness to the tragic fate all the tribes that fled the States had suffered. Macleod and Prime Minister Mackenzie Bowell hoped they would return for the buffalo herds were running low and they feared unrest on the prairies if food became a problem.

Walsh came into possession of a 7th Calvary survivor, a grey gelding he named 'Custer.' He wrote to the army and offered to return the horse but was pleased when the reply came back that he could keep it. Walsh and his 'B' division (note name change) were kept busy as the Sioux crossed the border to hunt buffalo and sometimes steal horses. Walsh and his men diligently rounded up the stolen horses and returned them to their rightful owners but Walsh was not too happy that Sitting Bull turned a blind eye.

With Sir John A. Macdonald again at the helm, 'Old Tomorrow' wanted Sitting Bull to return to the States. The buffalo herds had all but disappeared and the shortage of food made things desperate. Walsh shared some of the division's supplies and even gave scraps from their table to the women and children. Still Sitting Bull demanded more food and Walsh literally kicked the chief out of his office he was so upset with the situation.

Walsh was transferred to the farming community of Fort Qu'Appelle and Macleod resigned from the service. Sitting Bull was devastated by the change but met with Walsh before he left.

Sitting Bull handed Walsh his war bonnet, his most priceless possession. "Take it friend. And keep it. I won't need it again. Every feather marks a deed of bravery done in war when the Lakota were strong." Walsh was deeply touched by the offering.

Walsh spent only five days at Fort Qu'Appelle before departing for home. He was suffering from erysipelas and his health was deteriorating.

The new commander of the fort was Paddy Crozier and he first visited Sitting Bull in February 1880. By now some 3,700 Sioux had returned to the States in small numbers, as Walsh had predicted. With only 1,200 left, Sitting Bull still refused to leave and waited to hear from Walsh whom he trusted implicitly.

Walsh was overjoyed to see his wife and daughter Sarah, who was now eight. Soon after, he was intent on having a meeting with Macdonald. When he met the Prime Minister he was thankful to be able to remain on sick leave and was asked to not contact Sitting Bull who was so disappointed he journeyed to Fort Qu'Appelle to meet with White Forehead. He was not there and Sam Steele encouraged him to return to the States.

On his own Walsh went to see General Hammond, got assurances and sent a letter to Sitting Bull that he would be treated well if he returned to the States. This was the assurance Sitting Bull was waiting for.

July 19, 1881 Sitting Bull surrendered to Major Brotherton at Fort Buford. He composed a surrender song then was confined at Fort Randall until 1883. He then became the main attraction in Buffalo Bill Cody's Wild West Show for a time.

Sitting Bull continued to fight for Sioux rights but was shot and killed with his son Crowfoot and six followers by the tribal police and soldiers at Grant River, South Dakota on December 14, 1890. He was spared the heartbreak of hearing about the slaughter of over 200 Sioux and their Chief Big Foot in South Dakota two weeks later.

Walsh impressed the president of the CPR Cornelius Van Horne when he returned to Fort Qu'Appelle. He retired two years later and provided coal for the CPR becoming prosperous.

In 1897 Walsh was appointed the Commissioner of the Yukon during the Klondike Gold Rush. He saved many lives when he mandated a full camp as well as 1,150 pounds of food were required to enter the area. In less than a year he stepped down and Sam Steele succeeded him. Walsh retired to his home he named Indian Cliff in honour of his favourite rock outcropping in the Cypress Hills. He died July 25, 1905 at Brockville, Ontario.

Sitting Bull's war bonnet was passed on to Van Horne and his family donated it to the Royal Ontario Museum.

The mission of the North-West Mounted Police was to keep the peace and 'maintain le droit' - uphold the right. Walsh recommended the buffalo as a fitting symbol for their crest and to this day it is the centrepiece of their badge.

Angus Walters
Captain of the *Bluenose*

Angus Walters was born June 9, 1881 in Lunenburg, Nova Scotia. He was one of twelve children. His dad wanted his children to get a good education and Angus waited until he was 13 to work the cod as a 'throater', cutting the heads off the gaffed fish.

By age fifteen he was out in the dories by himself. His first journey was almost his last as a thick fog enveloped him and as night fell he feared his fate would be like so many before. He was lucky that night, the fog lifted and he found the red and green lights of their schooner. A few years later Angus was on the deck at night when, in high seas, a wave washed his brother, John, off the deck. The rails were built low to allow fish to be easily gaffed and to throw the catch from the dories on board. Angus showed his flair for command when he heaved about and yelled for a dory to be lowered over the side. Thankfully John caught a line hanging from the dory and was saved.

In 1904 he took command of the *Minnie M. Cook*. He was already a veteran of the Atlantic cod fishery. Those who sailed with him remember him as extraordinary. He was small but mighty. Though he could be fearsome his sailors came to love him. He was respected and when he said, "We'll do such," that such, whatever it was, was done. He was a 'sail dragger', a skipper who liked to pile on the sail and push her hard. Whether out bound or home he'd get on the megaphone and cry, "Let's have a hook (race)." All hands on deck cheered and yelled taunts back and forth. They sailed dangerously close to capsizing and looked for the tiny bit of speed that would over time bring her home or to the fishing banks ahead of his competitors. Racing was not only great sport but increased the profit margin for the first ship home always got the highest prices for their haul.

He married Maggie Tanner in 1906 and had three sons over the next seven years, Gilbert, Spike and Stewart. Their dad was at sea as much as he was at home and built a reputation as a highline skipper who brought home huge catches. He commanded *Muriel B. Walters*, named after his mother, and got a hell of a reputation whenever they went for a hook, which was at every opportunity.

In 1919 the New York Yacht Club postponed the America's Cup because there was a 23 mile per hour gale. The *Halifax Herald* editor/senator William Dennis laughed for he knew that was barely a tickle for the sail of a Nova Scotia salt bank schooner. He decided to create the *Halifax Herald* North America Fisherman's International Race.

For generations the 'Yanks' and 'Novies' had raced but now it would be formal.

On October 11, 1920 the pre trials took place and Angus in *Gilbert B. Walters* was leading down the stretch when on the last leg the topmast broke and he lost to the *Delawana* skipped by Tommy Himmelman. A week later the *Delawana* faced the Yankee schooner *Esparanto* captained by Nova Scotia born Mary Welch. The *Esparanto* won 2 out of the 3 races and claimed the trophy and $4,000 prize, a handsome sum in those days.

Not to be outdone, Senator Dennis put together a consortium of businessmen and approached Walters with a proposal to build a better schooner. Angus drove a hard bargain and soon yacht designer William Roue had the *Bluenose* on the boards. Walters watched closely as the ship was built. He pushed for the forecastle sleeping quarters to be elevated, much to Roue's dismay, but he felt the men in his command needed the room for it was where they slept. Interestingly enough modern ships now have this bulbous design at their bow for it is more efficient.

On March 21, 1921 the *Bluenose* was launched. The days of the salt water schooner had left their greatest days behind as vessels were now turning to steam power. The waning days of great sailing ships would go out with a flash.

In the International Fisherman's Race that year, the *Bluenose* under the able command of Angus won the first race against the *Elsie* by 13 minutes and took the second by three miles. Overnight the *Bluenose* became a national symbol and 'Champion of the Atlantic.'

In 1922 in the same race they faced the *Henry Ford* and won handily.

In 1923 they faced a newly designed and outfitted schooner the *Columbia* under the command of Captain Ben Pine. The race was marred by a collision on the course, a protest and controversy. The *Bluenose* won but the judges ruled Walters went on the wrong side of the buoy though it was not stated in the rules of engagement. Walters and his crew packed up and left. Pine refused to accept the trophy or prize money for he felt they had not won. Later that year the *Bluenose* landed a record 646,000 pounds of cod in one haul.

The International Fisherman's Race went uncontested for years under a spell of gloom. In 1925 the *Bluenose* spent 4 days on the rocks near Placentia Bay, Newfoundland and had a hole knocked in her but it was soon repaired.

April 7, 1926, Walters was surprised by a blizzard south west of Sable Island, the 'Graveyard of the Atlantic.' The wind blew them toward the shore. Angus sent the men below and lashed himself to the wheel and fought the gale for 8 hours. He sailed under a jumbo double-reefed foresail and a riding sail until she cleared the point. No trophy was awarded that day but Walters claimed it was her greatest race.

On August 24-25, 1927 off the coast of Nova Scotia and Newfoundland, nine schooners including: *Joyce M. Smith, Clayton Walters, Mahala, Columbia, Vienna, Loretta, Balena* and *Una Corkum* were lost off Newfoundland and Nova Scotia and 87 men lost their lives. The *Bluenose* proved her worth riding the fierce gale in deep water under the eye of Angus. There was deep grief at the great loss of life.

In 1930 Ben Pine challenged Walters. The Thomas Lipton Tea Co. agreed to put up the prize money. A ragged, tattered *Bluenose* lost to the *Gertrude L. Thebaud*. Angus took all the blame for the loss and was determined to avenge the defeat.

In 1931 the Fisherman's Trophy was again contested. The *Bluenose* beat the *Thebaud* in the first race by 3 miles and in the second by 2. After the convincing victory Walters exclaimed, "The wood ain't growin' yet that'll beat *Bluenose*."

The *Bluenose* went to the Chicago Exposition in 1933 and visitors were amazed to see such a large wooden vessel. In 1935 they went to King George V's Silver Jubilee. They joined in a race around the Isle of Wight and the *Bluenose* placed a disappointing third.

On September 2nd, 1935 an unnamed category 5 hurricane hit the Florida Keys with a barometric pressure of 26.35 inches, only surpassed by Gilbert's 26.22 inches in 1988. There were 408 deaths. The *Bluenose* sailed right into the remnants of this storm on September 11. They fought it for three days. At one point she keeled right over and stayed down for 5 minutes, mast and all, then she shuddered and righted herself again. It took months to refit her.

In 1937 Walters wife succumbed to a disease and the *Bluenose* was cast on the dime by the Canadian mint. The last Fisherman's Cup was up for grabs and again they faced *Gurtrude*. This time it was best of five. They were deadlocked after four races. In the final race the *Bluenose* lost her mizzen topsail halfway through the race. Angus got the boys working like they never had, got a line on her and cleared the mess. The *Bluenose* looked her age and coming around the last buoy Walter pleaded, "One more time old girl, just one more time." She responded and won by three minutes. She clocked an average speed of 14.15 knots, the fastest ever recorded over a set fixed course by a canvassed vessel. It was the end of the grand age of tall ships.

The *Bluenose* should have retired as the queen that she was but unfortunately she was sold in 1942 to be used as a scow. On January 28, 1946 she struck a reef off the coast of Haiti and sunk. Walters cried when he heard of her final resting place and wanted to salvage her.

A Halifax brewery that bottled 'Schooner Beer' put up the funds to build *Bluenose II*. She was launched July 24, 1963 in Lunenburg. The hull and rigging was identical to the original but the interior was designed for passengers rather than cod. Walter's grandson Wayne Walters became the captain. Walters took her out but she wasn't the same. The old man of the sea died August 12th, 1969 and passed into folklore and history.

John Ware
'Bronco Busting Cowboy'

The first slaves in the English-American colonies were twenty African Negroes brought to Jamestown, Virginia in 1619 and sold to the highest bidder. They brought only slightly higher prices than mules. Queen Anne of England was said to be a prominent shareholder in the evil operation and even Christian churches in the south did little to oppose the trade. In 1750 the British Parliament legalized the trade in slaves.

John Ware was born a slave in Georgetown, South Carolina in 1845. His mother, like all the other cotton plantation workers, was restrained in everything except propagation. Education was a foreign concept never entertained and John went to work at the age of eight alongside the adults. To salvage their souls they were released from labour on Sundays to attend services for Christian instruction. They often showed more faith than those who preached and sacred songs brought comfort to them at any time. Spiritual songs echoed through the magnolia groves filling the fields with woeful melodies.

John, with a smile as continuous as the toil he faced, could out run and out jump all the others. For the amusement of his visitors their master Mr. Chauncey staged a mass fight of fifteen Negro boys from twelve to fifteen. A rope enclosure was fashioned. The rule was that any boy who was knocked down was to remain down. The last boy standing would win a pair of shoes. The free-for-all began with no ill feeling among the contestants. One by one the boys dropped until only John and Mose remained. Mose had been sick a lot and was hardly worth keeping. John didn't finish Mose with one blow instead he missed him every time. Mose landed a light blow and Ware went down. Mose helped him to his feet and John smiled wiping blood from his face. "Dem shoes'll go on yo feet Mose I don imagine any shoes'd be big 'nough for ma feet. Sides yo ma was awful good to ma mammy when she was sick."

Now Chauncey was a hard master, harder than most. He was rarely outside the house without his black-handled whip with the six-foot lash. One day he was in a black mood and thought the hoes were moving too slowly. He lashed a man who was feeble from old age. No one retaliated for to do so would bring reprisals. He went too far when he whipped a mother taking time out to nurse her baby and then he struck a girl, John's sister. John stepped forward and warned him not to do that again. Chauncey took exception and swung the whip bringing it down on his shoulders. Ware grabbed the man's coat and demanded the whip.

Chauncey struck the 'boy' in the face as hard as he could. John could restrain himself no longer and his fist came up knocking him violently to the ground. The men whispered admiringly and the women wept knowing the trouble it would bring. In the afternoon their master appeared with two pistols hanging from his belt and announced John Ware must present himself to be tied to the whipping tree. John submitted at once knowing all would suffer if he didn't. He gritted his teeth as he received ten lashings and blood oozed from the welts. His mother tenderly applied pork grease and the next day John was at work with all the others.

In 1860 Abraham Lincoln was elected President. The North was conscious of the injustice of slavery just as the South, with four million slaves, saw their financial benefit. The Ordinance of Succession passed in Charleston on December 20, 1860 was the first step toward a separate government. Many other states followed suit and on February 18, 1861 the Confederacy was given birth. Jefferson Davis became the president. The American Civil War was soon on. January 1, 1863 Lincoln signed the Emancipation Proclamation freeing the slaves. The turning point in the war came on July 3, 1863 when General Lee's Confederate troops were soundly defeated at Gettysburg. Lincoln was assassinated on April 14, 1865 with the Civil War reaching its conclusion. Half a million lives were lost.

General Sherman set fire to the Chauncey plantation. Ware left but not before confronting his master and pinning him to the whipping tree. He told him he could finish him right then and there but he was nobler than that and let the creep go. John was lucky he wasn't shot in the back.

John left his mother, father, ten brothers and sisters and traveled to Texas. It was cattle country and he landed a job with Old Murphy Blandon. He could do the work of two men and he was too good to let go. He had a hankerin' to ride a horse so they bridled a colt and John jumped on like a cat would pounce on a mouse. He was a huge man over six feet tall and 230 pounds. The horse had no saddle and immediately bucked then took off clearing the deadfall that formed a four-foot fence. They streaked away toward Mexico, dropped from sight in a ravine and came into view on the other side and finally disappeared in a belt of trees near the river. Young Murphy found John still on the horse making his way back to the corral. They named the horse Ol Hound Dog as suggested by John. He would soon win a race with big John on board at Fort Worth.

Longhorn cattle are the descendants of Spanish stock. Over the years they had multiplied. The Republic of Texas declared them public property in 1845 hence they belonged to anybody who could catch and brand them. They had little cash value in the state but in New Orleans or Chicago they could give a cowboy a good 'poke.' There were estimated to be two million before the Civil War and at least four million after.

John was filled with envy when he watched Young Murphy ride away on a cattle drive. Only the most seasoned and experienced cowboys were wanted for the trail could be dangerous with warlike Indians, heavily armed bandits and irritated settlers.

John could soon ride and rope with the best of them and was recognized as an expert horseman. His big chance came in 1879 to ride with a big trail herd. Old Murphy was sad to see him go but gave him a saddle and Hound Dog. Twelve cowboys, a cook and remunda of eighty horses started out with 2,400 bawling, ill-tempered Texas cows.

The first day they drove hard, twice as far as any other day to tire the herd so they would settle down for the night. They called it 'trail breaking.' The favoured position was the point of the herd. Of course John rode the rear drag position where they had to prod the cattle and eat dust. With his good nature he accepted the long days and men who resented him at the beginning found themselves attracted to him by the end.

John got the night shift but he took it all in stride. He would sing for he loved the hymns he sang as a child. Singing helped keep him awake and it identified his presence all the time and there was less chance of a night stampede, the greatest fear of all cowboys. One night on his rounds he spotted something inching toward the herd but it dashed to the trees as John approached. He thought it was human but wasn't sure so he reported it to the boss who dismissed it.

Shortly there after a shrill Indian scream cut the air and instantly 2,400 cattle were on the move. It was an old Indian trick to start a night stampede so they could pick up the strays for their tribe. John had his horse saddled and he was soon on Hound Dog racing to reach the leaders. He pushed his beloved horse on knowing the dangers. A badger hole could trip a horse or the thundering column of beef could trample horse and rider in their blind dash.

John urged Hound Dog on to the front of the herd and tried to turn them. They couldn't see him or ignored him. He swung his lariat and shouted to no avail. At last he drew his revolver and fired at the horn of the nearest cow. The horn was shattered and the cow turned sharply turning the herd. He repeated this five more times emptying his gun. It worked, the herd was now running in a circle. Their speed slackened and the panting cattle soon stopped. When the foreman finally caught up to him with the rest of the hands they couldn't believe John was dismounted and lying peacefully watching the herd graze. Damn if he hadn't stopped the stampede all by himself and in such short order.

After four months and nearly 2,000 miles of travel the herd was delivered to Montana. Some of the boys decided to go looking for gold, including John and Bill Moodie. They didn't find any and soon parted. John hunted some big game animals like deer, elk and grizzly bear but soon tired of that. He was grief stricken when Ol Hound Dog died and he was relegated to travelling on foot.

In 1882 he found his old friend Bill Moodie and hoped they would ride home to Texas together. A man named Abe Cotterell intervened and changed the shape of their destiny. He was driving a herd north. There were rumours of cheap land and ocean-like expanses of unoccupied grass. Abe tried to hire Bill for the trail ride. He was reluctant for he had promised Ware he would ride with him back home. Bill persuaded Abe to hire John. Tom Lynch didn't want the coloured boy. He knew they were not good cowboys and seein' as he didn't have a horse they weren't even sure he could ride. Bill stuck to his guns and got his friend signed on with the North West Cattle Company.

They had 3,000 cattle to drive and John's first job was peeling potatoes for the cook. He was given a dilapidated saddle with rope for stirrups and a broke down old nag.

Though a better cowboy than most he concealed his resentment. Life had taught him patience so he waited. When he finally got tired of the old nag they'd hoisted him with he said ironically, "Boss ah was jist awunde'n if yo'd give me alil betta sddle and a lil wuss hoss, cause ah thinks ah can wide um."

The gang thought they have some fun so they brought out the worst tempered horse they had. It had taken the conceit out of more than one seasoned cowboy. It was an event and all hands were present including the cook. Moodie said nothing. John got on the mean critter and it bucked, reared, jolted, sunfished and swung his massive bulk around the corral for twenty minutes before grinding to a halt. The cowboys forgot their plot as they looked on in silence. They knew they were seeing an exhibition of rough riding such as to fill everyone with awe and admiration.

The once-untamed bucking horse stood in subdued quiet. John dismounted saying with a grin, "Thanks boss. Ah'll keep this hoss - if'n it's ahwight whit yo."

The foreman said, "Keep the horse? Sure you can keep him, nobody else wanted him anyway. He's your pony John. That was a great ride."

He was promoted to the day crew near the point and never had to take a night shift again. Never again was there any doubt about his ability or skill as a horseman. They made between twelve and fifteen miles a day. They didn't want to drive the herd too hard for they would arrive too skinny to survive the hostile Canadian winters.

Midway between Fort Benton and the Canadian border Lynch suspected some cattle were cut out and he sent John to investigate. Sure enough in a draw to the west he discovered two desperados heating a branding iron beside a crude corral holding some cattle. John rode up close and they drew their guns. They expected the intruder to retreat but he neither drew or retreated. He showed no fear or emotion as he addressed the men, "Anywher rond here a thirst man can git a drink of wat'r."

Before they could reply John spurred his horse and the animal leaped forward upsetting both men. He leaped from his mount and seized both guns and overpowered the rustlers. He had the guns and the men. The boys witnessed a strange sight as a lone rider approached driving the stolen cattle and leading the two terror-stricken men at the end of a thirty-foot rope. The men knew the penalty for their crime was hanging. They were given some sound advice and released on foot without their guns.

Their destination was Highwood up in a territory that would not become Alberta until the year John died. Fred Stimson, the manager of the Bar U Ranch asked Lynch, "Any boys I should keep for the ranch work."

"You'll be a fool if you don't hang onto that coloured boy. Almost didn't bring him but by dang if he didn't turn out to be the best of the bunch," was the reply.

Fred offered Ware $25 a month. John hoped this would happen for he liked the frontier spirit and felt this country would give a fellow an honest chance to be a man. Never the less he replied, "Wall Boss, ah neva thout ah'd a be so fa fom Ca'oline or Texas, but ah so't a likes this heah country. Tell you what ah'll do. Ah'll take yo job on the condition that yo hiah my fwiend Bill Moodie too." Lynch snickered recalling the day he hired Moodie.

Stimson looked puzzled as he replied, "All right John, it's a deal."

His first winter in Alberta was extremely cold and harsh. It was something new for this boy from the south who had rarely seen snow and certainly never the freezing temperatures he now encountered.

John liked a hard bed, tough meat and fancied a horse that began the day with a bit of a buck. In 1883 they were camped north of Old Man River when a greenhorn asked if John could break Mustard an unusually docile black gelding as long as no one was on board. He jumped on and the show was on. With all the fury he possessed Mustard leaped into the air with head hung low, mouth open, nostrils flared and back arched showing the demon in him. The onlookers were horrified as Mustard and John fell off the river bank cliff. The animal cleared the bank and landed perfectly horizontal in deep water with John still stuck to his back. He guided the dejected horse out of the water saying, "Yo god a good hoss theah causin' 'taint evr'y hoss that can buck and swim at the same time lak that fellah."

In '84 some of Ware's friend were talking about gold. Every frontiersman was part prospector and gold pans were as common as Winchesters. He went looking for the lost Lemon mine with Dan Riley and Lafayette French. The story was told how Lemon murdered his partner Black Jack so he could have the gold nuggets that were strewn on the gravel bar like hail stones after a storm. However he went batty and could never relocate the treasure. Many have since tried. Some died and evidently the find was never found.

In 1885 he signed with the militia but he undoubtedly felt a kinship to the beleaguered Métis who like him were free but with few effective rights. The Indians called him *Matox Sex Apee Quin* that means 'bad black white man.'

He struck off on his own and soon had a cabin built and a herd of 75 head with the 9999 brand he registered May 25, 1885.

Horse stealing was commonplace and it wasn't uncommon for the Snake Indians to be driving Peigan horses southward only to meet Peigans driving Snake horses in the opposite direction. John could attest to the fact that horse rustlers south of the border were usually lynched for he had seen the cold eyes, blacked faces and protruding tongues of bodies dangling from tree branches. It didn't happen in Canada though. But pitched battles did occur like in 1886 when the Canadian Blood and Montana Gros-Venture squared off in Sweet Grass in one of the bloodiest tribal battles in history.

Mosquitoes could come in murderous waves and John like to kid that when he built a smudge to protect the animals he had to shoot a hole through the clouds of 'skitters' before any smoke could get away.

When some British Lords and high fallutin' men visited Tom Lynch in '86 John impressed them with all his skills including his singing. Lord Harold was so impressed he sent Ware a tailored jacked from London.

The winter of '85 was brutal and only the Indians, coyotes and wolves fared better than usual on the thousands of cow carcasses that littered the range. John lost half of his herd. Horses fared much better for they could dig for their food. One enterprising rancher tied a horse to every cow he had and they all survived.

November 7, 1886 fire raced through fourteen tinder-dry log and wood framed buildings in Calgary and that led to some fire resistant buildings being constructed out of sandstone from the near by quarry. When John and the Bar U boys went to town they were arrested for drunkenness but John was not drunk and refused to go. After rounding up the other fellas the two officers came to take Ware in. Instead John grabbed them by their collars and went to see his boss Billy Holmes who suggested he submit to the collared officers. He went and spent the rest of the night in jail. The next day the magistrate eyed him resentfully for there had been another Negro who had recently been convicted of murder and hung. This seemed to stain Ware's reputation in the city.

John claimed he wasn't drunk and Holmes confirmed his statement. The magistrate asked if he was a cowboy and Ware confirmed this. The judge asked if he could break horses and Holmes spoke up saying, "Probably the best horse breaker in the country."

The judge dismissed the case and the entire courtroom was soon off to the judge's house for he had an unbroken brown gelding he wanted tamed. John mounted the steed and the horse was soon bucking his way toward the Elbow River. They disappeared into the valley and soon appeared on the other side with the struggle now slackening. He soon returned with the gelding subdued. The magistrate was won over and asked Ware to dinner and his wife said as he was leaving, "Any time you're here, you might drop in and see us. We'd like to get to know you better."

John seemed to have a way of getting people to like him with his easy way and smile that was as wide as the horns on a Texas longhorn. His feats of horsemanship and legendary strength endeared him to all but the most crusty cow puncher.

He loved dogs almost as much as horses and when his young pup Moses disappeared he rode into an Indian camp and brazenly searched every tepee before finding the little critter. He faced the whole tribe defiantly and admonished them for stealing his hound before he rode triumphantly down the trail.

He met a young nineteen-year-old black gal named Mildred Lewis. While courting her he took her out in his wagon. A storm was brewing and lightning struck knocking his two horses dead in their tracks. John unhitched them and dragged the wagon with Miss Mildred aboard back to her home. Nothing seemed to faze this grand cowboy.

He married Mildred February 29, 1892. When he returned to his home with his bride they were surprised and frightened to see candlelight in the window. They were relieved to find their neighbours had gathered to bid the new couple a happy future. March 9, 1893 Jeanette was born but she went by the name of Nettie. Robert was born the following year on November 9.

In '94 when drought hit the area he dug a ditch from the creek to water his fields. The next two years were not much better.

One day in a corral John was caught unaware when a bull charged him. He jumped like a startled cat and seized the widespread horns and drew himself to a position behind the left one. The critter dragged him for some distance but John had him stuck like a weasel on the throat of a rabbit. He grabbed the animal's muzzle, twisted the steer's head and threw it off balance rolling it on its side. Onlookers were surprised, relieved then amazed and broke into a great cheer. After this he received requests to wrestle a steer but John didn't like to show off too much.

'97 looked like another drought year but it turned to raining and the rivers raged. His neighbour E.D. Adams built too close to the creek and his log home was washed away. As usual it was John to the rescue. He came to be of whatever assistance he could. There were a group of hungry cattle marooned on a spit of land amid the torrent. Ware handed Adams his revolver and launched his horse into the treacherous water. It was not easy to persuade the herd from the island but with Ware's experience forcing trail herds across unfriendly waters he soon had the unwilling beasts swimming to safety. Adams recalled, "That was why neighbours loved John Ware."

There was a declining market for horses. It was reported that people in Ottawa rode bicycles, mules pulled the wagons, streetcars were run by electricity and jackasses ran the government, so there was no need for horses there. When a friend asked John when he was going to buy a bicycle. John replied, "When the last hoss is dead."

There were more cattle than ever with over half a million by 1900 compared to 132,000 in 1891 and a mere 13,000 in 1881. Homesteads entries were rising with 7,426 in 1900 alone.

By the turn of the century John found the quiet remote place he loved being over run with settlers so they moved to a place twenty miles north of Brooks by a stream. Mildred was pregnant again and she found the move difficult but she made the most of it. Soon a small cabin was erected with the help of many hands he had helped over the years.

In 1902 the creek flooded and carried away his home. It is now called Ware Creek. As luck would have it a boom of logs destined for a sawmill broke loose and good spruce logs came floating by. Ware lassoed them and dragged them ashore single-handedly. When additional logs were needed he cut a near by stand of poplars. Once again in no time a structure was completed albeit with a sod roof and dirt floor as well as a safer distance from the creek.

Mange, a parasite that spread amongst the cattle, was rampant and to combat it the cattle were run though a tank with a sulphur solution. The Stock Growers Association, of which John was a member, approached him about building a dipping vat just below his house. John was only too obliging and as usual gave his mighty strength to the project. Even before he had built a stable or dug a well, herds of cattle were dipping in the tank. John helped all and became an expert on the disease and the remedy.

April 29, 1903 millions of tons of limestone crashed from Turtle Mountain and buried the town of Frank in the Crowsnest Pass killing 76. It was the most shocking news of the time. On May 16 a rain turned to snow during the night and didn't let up for four days. John was in Calgary getting some medicine for Mildred as she was not well since the last baby was born and unfortunately died. He was advised to postpone his journey home but he would not listen. He took his horse into the blizzard but it balked at the prospect and refused to make progress despite John's spurs raking her flank. He returned to the stable and left on his own. He walked the 25 miles and after seven hours of battling the unrelenting storm he arrived home. Mildred embraced him then tenderly scolded him but she knew him well as she had placed a lantern in the window as a beacon.

John lost at least a hundred head including calves and the dead corpses raised a horrible stink.

By 1905 the number of homesteads soared to 30,891. Open range was a thing of the past and barbed wire became as much a part of standard ranch equipment as stock saddles.

In April of 1905 Mildred got typhoid and pneumonia and was transported to Holy Cross Hospital in Calgary. She died and John sent the five children, Nettie, Robert, William, Mildred and Arthur to their grandmother and he stayed alone in the empty cabin.

September 12 he went riding with his son Bob. Ware had ridden half a million miles in his life. As John turned the grey mare he was riding, she stepped in a badger hole and fell awkwardly right on top of him. He remained motionless and the mare got up and walked away. Bob tried to rouse is father but there was no response. He rushed to get help and when they returned there was no doubt that John was dead.

That big black guy fondly known as 'Nigger' John had earned such respect and renown that his funeral was the biggest Calgary had ever seen.

Mike Weir
Becoming a Master

Mike Weir was born on May 12, 1970 in Bright's Grove, Ontario. He graduated from Brigham Young University. Mike earned his PGA Tour card in November 1998 and posted his first PGA Tour win in 1999 taking the Air Canada Championship in Surrey, British Columbia. This victory made him the first Canadian to win a PGA Tour event in Canada in 45 years.

In 2000 Weir won the season-ending American Express Championship in Sotogrande, Spain. It was worth $1 million U.S. and boosted his earnings to sixth-best on the tour that year.

He lives with the wife Brica in Draper, just south of Salt Lake City, Utah. They have two daughters Elle and Lily. Though in many aspects of his life he is right handed, in golf he is a lefty.

Mike Weir entered the 2003 Masters Championship a definite underdog. But when the final day came on April 13, he was in the running at the August National Golf Course. At the end of regulation play Mike was tied with Len Mattiace and won it on the 72nd hole with a dramatic pressure-packed 8-foot par putt. He is the only Canadian to have won the prestigious tournament. George Knudson placed second in 1969. Mike also won the Bob Hope Chrysler Classic and the Nissan Open the same year. He won the Nissan Open again in 2004.

Canadians hope their diminutive champion; he is only 5' 9" and 155 pounds, snares a few more titles from the goliaths of the golf world.

Percy Williams
World's Fastest Man

The 1928 Olympics caught the imagination of the world and the promotion and coverage was better than ever. The hero of the games was the great Finnish distance runner Paavo Nurmi having won two gold medals in the 1924 Olympics in the 1,500m and 5,000m events. 'Flying Finn' would win the gold medal in the 10,000m event and the silver medals in the 5,000m and 3,000m steeplechase. However a new hero would emerge during the games and he was a Canadian by the name of Percy Williams.

Percy Williams was born in Vancouver, British Columbia on May 19, 1908. If ever there was an unlikely Canadian sports hero it was Percy. He was small - only 126 pounds at the peak of his athletic career. In 1926 Percy accepted a challenge from Wally Scott, Vancouver's sprint champion. Scott's coach Bob Granger watched as Percy ran his boy to a dead heat. From that moment Bob took Percy under his wing.

Under Bob's coaching Percy began to develop and by 1928, when the B.C. Olympic trials took place, he tied the Olympic record of 10.6 seconds in the 100m event. As an unknown, he went to the Olympic trials in Hamilton, Ontario and won the 100m and 200m events and a place on the Canadian Olympic team.

Percy was on his way to Amsterdam but his coach did not accompany him, as the Olympic committee could not afford to pay his fare. On the voyage Percy practised his starts by putting a mattress up against the wall and running into it. Bob Granger managed to raise the necessary funds to cross the Atlantic and arrived at the hotel in Amsterdam three days after the team.

In the first heat of the 100m event Percy won easily. In the second heat he had to clock his fastest time of the games, 10.6 seconds, to qualify for the semi-finals. The next day in the semi-final, Percy got a bad start but came from behind to finish second and qualify for the final. The skinny twenty-year old from Canada was a decided underdog but had captured the fancy of the spectators.

On July 30, 1928 at 4:00 P.M. 80,000 spectators came to see the world's fastest human. The diminutive Canadian, sporting the red maple leaf, appeared a child among the men he crouched beside. The tension was too great. Wilfred Legg of South Africa broke with a false start and the entire field jogged off down the track bouncing and shaking their arms to reduce the tension. They entered the starting pits, they did not have blocks back then, and the gun was up. Once again there was a false start, this time it was Frank Wykoff of the U.S. Williams jogged back and forth appearing very cool. Again, everything was ready. The gun was up and its crack signaled a good start.

Williams made a perfect break coming out in front with Jack London of Britain just inches behind. He settled into his mid-race pace and found Legg and Wykoff flanking him; but the red maple leaf blazed ahead. London came up and made a tremendous challenge, but Williams shifted into his famous finishing explosion of speed and crossed the line first by a yard. He had won the gold medal and the title 'The World's Fastest Man.' He became the smallest man to ever win the 100m event at the Olympics.

Williams was mobbed by the ecstatic Canadian team and was carried aloft around the infield. The British fans were jubilant as London of Great Britain placed second while George Lammers of Germany took the bronze medal. The women's team sent Percy flowers.

Williams' effort astounded the experts and he would continue to do so with his efforts in the 200m event. He won his first two heats. The crowd now adored him and every accolade was heaped upon his shoulders. In the 200m event, coach Grange marked Helmut Koerning of Germany as the man to beat. The gun was up and the field broke cleanly and once again Williams got a good start. He ran neck-and-neck with Koerning up to the final 50 metres where he made his famous 'shift' and drove past Koerning to his second gold medal in a time of 21.8 seconds. Williams also ran in the relay event but unfortunately Canada was disqualified due to a poor baton exchange.

When Percy Williams returned to Canada, it was to a tumultuous welcome. He received accolades and gifts as he crossed Canada from Québec to British Columbia. In Vancouver he was mobbed at the train and at a reception at Stanley Park he was presented with a sporty blue Graham Paige automobile and a trust fund of $14,000 for his education.

Touring the States he ran twenty-one races in twenty-two days and won nineteen of them. Sports historian Bill McNulty called it the Tour of Guts. In 1930 Percy set a new world record in the 100m in Toronto with a time of 10.3 seconds. The record would stand for eleven years. Later in the year, at the British Empire Games in Hamilton, he tore a muscle in his thigh and although he won the race he was never the same.

Percy donated his Olympic gold medals to the Vancouver Sports Hall of Fame and within a week they were stolen and never recovered. To celebrate his Amsterdam gold medals he was presented with the starting pistol that he unfortunately chose to kill himself with in 1952.

The saga of 'Peerless Percy' was over but those moments of glory live on through pages like these.

Canada
'The Promised Land'

Long days ago in our short history past
Our shores saw many furled sails of foreign ship's mast
The British and French, Spanish and Dutch
Most came to fish and didn't take much

Unlike the Aztecs no gold did adorn
To our natives, diamonds and gems were totally foreign
They simply treasured nature that was abundantly found
Throughout their land unrestrained and unbound

The white man came hunting for the treasure of lands
And simply took it from each successive first nations bands
It was no contest disease was their plague
Reduced to shambles and then forced to beg

Then came the tracks and more people by rail
Most of them fair skinned and comparatively pale
Gone were the buffalo their sustenance of life
Cast into poverty to suffer strife

This great land was conquered on the backs of great men
In a time and a land a long way back then
Brought were the laws of our great nation
For the people of the world it was their destination

The country great spread shore to shore to shore
So many people came to knock on our door
What do we have, what do they want?
What do they look for, what should we flaunt?

Is it our freedom, our peace and our space?
As a Canadian I know I am in a treasured place
So thanks to the pioneers who settled the land
And made our country the promised dreamland

Christmas 1792

*T'was Christmas here in New England
Indians were hootin' and soldiers were singin'
They had a party in Boston Bay
To object to the taxes ... they had to pay*

*Some people starved it was hard to survive
They celebrated just being alive
Indians cried, soldiers shoot
They fight and they kill and don't give a hoot*

*It was a hard way to suffer through life
Surviving the odds, suffering strife
Only the strong lived to survive
Christmas was a party of just being alive*

*After Thanksgiving the larder was low
Little to eat and no where to go
So far away from kin and their friends
To the end of the earth and at their wits ends*

*A New World was born for all had to pitch in
Small were the gifts given to new found friend kin
Christmas was low key, they didn't have much
A trinket, a tasket a crumb was it such*

*As it was they really had lots
Heart rendered spirit that's what they got
Of little value but treasured much more
As neighbours and strangers trod through their door*

*They did what they could and gave from the heart
Mostly they just shared of themselves a warm fuzzy part
Sharing from misery far from their home
Over an ocean of waves that seethed rolling foam*

*Yes it was hard, of that there is no doubt
But wasn't that what settling the New World was about
Perhaps we should thank those brave pioneers
As we toast with wine glasses and large steins of beer*

Canada's Peace Poem

1496 that was the year
John Cabot sailed over here
He was one of the first but far from the last
The fate of our future was then cast

From all over Europe many men came
It was a New World, for them to tame
Oh so beautiful, it was quite a sight
They came over here to try to make all things right

Poverty despair such a gloomy past
Now they saw hope on that tall spar wood mast
English and French came to our shore
They came with hope of oh so much more

No landlord to be found, yes the land was free
Not a single building or factory could one see
But there were many men who had staked a claim
These were the savages the gun came to tame

The English and French had the bloodiest wars
The brave red skins died by the scores
Not so much by bullets or by the sword
White man's diseases silently ravaged the hoard

On the Plains of Abraham the French they did lose
Their leader, Montcalm and a future to chose
A bloody past that was our fate
We fought and hurt and killed .... But wait

What has now happened in this mighty land
Across the centuries of times shifting sand
The men of war have left and gone
Lives were saved with a delicate peace song

Armistice, treaties and much more debate
No more bullets of revenge or of hate
Still we must talk it can never end
Both sides must be willing to listen and bend

How did we do it, does the world care?
How we found peace, we really should share?
That is the point, we must not be greedy
That is the seed in the poor and needy

We must be fair and listen to their voice
Letting them know that they have a choice
Negotiations that never stop ... that is the key
The fabric, the linen ... of a peaceful society

Hockey

Though lacrosse is Canada's national game
It is hockey that has garnered wide spread acclaim
Back in the 1800's they played Hurly on Ice
Rickets or shinny was a fun winter exercise

In 1892 Lord Stanley donated the cup
Though he never did see a game played real close up
Ever since then teams have competed for honour
To win the cup in a playoff sudden death boiler

No wonder we're proud for in 1920 we won
The first Olympic gold medal in hockey, my that was fun
The Winnipeg Falcons did it for us
They were just juniors that caused all the fuss

We won again in 1924, we were on a tear
Our team though just juniors, were simply premier
Toronto Granites took it in 1928, oh my, ho hum
In '32 the Winnipeg Monarchs continued the run

In 36 we lost the gold to Great Britain, silvers not bad
When we won gold in 48, we surely were glad
1952 the Edmonton Mercurys continued the streak
But after this time for us Olympic hockey looked bleak

Still we were happy we had the Rocket
And his little brother who they called the Pocket
Montreal Canadiens took claim of the cup
They won it so much I thought it was stuck

In the French province with all of their stars
La Fleur, Beliveau, Boom Boom they were czars
At the Olympics we couldn't win gold
It seemed the Russians had a strangle hold

Still in the NHL Canadians played with acclaim
Bobby Orr, Wayne Gretzky, Mario Lemieux, each had their day of fame
The Canada Cup with the very best that we had
Crunched in game one we just played so bad

But in the final game Paul Henderson rose
And still his legend grows and it grows
Finally at last with Gretzky in the wings
In 2002 we won gold and all the acclaim that it brings

But what is this, a hockey standstill
They took a year out to fight and to chill
No "He shoots, he scores" to ring round with a cheer
Instead we just mumble and cry in our beer

Our stars on ice are certainly well paid
But it could be the fans that have the final grenade
Hockey could blow up for how many are so driven
That their interest and attendance is a certainty given

We want our hockey to be our national pride
Do they care about the fans or are we just along for a ride
Perhaps the game is no longer a game
Now it seems to be who has the largest paycheque to proclaim

How Steep the Price?

Men of daring, men of do
Fought the good fight for me and you
Spitfires with their bull's eye wing
Can they help to save the king?

Heinkels, Dorniers droning heavy
Bringing goods but pay no levy
109s complete the cast
Bader thinks, this will be a blast

Hurricanes rush the bombers low
Spitfires find 109s to mow
Far out numbered, the odds are high
A dear cost for those who fly

The price was steep, the pay was not
But these young men so bravely fought
High above on vapour trail
Fighting till their steed did fail

Some of them could pop the lid
To bale on silk was the lucky kid
Too many were trapped in a flaming wreck
And rode the monster to the deck

Did they complain, not this lot
Exhilarated, they bravely fought
Not for glory, not for fame
Not for fortune, too many lame

Burned, disfigured, was many a fate
Far too young to never date
Would they care, I s'pose they did
What a fate to give a kid

We bow to them who gave their all
Those who lived should lead the ball
Those who died do have our prayers
I am sure we have shed a tear

Soon they will all be gone, memories fade
What of the sacrifice so many made
When the last survivor is finally lost
Will we forget the mighty cost

I hope not, for there are stories told
Of the brave and of the bold
Become informed about that time
Let those brave boys forever shine

This poem is dedicated to the likes of Willie McKnight and all the pilots that lost their life in both World Wars.

Yonder Hudson Bay

I am the Bay in which they left Hudson
I think he was some far off, very distant cousin
Never the less my shores became great
They once housed the home of the Hudson Bay gate

The mighty Hudson Bay in its long ago past
Displayed its rocky shores to many a ship's mast
Captains and traders established forts on my shore
They traded for furs with the Indians of lore

They traded for beads but wanted much more
They wanted the weapon that made the huge roar
The village women liked the cool cooking tools
Still too many traded for the liquid of fools

Plying the rivers in vessels of bark
In long ago days of images dark
The war of the white man with diseases they brought
He ravaged the natives with hardly a thought

Armed with the power of the mighty gun
The bow and the arrow was put on the run
A final surrender was their only hope
On a reservation is where they must now cope

A great land was conquered on backs of great men
In a time and a land a long way back then
The Hudson Bay traded throughout the great land
Once leading our country with a firm helping hand

Brought were the laws of our great nation
For the people of the world it was their destination
The country grew, it spread shore to shore
Many a people came to knock on our door

*What do we have, what do they want
What do they look for, what should we flaunt
Is it our freedom, our peace and our space?
As a Canadian I know I'm in a great place*

*So thanks to the Bay for getting us started
Even though days of yonder have parted
We know your still here manning your stores
That have scattered so far from my rocky shores*

Oath to Canada

October 30, 1995

*I was born in a country that was truly great
But the citizens watched until it was too late
Politicians argued and bartered with hard headed pride
They tore up the constitution, our country just died!*

*Our freedoms and rights were unfairly denied
The politicians lost and so was our pride
A country of peace and love of mankind
We lost it because we all were so blind*

*We did not see our country as it fell and it crumbled
We just carried on, nobody mumbled
We had a life and a very rich history
Few people cared, why, was a mystery*

*The English had their culture, so did the French
Each had an aim as they dug in their trench
Each minority group needed to have their say
They argued and fought until one fateful day*

*Everyone cussed and said, "Eh, what the hell!"
No one would compromise and our country fell
And it didn't take long to discover our fate
Citizens cried but by then it was too late!*

*The American's smirked as they rushed to our aid
It took little time to see the price that we'd paid
They raped and they plundered our resources with glee
Oh! should we be grateful? we paid them a fee*

*Decidedly weak we lost our last shred of will
The American eagle swept in for the kill
We sold out our country, the highest bid won
Oh what a shame! what had we undone*

We lost our country so free and once strong
Everyone asked themselves, "Where did we go wrong?"
Did you stand to be counted? Did you do anything?
Did you cry in the streets or did you do your **ostrich** *thing?*

Now it is all gone, Canada's a thing of the past
Québec went down first, the North was the last
Did my country fall in some way cause of me
Did I not sing "I stand on guard for thee"

Well don't be a fool and let our great country die
Rally and protest, shout and let fly
Your patriotic fever must reach to the 'Hill'
Fellow citizens of Canada we must send our collective will

My dear Canada, I'm on guard for thee
I value the priviledge of living this free
I will fight and I'll rally, shout and I'll vote
I'll do something, of which, the politicians will take note

Canada, Canada, Canada be
Canada Canada, I love you so free
Canada guard, Canada hope
Canadian politicians, **Canada**'s *my vote*

I love you Canada, please don't die

Bibliography

Adamson, Joseph. 1993 *Northrop Frye A Visionary Life*. ECW Press.

Anderson, Frank W. 1969 *Canada's Worst Mine Disaster*. Frontier Book

Asfar, Dan and Tim Chodan. 2003 *Louis Riel*. Folklore Publishers.

Aubin, Benoit. 2000 *Trudeau: his life and legacy*. Macleans.

Barnett, Don C. 1976 *Poundmaker*. Fitzhenry & Whiteside Limited.

Batten, Jack. 2002 *The Man Who Ran Faster Than Everyone The Story of Tom Longboat*. Tundra Books.

Beurling, Buzz with Leslie Roberts. 1943 *Malta Sptfire The Buzz Beurling Story Canada's World War II Daredevil Pilot*. Penguin Books.

Bishop, Billy. 1990 *The Illustrated Classic Autobiography of the Canadian World War I Ace Billy Bishop WINGED WARFARE*. McGraw-Hill Ryerson.

Bliss, Michael. 1984 *Banting A Biography*. McClelland and Stewart Limited.

Bliss, Michael. 1999 *William Osler: a life of medicine*. University of Toronto Press.

Brown, Cassie. 1999 *Death on the Ice*. Bantam Doubleday.

Brown, Jacqueline A. 2005 *Sir John A. Macdonald The rascal who built Canada*. JackFruit Press Ltd.

Brownlow, Kevin. 1999 *Mary Pickford rediscovered: rare pictures of a Hollywood legend*. Harry N. Abrams Publishers.

Bonic, Tom. *Jean de Brébeuf A Giant in the Land of Huronia*. St. Paul University.

Burton, Pierre. 1958 *Klondike: The Last Great Gold Rush 1896-1899*. Doubleday Canada.

Carrier, Roch. 2001 *Our life with the Rocket: the Maurice Richard Story*. Viking.

Clarke, Michael D. 1998 *CANADA Portraits of Faith*. Reel to Reel Ministries.

Costain, Thomas B. *The White and the Gold*

Creighton, Donald. 1952 *Sir John A. Macdonald: The Young Politician and Old Chieftain.* University of Toronto Press.

Edmonton Grads 25 Years of Basketball Championships 1915-1940.

Flemming, David B. 2004 *Explosion in Halifax Harbour The Illustrated Account of A Disaster that Shook the World.* Formac Publishing Company Limited.

Ford, Karen, Janet MacLean, Barry Wansbrough. 1885 *Great Canadian Lives: Portraits in Heroism to 1867.* Nelson Canada.

Gillespie, Gerald J. 1969 *Bluenose skipper: the story of the Bluenose and her skipper.* Brunswidk Press.

Goodall, Lian. 2003 *William Lyon Mackenzie KING Dreams and Shadows.* XYZ Publishing.

Goyens, Chrys. 2000 *Maurice Richard: reluctant hero.* Team Power Publishing.

Graham, H. 1997 *The Canadian 100, The 100 most influential Canadians of the 20th Century.* Little, Brown and Company Ltd.

Greenwood, Barbara. 2001 *Gold Rush Fever A Story of the Klondike, 1898.* Kids Can Press Ltd.

Grosvenor, Edwin and Morgan Wesson. 1997 *Alexander Graham Bell TheLife and Times of the Man Who Invented the Telephone.* Harry N. Abrahms, Inc.

Hacker, Carlotta. 1983 *The Book of Canadians, An Illustrated Guide to Who Did What.* Hurtig Publishers.

Hacker, Carlotta. 1999 *The Canadians Crowfoot.* Fitzhenry & Whiteside Limited.

Hansen, Rick and Jim Taylor. 1987 *Rick Hansen Man in Motion.* Douglas & McIntyre.

Harris, John N. 1958 *Knights of the Air.* Macmillan.

Hayes, Derek. 2001 *First Crossing Alexander Mackenzie his expedition across North America and the opening of the continent.* Douglas & McIntyre Ltd.

Henry, Lorne J. *Canadian a Book of Biographies.*

Hillmer, Norman. 1999 *PEARSON The Unlikely Gladiator.* McGill-Queens University Press.

Horwood, Harold. 1977 *Bartlett The Great Canadian Explorer.* Doubleday & Company.

Hume, Stephen Eaton. 2001 *Frederick Banting Hero, Healer, Artist.* XYZ Publishing.

Hurtig, Mel. 1985 *The Canadian Encyclopedia.* 3 volume set.

James, Donna. 2001 *The Canadians Emily Murphy.* Fitzhenry & Whiteside Limited.

Keller, Betty. 1999 *Pauline Johnson, First Aboriginal Voice of Canada.* XYZ Publishing.

Kidd, Bruce. 2004 *The Canadians Tom Longboat.* Fitzhenry & Whiteside Limited.

Lennox, Muriel. 1985 *Northern Dancer: the legend and his legacy.* Beach House.

Loudon, William J. 1930 A *Canadian geologist.* Macmillan of Canada.

McCaffery, Dan. 2002 *Billy Bishop Canadian Hero.* James Lorimer and Company Ltd.

McCaffery, Dan. 2000 *Tommy Burns Canada's Unknown World Heavweight Champion.* James Lorimer & Company Ltd.

McClelland and Stewart. 1999 *The Canadian Encyclopedia.*

Macdonald, Bill. 1998 *The true Intrepid: Sir William Stephenson and the unkown agents.*

McDonald, David. *For the Record, Canada's Greatest Women Athletes.*

MacEwan, Grant. 1975 *...and mighty women too.* Western Producer Prairie Books.

MacEwan, Grant. 1958 *Fifty Mighty Men.* Western Producer Prairie Books.

MacEwan, Grant. 1974 *John Ware's Cow Country*. Western Producer Book Service.

MacGregor, James G. 1975 *Father Lacombe*. Hurtig Publishers.

Mander, Christine. 1985 *Emily Murphy, rebel first female magistrate in the British Empire*. Simona & Pierre.

Manson, Ainslie. 2003 *ALEXANDER MACKENZIE From Canada by Land*. Groundwood Books/Douglas & McIntyre.

Margoshes, Dave. 1999 *Tommy Douglas Building the New Society*. XYZ Publishing.

Marin, Reva. 2003 *Oscar: the life and music of Oscar Peterson*. Douglas & McIntyre.

Marlo-Trump, Nancy. *Ruby Keeler, A Photographic Biography*. McFarland and Col Incorporated Publishers.

Marshall, Ingeborg. 1989 *The Beothuk of Newfoundland A VANISHED PEOPLE*. Breakwater Books.

Martin, James. 2004 *Irresponsible Freaks, Highball Guzzlers & Unabashed Grafters A Bob Edwards Chrestomathy*. Brindle & Glass Publishing Ltd.

McCaffery, Dan. 2000 *Tommy Burns Canada's Unknown World Heavyweight Champion*. James Lorimer and Company Ltd.

Metson, Graham. *Halifax Explosion*.

Neering, Rosemary. 1999 *The Canadians Louis Riel*. Fitzhenry & Whiteside Limited.

Nolan, Brian. 1981 *Hero: The Buzz Beurling Story*. Penguin Books Ltd.

Pearson, Lester B. 1975 *Mike, the memoirs of the Right Honorable Lester B. Pearson*. University of Toronto Press.

Pelletier, Jean and Claude Adams. 1981 *The Canadian Caper*. Macmillan of Canada.

Plante, Raymond. 2001 *Jacques Plante: behind the mask*. XYZ Publishing.

Quan, Holly. 2003 *Sam Steele: The Wild West Adventures of Canada's Most Famous Mountie*. Altitude Publishing Canada.

Quirk, Lawrence J. 1988 *Norma: The Story of Norma Shearer*. St. Martin's Press.

Raby, Ormond. 1970 *Radio's First Voice The Story of Reginald Fessenden*. Macmillan Company of Canada Limited.

Rawlinson & J.L. Granatstein. *T.C. Douglas*.

Ray, Renna. *Janis of City View*.

Reader's Digest. 1980 *Canadian a Book of the Road*. Canadian Automobile Association.

Reader's Digest. 1971 *In Search of Canada*.

Robbins, John. (editor in chief) 1957 *Encyclopedia Canadiana*. red 10 volume set.

Romain, Joseph and Jame Duplacey. 1999 *Wayne Gretzky The Great One*. Brompton Books Corp.

Rowe, Frederick. 1977 *EXTINCTION The Beothuks of Newfoundland*. McGraw-Hill Ryerson Limited.

Rubenstein, Lorne. 2003 *Mike Weir the road to the Masters*. McClelland and Stewart.

Sauerwein, Stan. 2004 *Pierre Elliott Trudeau: the fascinating life of Canada's most flamboyant prime minister*. Altitude Publishers.

Sawatsky, John. 1984 *GOUZENKO The Untold Story*. Macmillan of Canada.

Slade, Arthur. 2001 *John Diefenbaker An Appointment with Destiny*. XYZ Publishing.

Slocum, Joshua. 1997 *Sailing alone around the world*. Köneman.

Sluman, Norma. 1967 *Poundmaker*. Ryerson.

Smith, Beverly. 2002 *Gold on Ice: the Salé Pelletier story*. Key Porter Books.

Spencer, Ann. 1998 *Alone at sea: the adventures of Joshua Slocum*. Doubleday Canada.

Stevenson, William. 1976 *A man called Intrepid: the secret war*. Harcourt Brace Janonvich.

Stewart, Walter. 2003 *The Life and Political Times of Tommy Douglas*. McArthur & Company.

Strong-Boag, Veronica. 2000 *Paddling Her Own Canoe*. University of Toronto Press.

Sutow, M. Pauline Murphy. 1992 *Worse Than War The Halifax Explosion*. Four East Publications.

Tekahionwake (E. Pauline Johnson). 1997 *FLINT and FEATHER*. Iroquois publishing and Craft Supplies.

Tekahionwake (E. Pauline Johnson). 2002 *Collected Poems and Selected Prose*. University of Toronto Press Incorporated.

Towle, Wendy. 1993 *The Real McCoy The Life of an African-American Inventor*. Scholastic Inc.

Waite, Peter B. 1985 *The Man from Halifax Sir John Thompson*. University of Toronto Press.

Waite, Peter B. 1999 *The Canadians John A. Macdonald*. Fitzhenry & Whiteside Limited.

Wateston, Elizabeth. 1957 *Pioneers in Agriculture: Massey, McIntosh, Saunders*. Clark Irwin.

Watson, Patrick. 2000 *The Canadians Biographies of a Nation*. Volumes I, II and III, McArthur & Company.

Webb, Michael. 1991 *Reginald Fessenden Radio's Forgotten Voice*. Copp Clark Pitman Ltd.

Westrup, Hugh. 1994 *Maurice Strong: Working for Planet Earth*. The Millbrook Press.

Whelan, Ed and Pemrose. 1990 *Touched by Tommy Stories of hope and humour about Canada's most loved political leader T.C. Douglas*. Whelan Publications.

Wilker, Josh. 1998 *Wayne Gretzky*. Chelsea House Publishers.

Windler, Robert. 1974 *Sweetheart The Story of Mary Pickford*. Praeger Publishers.

Wise, Sydney Francis and Douglas Fisher. 1974 *Canada's Sporting Heroes*. General Publishing Company Limited.

Whitfield, Eileen. 1997 *Pickford: the woman who made Hollywood*. Macfarlane Walter & Ross.

Wood, Kerry. 1964 *The Great Chief: Maskepetoon, warrior of the Crees*. Macmillan.

ISBN 1412088976